Books by Kenneth Koch

POETRY

One Train   1994
On the Great Atlantic Rainway, Selected Poems 1950–1988   1994
Seasons on Earth   1987
On the Edge   1986
Selected Poems: 1950–1982   1985
Days and Nights   1982
The Burning Mystery of Anna in 1951   1979
The Duplications   1977
The Art of Love   1975
The Pleasures of Peace   1969
When the Sun Tries to Go On   1969
Thank You and Other Poems   1962
Permanently   1961
Ko, or A Season on Earth   1960
Poems   1953   1968

FICTION

Hotel Lambosa   1993
The Red Robins   1975

THEATER

One Thousand Avant-Garde Plays   1988
The Red Robins   1979
A Change of Hearts   1973
Bertha and Other Plays   1966

EDUCATIONAL WORKS

Sleeping on the Wing:
     An Anthology of Modern Poetry with Essays on Reading and Writing
     (with Kate Farrell)   1981
I Never Told Anybody:
     Teaching Poetry Writing in a Nursing Home   1977
Rose, Where Did You Get That Red?:
     Teaching Great Poetry to Children   1973
Wishes, Lies, and Dreams:
     Teaching Children to Write Poetry   1970

ON THE GREAT
ATLANTIC
RAINWAY

KENNETH KOCH

Alfred A. Knopf New York 1994

ON THE GREAT ATLANTIC RAINWAY

Selected Poems 1950–1988

THIS IS A BORZOI BOOK
PUBLISHED BY ALFRED A. KNOPF, INC.

Most of the poems included in this work were originally published in the following collections:

Black Sparrow Press: Poems 1952–1953 (1953) and *When the Sun Tries to Go On* (1969)
Grove Press, Inc.: Ko, or a Season on Earth (1960), *Thank You, and Other Poems* (1962), *Bertha, and Other Plays* (1966), *The Pleasures of Peace, and Other Poems* (1969)
Alfred A. Knopf, Inc.: One Thousand Avant-Garde Plays (1988)
Random House, Inc.: The Art of Love (1975), *The Duplications* (1977), *The Burning Mystery of Anna in 1951* (1979), *Days and Nights* (1982)
Tibor de Nagy Gallery: Prints-Poems (1953)
Viking Penguin: On the Edge (1986) and *Seasons on Earth* (1987)

An extract from *The Red Robins: A Play* (*Performing Arts Journal*, 1979), is reprinted by permission of The Johns Hopkins University Press, Baltimore/London.

Library of Congress Cataloging-in-Publication Data

Koch, Kenneth,
        On the great Atlantic rainway : selected poems, 1950–1988
        by Kenneth Koch.—1st ed.
            p.   cm.
        ISBN 0-679-43418-6
        I. Title.
PS3521.027A6   1994
811'.54—dc20   94-28070
                                                   CIP

TO JESSE KOCH STATMAN

A NOTE ON THE TEXT

Except for a few slight displacements, everything is here in the order in which it was written. There is a good deal of it—about half the book—that didn't appear in *Selected Poems 1950–1982*. This includes work written and published since 1982, as well as selections from long poems (*When the Sun Tries to Go On, Ko,* and *The Duplications*), some plays and scenes from plays, and some uncollected poems from the 1950s.

I am very grateful to those who have helped me to write what is in this book: Janice Koch, John Ashbery, Frank O'Hara, James Schuyler, Kate Farrell. To have had such readers and such friends is a great good fortune.

CONTENTS

ON THE GREAT ATLANTIC RAINWAY

On the Great Atlantic Rainway

I set forth one misted white day of June
Beneath the great Atlantic rainway, and heard:
"Honestly you smite worlds of truth, but
Lose your own trains of thought, like a pigeon.
Did you once ride in Kenneth's machine?"
"Yes, I rode there, an old man in shorts, blind,
Who had lost his way in the filling station; Kenneth was kind."
"Did he fill your motionless ears with resonance and stain?"
"No, he spoke not as a critic, but as a man."
"Tell me, what did he say?" "He said,
'My eyes are the white sky, the gravel on the groundway my sad lament.'"
"And yet he drives between the two. . . ." "Exactly, Jane,

And that is the modern idea of fittingness,
To, always in motion, lose nothing, although beneath the
Rainway they move in threes and twos completely
Ruined for themselves, like moving pictures."
"But how other?" "Formulalessness, to go from the sun
Into love's sweet disrepair. He would fondly express
'Rain trees'—which is not a poem, 'rain trees. . . .'"
"Still, it is mysterious to have an engine
That floats bouquets! and one day in the rear-vision
Mirror of his car we vowed delight,
The insufficiency of the silverware in the sunlight,
The dreams he steals from and smiles, losing gain."

"Yet always beneath the rainway unsyntactical
Beauty might leap up!" "That we might sing
From smiles' ravines, 'Rose, the reverse of everything,
May be profaned or talked at like a hat.'"
"Oh that was sweet and short, like the minuet
Of stars, which would permit us to seem our best friends
By silver's eminent lights! For nature is so small, ends

Falsely reign, distending the time we did
Behind our hope for body-work, riding with Kenneth."
Their voicing ceased, then started again, to complain
That we are offered nothing when it starts to rain
In the same way, though we are dying for the truth.

The Bricks

The bricks in a wall
Sang this song:
"We shall not fall
The whole day long
But white and small
Lie in abandon."

Then the fair maid
Passed with her love
And she to him said,
"There are stars above
Where they have been laid
Let us lie in abandon."

Then the wolf came
With his teeth in abandon
And the lion came
With his teeth in abandon
And they ravaged and he came
To the white stone

And he kissed the field's grass
And he lay in abandon.
"I forget if she was
Or he was the stone
Or if it was the animals,"
And, "Everything comes soon."

Ma Provence

En ma Provence le blé est toujours vert
Et les filles sont jolies
Elles ne meurent pas elles vous aiment à la folie—en ma Provence.

Bills break the breakfast teacups and the sun
Shines darkly over the bill-ware.
She writes it out in enervating prose
"In my Provence, my rose."

The Brassiere Factory

Is the governor falling
From a great height?
Arm in arm we fled the brassiere factory,
The motion-boat stayed on the shore!
I saw how round its bottom was
As you walked into southern France—
Upon the light hair of an arm
Cigar bands lay!
I kissed you then. Oh is my bar
The insect of your will? The water rose,
But will the buffalo on
The nickel yet be still?
For how can windows hold out the light
In your eyes!
Darling, we fled the brassiere factory
In forty-eight states,
Arm in arm,
When human beings hung on us
And you had been arrested by the cloths
Were used in making, and I said, "The Goths
Know such delight," but still we fled, away
Into a dinner atmosphere
From all we knew, and fall asleep this day.
O maintenance men, with cruel eyes,
Then arm in arm we fled the listless factory!
The music changed your fingers' ends to pearl,
I punched you, you foolish girl,
For thanks to the metronome we got out alive, in the air
Where the sun filled us with cruelty!
There's what to do
Except despair, like pages! and laugh
Like prawns, about the sea!
Oh arm in arm we fled the industry
Into an earth of banks
And foolish tanks, for what bare breasts might be.

Summery Weather

One earring's smile
Near the drawer
And at night we gambling
At that night the yacht on Venice
Glorious too, oh my heavens
See how her blouse was starched up.
"The stars reminded me of youse."
"His lip sticks out. His eye is sailing.
I don't care what happens
Now," she says,
"After those winters in Florida!"
As for a pure dance
With oranges,
"All my factories
Need refilling,"
The corpse said, falling down between them.
"Okay okay
Here's a banana and a bandana
The light on a bright night,
With which, to finish, my personal challenge."
Oh how she admired him!
Lovely are fireworks;
Given, the shirts have a sale
To themselves; but
The wind is blowing, blowing!

Sun Out

Bananas, piers, limericks!
I am postures
Over there, I, are
The lakes of delectation
Sea, sea you! Mars and win–
Some buffalo
They thinly raft the plain,
Common do

It ice-floes, hit-and-run drivers,
The mass of the wind.
Is that snow
H-ing at the door? And we
Come in the buckle, a
Vanquished distinguished
Secret festival, relieving flights
Of the black brave ocean.

Your Fun is a Snob

Amnesty store by the facing machine
In the winter of glove
Raiding Western minutes
She spoke low, as a dram,
"On the hinge of a dainty glue
Hundred daisy become a fox
Listen, to what these pin-stripes bore
A sin from firewood, up this day
Stump, wheat, end! at my mule team passes
In with love Death Valley."
Through, goodbye mainland!
"These tears, I'm stacking way,"
She whirling smiled, "goodbye," is the plan
Of aspen, rain-tinned sunlight, on, "ahem!"

In the next minute the feature is oh
I am backing, science
Halve the apple, plates, come too.
She is reading in her silk stocking,
La la: "I've got a famous apartment
In cooking. Religion
In the worst ways, that leaves to the basement,
What I know
The hand-made height is made you
Is fun, but your fun is a snob."
Agrees, to walk out, illness, the wax taxis,
Reading, "Hopeless mints of lead. . . ." So her
Shy lends night, a helpless manner
Without, in leaflets, to within, often "we're," the crib.

Where Am I Kenneth?

1

Nail Kenneth down
For I fear the crying bloomers
Of a gnome race
They come yessing among the trees
Like your Boston survivor
Nail Kenneth down

Pick Kenneth up
For it is necessary that the sun
Will be a comb of the blue trees
And there's no cough to race
The tumbling seething jenny
Pick him up, put him to work

Amid the freed trees. Is this Boston?
Look around you. Am I Kenneth?
"The changing sighs of her disgust,"
A young man said, "am blue-kneed dust."
Kenneth waddled into a store and said
"Pick me up," and said "Apples, down."

2

Beyond the costly mountains
Some pills are going to sleep
Frank will cover them with blinding bloomers
Janice appears from multiple nowhere
The sun was a hot disk
How do you spell "dish"?

"The young Ann falls off lie zoom
January ends a room
I am afraid life in a tomb,"
Shouted to dusk.
The Doc comes in. "Hi, disk."
"Halo Kenneth, the sunlight is a factory."

Nail Kenneth down
For I fear the shades have gone to sleep
Throw the windows, and hey!
Grace comes, it is a rabbit
A rabbit discovers the triumph's lips
And a tuneless campus is deader than ships,

3

With the object of a displaced foot.
Kenneth is reading a novel
Nail us down
Skip the air
The sea is a ship,
And yet a ship of consultation!

So hail the worlds down, but lead in the air!

(Blue is the air above concentric Lambeth.)

Pericles

SCENE 1

FRIEND
I stop and go, Pericles.

PERICLES
Because we have come to find this land

FRIEND
In the midst of truth,
climates, guitars

PERICLES
This breeze is smaller than my mouth.

FRIEND
O Pericles
what is a leader?

PERICLES
How we have grown, dears, since we've
been from Greece!

FRIEND
How tall a music

PERICLES
Lies wasting on the shore.

SCENE 2

ANOTHER MAN
Here I sit.

SCENE 3

A WOMAN

Not that the gnat of smallness itself
has anything to offer the beach
with and through, without our tears
as if some tea had raised a blind
into the concussion of nonsense,
and a coughing death.

In Athens I saw twenty-nine old people
and the sidewalk was faery.
Oh everywhere the rats struck down ribbons,
heaven. A slave-ship hides my ears.

O friends
amid the fornication of signposts
I saw a new Greece
arise!

SCENE 4

FRIEND

You know. And yet
he is bothered by the misery of pebbles
which hat the lovely show
in which he dies and does appear.
He: "Take me back to the faucets
of truth; my mind is a mass."

PERICLES

Here is freshness and the shore's timeless teeth!

SCENE 5

FRIEND

There's no midnight mystery
and no coconuts here to see,
nothing but the ocean's sea
which will wash history's tattoos from me;
I hope to live satisfactorily
like a capon that's struck by a tree
and does die gladly
bereft, O large, of his sexuality.
Oh as honey fills the bee
while the waves' orchestra's business spree
sticks its night in your head like a country,
and as the madman throws the flea
to music, helplessly,
here always shall I be
and not in idolatry,
but yet superfluous as a ski
in a barge; while the withered air
reduces baneful boughs to everywhere.

PERICLES

Goodnight, the parachutes have gone to sleep.

FRIEND

I stop and go, Pericles.

SCENE 6

PERICLES

The air is Chinese!
I felt so strange
the day after tomorrow.
The stops have been removed
and the bottle is filled with leeks.
In the forest a sparring partner

whispers, "We grow."
O maidenhead of today
O maidenhead of yesterday

FRIEND

My lord, I found this face in the sand.

PERICLES

Drop it!

FACE OF ANOTHER MAN

Help!

CURTAIN

EPILOGUE

(Spoken by the conductor of the orchestra)

And would it not have been too late
The gas goes on the gas goes off
And we stood there with pure roots
In silence in violence one two one two
Will you please go through that again
The organ's orgasm and the aspirin tablet's speechless spasm.

From When the Sun Tries to Go On

And, with a shout, collecting coat-hangers
Dour rebus, conch, hip,
Ham, the autumn day, oh how genuine!
Literary frog, catch-all boxer, O
Real! The magistrate, say "group," bower, undies
Disk, poop, "Timon of Athens." When
The bugle shimmies, how glove towns!
It's Merrimac, bends, and pure gymnasium
Impy keels! The earth desks, madmen
Impose a shy (oops) broken tube's child—
Land! why are your bandleaders troops
Of is? Honk, can the mailed rose
Gesticulate? Arm the paper arm!
Bind up the chow in its lintel of sniff.
Rush the pilgrims, destroy tobacco, pool
The dirty beautiful jingling pyjamas, at
Last beside the stove-drum-preventing oyster,
The "Caesar" of tower dins, the cold's "I'm
A dear." O bed, at which I used to sneer at.
Bringing cloth. O song, "Dusted Hoops!" He gave
A dish of. The bear, that sound of pins. O French
Ice-cream! balconies of deserted snuff! The hills are
Very underwear, and near "to be"
An angel is shouting, "Wilder baskets!"

For, yes! he helped me collect our bathers
At the white Europe of an unchanged door
Sea, the pun of "chair"
Lowing the flight-seducing moderate
Can. Treat. Hat-waitress city of water
The in-person tunes, drum flossy childhood
Banana-ing the change-murals off winter
Shy. Hay when when shy. Sick murals. Each
In call tone returns his famous cigarette
In labels the Easter cow stubbed man
Is winter the water treats its gusts, we

Love, up! sigh there is a daw truth, the
Manner singing, "Doe, O flight of pets
And hen of the angel!" black sobs to your poets.
Soda, as Wednesday of the east
Vanishing "Rob him
Of the potato's fast guarantee, court
Of Copernican season planes! O bland
Holly!" The breathing semblance of batteries
To five youth-artists . . . "Is it this inspired
That he runs the tree of bather? Watchman?
Glue." It is, fashion, they have up timidity
South, and the lain thorn, too. A lover's decency
In, bank! We: four: "Paint was everyone's top!"

Bomb, thank you for writing to me.
Oat sad, it was a day of cursing blue
Fish, they reunited so the umpire to finish
The exhaustion of the Packard and tarantula
Parallel excursion. O black black black black back,
Under the tea, how a lid's munificent rotation
Is that, he cries "The daffodil, tire, say-so,"
O manufacture-clams building! Some days are
A fox of coolness and crime. Blot! Blot!
The wind, daisy, O "Call me up, I am
Listing beneath the telephone bat, hum
Hum, death and resurrection," what hay ballpark
To forward the punch-mints! O hat theory
Of the definite babies and series of spring
Fearing the cow of day admonished tears
That sigh, "Blue check. The tan of free councils
Cloaks the earth is hen blonde, oh want
The dye-bakers' coke and hilly plaza, too
Sunny, bee when halls key tuba plaza corroboration
Mat nickels." O tell us the correction, bay
Ex-table, my cocoa-million dollars! Next
To. O dare, dare-pullman car! The best way
You howling confetti, is "Easter tray,
As moat-line, promise." How teach the larks!

And, dame! kong swimming with my bets,
Aladdin, business, out Chanukah of May bust
Sit rumours of aethereal business coo-hill-green
Diamonds, moderns modesty. "There sit
The true the two hens of out-we-do maiden
Monastery belongs to (as! of!) can tin up off cities
Ware fizzle dazzle clothes belong (hand) the hearse
Walls bee bleed, pond ancient youth!" Who're
The den from coffee hanky hofbrau, at
Hint-magistrate. O bursar, off
Dollar rainwear, the itch; majesty summer that
Cough lady climate. Magisterial dandy. Apes. Ducks.
"Wanting, Satan, to mark glow-Virginia
A stair, this doe, Virginia. The sea cots
Magisterial lent 'who're' dodos. Aga Khan!
Mutt! the saint of perfect 'more oh' limpidity
Sand, 'bower,' hot, lens, O jetties
And sun-rows, calming the Endymion, fair, peaches'
Aspirin" hare, "lewd 'ain't him' summer hat hit
Dulls." They are bottles looser than, pow! hair
Open-necked Kokoschka, leaf, deers, and.
Ashes. Lights. Who bouquet of till stomach
Lama-periwinkle, engine! as under the
Lore "happy mew" inventive "haven't" stalls sprint.

"O goddess handkerchief quartette and the pyramids
How uncommon is your silence amid the pimples
Of today where a skirt pencils your dismay
To the blankets of seemly wind, log-rolling
Foolishly the polka-dots of this purged atmosphere
From everywhere, darling time-limits! she-planes, and
Pear-planes! O closet of devoted airplanes
How dismissed the reciprocating Congo has to seem
Amid these pans! Ha ha they are the pyramid
Of my strings' dorothy weak hell of youth
Mango, cob, district, lode, shimmy, charmed banks
On a bin of streets." Is Moscow walk,
O lacks? I noticed you on an
Unbearably fast pullman train, you
Muttered, "India," and bicycles parked in snow

Near the pancake's face, graceless perimeter
Of Count "Blotter," and Prince "Dit-
To," O "O pray"-rhyming cow-manufacturer,
Began to wear, science and youth, oh
A pin's aspect, "The Merchant of Venice." O sods
Of the blameless Atlantic! O murder of the tools
The cosmopolitan lint. Now. Rose bastardy
Millions and millions. She lends me the
Militia of. Bent cow pastures cough grape lights.

A horse is waiting for the submarine's
Feathery balcony. The hollow castle, like a boat
Filled with silliness, is more sand than flag, its
Loose earl phones, I am dedicating this stanza to you
Marching prince of hacienda quoits. In each bank
An October of pitiful sand is going to be hidden,
Like the mid-afternoon quietude of the elephant
Who wishes to be indentured, the foolish cosmos
Of the conch for a "soon patter" 's ear life, lad
Of penny, ear, and dock roses, and went to
Ran, sheep, kindness! O black kindness of the hot
Bugle sea-pal ditch-mite hem-location of
Pre-glove. Each birthday momentous peach stanza
Its bother. Lama lama lama lama lama, D,
A, B, O, F, C. Guns
Of pill-will! Lint! Where it shows sane
Cat air bench, yas, dash, hoop, "Hamlet"
Of dirty cow-epigram refills, O why are we here?
Bench, dirt, majesty, science, flu, pier,
Sin of "at"s, boo, billboard's ragged canto
Ocean, bitch! "Lousy mineral that makes me shy
Of steering hot flags, mud, who, tin, blue
E calm April hat sky." Hour of. The. Hour
Bong! spins of denying catechisms, Persian pins!

Guinevere or *The Death of the Kangaroo*

(A street, a plaza.)

GUINEVERE
Oh solids!

GIRAFFE *(moving along the sidewalk):*
Yes, and you know, last evening there were junctures of drunken breath's
dear pink flowers on my lariat. He put around me. They said,
"Denmark and the vitrines! nameless one!"

WEISSER ELEFANT *(crossing the street toward the GIRAFFE at right angles):*
I remember.

GUINEVERE *(sings):*
With soles on her shoes,
She takes the gyroscope
Between her fingers,
And, quietly, it spins.

KANGAROO *(waiting at point where the paths of the GIRAFFE and*
WEISSER ELEFANT *cross):*
The. O the the. The. I gave the pillow a cussing sandwich. America said,
"A tree." The manager lay dead. Cuff links.

GIRAFFE *(pausing):*
Listen. Do you remember when Chicago was only fingertips?

ALL *(sing):*
Though circumstances may collect our iced man!

MAN *(who enters):*
Unpin these benches that you may descry
The leafs beneath them. Lovers know my voice
As that which is or was most at the docks

Before they stopped shipping roses to say "vivre,"
O macadam. A child sicklier than restaurant
Waits for the marrying blue of a stiff morning.
We seem to go to run about in a stiff roustabout,
Cuter is the pear of string. Common last touch
Is to die at the nest. Roommate, charm bracelet,
Oh I swear, this is Mexico City.

CHIEFTAIN:

He is falling toward me like the charm bracelet
I saw laughing out of the window. At this minute a giraffe
Knows the cow who is offering night my atlas.
The wind, curving from Chinese charm bracelet
To charm bracelet, seems to counsel me, "Dollars,
Feenamint, dollars, gunsmoke." After one night
With Dolores, I visited the Huguenot people.

CAPTAIN:

Anchors aweigh!

> (*The plaza with all its occupants floats away;* VENUS *rises from the waves*).

VENUS:

Listen. Listen to the bouquet.
Baby, that placing powder in the pistols,
Married, and placing pistols in the bouquet,
Left me to be long ago at this moment,
Lively, the goddess, a headache. A market
Of fleas!

> (*It is Paris*, a place. VENUS *disappears.*)

FIRST FLEA:

Let go of my left elbow.

SECOND FLEA:

That's your pot belly!

A PINK GIRL:

I chanced to find these two
Arguing. There were sadly smoke,

Giant cow-guns, shoguns; and, it appears,
A glass page blonder as a neck of blue jeers.

GIRAFFE & VENUS *(entering together):*
Aren't we a stray couple
From No Land? Oh when
Will catching diseases fly in our plane?

PILOT:
Never! Take everyone a box.

(He passes out little boxes, which, when they are opened, reveal white pieces of paper.)

WEISSER ELEFANT *(reads):*
"The bench you are sitting on is made of orange boa constrictors which have been treated with piratical chocolate Georgia-bannisters. The Maryland of your face. Despite what you have been, ho ho, the incinerator is not a call-girl. Depart before the ice cream melts." Mine is about food!

GUINEVERE *(throwing herself on* WEISSER ELEFANT *):*
O my lover, my lover!

PILOT:
Wait a minute. Read yours.

GUINEVERE *(gazes into* VENUS'S *face):*
"Your head may be paralyzed by lint." Orchids! buzz saws!

ORCHIDS:
This is not blood. This is an orchard.
Through which you may walk. Like a bug.

BUZZ SAW:
Everybody: one, two three!
Plywood!
Goldsmith!
Sun glasses!

(The plaza splits in two like an orange. WEISSER ELEFANT *eats one half of it. On the other half,* GUINEVERE *is playing a guitar to*

the KANGAROO, *and playing cards are falling from his pocket. In the slight breeze one can just make out the chorus of neckties. It seems as if the Old World had become the New. A* MOUSE *enjoys this séance.)*

MOUSE:
God plays the guitar
And Religion listens.
The weary squash
Lurks beside the lotus.
See! the glass buildings
Decide nothing.
We are the sobbing world,
Just as they are in the nude.

GUINEVERE *(very loud):*
Photomatic bad living
Gigantic prisms. Beaued. Gee. Leaves!

KANGAROO *(softly):*
Pretty Geneva, pretty Southland, beloved orchestra!

GUINEVERE:
I am pink in the nude.

KANGAROO:
Yes yes.

GUINEVERE:
O Joy!

KANGAROO:
Listen. Baccalaureate. Is that
Prometheus?

MAN *(he is wearing a large mouse head, and plays the guitar):*
Only the bathroom knees would care
And the table of good red air
Seriously affronts the car
With the yellow daffodils of today.
Somnolent I see an amethyst

Clearing the way for future
Eons, the ragged hoop
And the dippy Fragonard of fluffier days,
Played to the tune of our pablum violin.

GUINEVERE *(throws herself, kissing, against a statue):*
O you, concede that I am the airport!

MAN WITH MOUSE HEAD:
America is like an elephant whose baseballs
Are boundaries
Of sunlight. *This* is peppermint,
That billiard shore. Now she gets,
Like horror, the main idea, a stove that is
Brilliant as the curling raspberries and move to his heart.
O olives, I know your reputation for fairness,
And every pipe dreams of a shirtwaisted kimono
Beyond the callow limousine of the funnies; but Nugent
Drank the coca-cola, and Allen left the boudoir
Where Jane lay thrown like a saint, the music of a thumb
Daring the elate, childless strings.
O mothers, weevil, market-place of the Sixties,
What is the road to Gary, China?

GUINEVERE:
Should industry delay,
Or mice parade? Is that a youth group
Signing: "Daft, weird, kind pennons,
Yo-yos and hills, shirts and displays"?

MAN WITH MOUSE HEAD:
O Germany of sofas,
Are we so clear
As beer is harmless?

GIRAFFE:
A shoplifting land of railroad pajamas
Passed my door, evil filmstars.
Huguenot! evil girls of filmstar plantation!

HIPPO:

 Yes because we meant to spend the summer;
 But now we see the human element
 Is merely a white bear, tipping stars
 By the briefcase of a violet hand
 Meant to inform and believe concatenated
 The surface of a wheel-lake, or "morgen"
 Meaning "morning" in German. Yes I meant
 To thumb a ride along the Champs Elysées,
 But the sunny stars.
 Bid for the swinging of my door, and lo! I lay,
 The Hippopotamus, sweating as if funny
 Water may come true even in the summertime And—

   (Bang! The HIPPO falls dead.)

SOMEONE:

 Pure Pins the lobster!

   (YELLOWMAY comes in and takes off all Guinevere's clothes;
   GUINEVERE puts her clothes back on.)

GUINEVERE:

 The shortest way to go home yesterday
 He always called the best way.
 There's no suffering in a limeade
 Of clearer captains, carpenters, and shipwrights
 From brains solidly
 In the pier. O the white shore, the red sea—

   (YELLOWMAY takes her hand; they walk along the seashore.)

YELLOWMAY:

 And the works of pineapple.
 I have often been a shipmaster
 But never a ship. The blow from Tangiers
 Never came.

GUINEVERE:

 Soldiers waiting at my hammock

Counseled me, "Be as back as soot."
Oh nuts, the chairs have gone away.

YELLOWMAY:

Paintings of the sea, I won't reveal to you my name is Yellowmay.

MAN *(without mouse head):*

Or the lobster
That oval
Which I often noticed.
I think,
"Is this a cigar
Or, baby! maybe
The license for a white cigarette,
Given by the shields."
And when the frog becomes a bicycle,
Dear days of pineapple,
Lilac where the giant ripple
Rushes, as past a kangaroo.

KANGAROO:

O mournful existence within the matchbox
With a sullen cockatoo
Whose brain beats its own division
And dandy "wawa"—

OCEAN:

Oh Sweden is endless! the earliest time to drink.

YELLOWMAY:

Are we drinking in chairs like a column!

GUINEVERE:

Oh yes, master. Come jinx with the merry columbine!

> *(Suddenly it is spring. The* HIPPO *appears,* solus, *covered with garlands of flowers.)*

HIPPO:

Decency of printemps O

Knocks on my pillow!
Houses without a door!
Suitcases which miss my sleeves!
O bears, you too, on the misty shore
Of the sea, in whose elbows
I hear a moth beginning
To mourn on a blue, beautiful violin.

> *(The* SKY *descends, covering all with blue; from the empty stage comes a song.)*

VOICE FROM EMPTY STAGE:
Who cares about them
In a grouping again
Or the poking amethyst
And delicious anthem?
The bread in the butter box
And a dictionary—
The day fears to tell me
Of white screams. Oh, don't you know it,
The marriage of blue
Bells, America, generous, as white screens
Failing, the magazine basement
Of archways. Water
The generous magazines!

Summery blue daylight,
The manner of machines,
Daguerrotype, cigarette store.

> *(The dead body of the* KANGAROO *is dragged across the stage by a two-horse cart.)*

En l'an trentiesme de mon eage

O red-hot cupboards and burning pavements, alas it's summer; my cheeks
    fall into somewhere and alas for the Rainbow Club.
Flowery pins bluejay introspection anagrams. On this day I complete my
    twenty-ninth year! I remember the lovely margarine
And the ack-ack of the Chinese discomfortable anti-aircraft bullets shouting
    into the clay weather like a beachball in *Terry and the Pirates,*
A canoe in shorts, or a laughing raincoat of Bessemer steel. What lightness it
    is to be still
Here, among the orange living, like a spine faculty in the harvest diversity
    cup, a red Chinese giraffe that imitates a rose
Like a lover of steel mittens in collarbone harness time, blimp-lovely, and
    hooky-players in the green shark
Museum, the sand everywhere around, forming a coat for the naked pencils;
    the last laugh is on me, says air—
O spring! no, summer! O winter!

The coconut magistrate adopted my little sister, "Cousin."
She had always wear a green sweater and toy play in the sybaritic air.
I am trying to clean up the loft, so that if you will please remove
The red hayloft from the lost, I can do it a lot easier, with blue air
And red seagulls and green crashes. "Cousin" was put among the simple
    cases,
And when she came to see me (that was during my sixteenth summer) I said,
Cousin are you glad to be home? and she handed me a lime swimmer.
Boys often ask me my advice on how they can become more sensitive
To orange wagons sunning themselves beside green curbstones, but
    "Cousin" said,
Take this lime advance. Shoebox. We are swimming toward a coffee aspirin
    tablet.
I didn't know what it meant at the time; and when "Cousin" was packed
    away
With the other Christmas ornaments, she asked me once more, California
    lime Swinburne?

But mother and I laughed at her little cookies, and went home. What does it
   mean?
"Chorusgirl" was the name of a dog I had aged seven. I kept him until I was
   nineteen. In nineteen forty-four he reappeared as an ancient cook. But
   one could see the laughing young eyes beneath her (his) grey hair.
And then I touched Coffee Silverware in the Park on her lime-colored
   shoulder, and we kissed
After eating close to a million hamburgers, and drinking bourbon out of little
   hollow glass trees.
That was the advantage of living close to Kentucky! The sedge laboratories
   closed down over New Year's
Day, so Kent and I had to search the barnyard for a light blue accident
Machine; he went to Texas in the same year and founded a shortage hospital
Of pure ice, toward which lovely secret purple ladders fell. I sandwiched
In seeing him while I was canoeing through there in the army. Our
Regimental insignia was an ordinary, clean polar bear looking at the sun
As if he were surprised to be in a war. . . . To not hear coconut music
Was all right, but once I did. . . . ! O dreams! O nostalgia! A campus of
   cotton roses to detach my wristwatch
Was my dream, and matchsticks the color of yellow real estate, with white
   bearskin gloves
To hold a pink apple! It took place on a bed in New York, a rich
   neighborhood, O coffee-covered sentimentality!

What is your knowledge of the novel? is it happy? are you trying to cover up
   for the green ants? When will the popcorn graduate? The peach's
   mother and father came down to the wedding in fuzz.
Grasping for the boat-rail I inquired after "Cousin," and was showered with
   green lemons. I didn't know you were in love with her! I said to
   Raspberry Corpuscle. He shoved me out into the water.
Amid this blue clothing was I dying or living? how old was I? I had not yet
   published "Fuel Bedrooms," so let me see. . . . Nancy's hands were
   covered with glass sandwiches. She offered me seventeen. I said,
   They're green! She said, Gondolier!
The towers fell down. Mr. Howard, Mrs. Raspberry. Rosemary
   Character Study was holding the candy door wide open
   for me. . . .

Clean up the happy boats, my son, for we're going to take a vacation
    manuscript. Doctor "Raspberries" to tell me I'm crazy still in the future
    like a white plywood
Airplane. But Jane bought paints! We fractured the coffin-balloon. She wore
    a redbird hat. Alice favored the Cubs. Together they fought with tinfoil
    spoons. A glass of beer-water please!

September. The red photograph-milkmen's clay hods
Plant sybaritic green clay roses through the center of Cow
Museum. "Peanut" arrives in a fur coat. Some more clay?
No thank you, I have to miss the detestable passenger plane
Of agoraphobic candy, which thousands consider a Mississippi
Hairline. Isn't it customary to Presbyterian Hospital? Larks in a motor.
Water, water, water! Heavenly December. O my sovereign, the railroad
    illness!
Aerate the detached choochoo! The leaves fell, greener than grass-
Colored leather. Can I sell you the wheels, sweet European doctor?

Argentine. Italy. Cairo. Myopia. The Last Supper. My twenty-sixth birthday.

Nudity Silex Kleenex bells June The Empire State Building.
Do you remember France? Can ants be a peasant? When did the daughter of
    Wendell Willkie walk like green lipstick toward the frogs?
Oh why is the weather no signal of gloom, sweet February twenty-seventh?
    The restaurant would not serve licorice, you remember,
To persons under the age of five, and still I love news! Sweet music of
    cement,
Am I a has-been? What? The water is feeling very pretty and green. The
    gunpowder is coughing beside the submarine archway
Of my twenty-ninth birthday, sealion, cloudburst November! Did the
    bullfrog say he had something he wants to celebrate? Well, come on!
We can't stand here forever smoking bumblebee cigarettes!

Desire for Spring

Calcium days, days when we feed our bones!
Iron days, which enrich our blood!
Saltwater days, which give us valuable iodine!
When will there be a perfectly ordinary spring day?
For my heart needs to be fed, not my urine
Or my brain, and I wish to leap to Pittsburgh
From Tuskegee, Indiana, if necessary, spreading like a flower
In the spring light, and growing like a silver stair.
Nothing else will satisfy me, not even death!
Not even broken life insurance policies, cancer, loss of health,
Ruined furniture, prostate disease, headaches, melancholia,
No, not even a ravaging wolf eating up my flesh!
I want spring, I want to turn like a mobile
In a new fresh air! I don't want to hibernate
Between walls, between halls! I want to bear
My share of the anguish of being succinctly here!
Not even moths in the spell of the flame
Can want it to be warmer so much as I do!
Not even the pilot slipping into the great green sea
In flames can want less to be turned to an icicle!
Though admiring the icicle's cunning, how shall I be satisfied
With artificial daisies and roses, and wax pears?
O breeze, my lovely, come in, that I mayn't be stultified!
Dear coolness of heaven, come swiftly and sit in my chairs!

To You

I love you as a sheriff searches for a walnut
That will solve a murder case unsolved for years
Because the murderer left it in the snow beside a window
Through which he saw her head, connecting with
Her shoulders by a neck, and laid a red
Roof in her heart. For this we live a thousand years;
For this we love, and we live because we love, we are not
Inside a bottle, thank goodness! I love you as a
Kid searches for a goat; I am crazier than shirt-tails
In the wind, when you're near, a wind that blows from
The big blue sea, so shiny so deep and so unlike us;
I think I am bicycling across an Africa of green and white fields
Always, to be near you, even in my heart
When I'm awake, which swims, and also I believe that you
Are trustworthy as the sidewalk which leads me to
The place where I again think of you, a new
Harmony of thoughts! I love you as the sunlight leads the prow
Of a ship which sails
From Hartford to Miami, and I love you
Best at dawn, when even before I am awake the sun
Receives me in the questions which you always pose.

In Love with You

I

O what a physical effect it has on me
To dive forever into the light blue sea
Of your acquaintance! Ah, but dearest friends,
Like forms, are finished, as life has ends! Still,
It is beautiful, when October
Is over, and February is over,
To sit in the starch of my shirt, and to dream of your sweet
Ways! As if the world were a taxi, you enter it, then
Reply (to no one), "Let's go five or six blocks."
Isn't the blue stream that runs past you a translation from the Russian?
Aren't my eyes bigger than love?
Isn't this history, and aren't we a couple of ruins?
Is Carthage Pompeii? is the pillow the bed? is the sun
What glues our heads together? O midnight! O midnight!
Is love what we are,
Or has happiness come to me in a private car
That's so very small I'm amazed to see it there?

2

We walk through the park in the sun, and you say, "There's a spider
Of shadow touching the bench, when morning's begun." I love you.
I love you fame I love you raining sun I love you cigarettes I love you love
I love you daggers I love smiles daggers and symbolism.

3

Inside the symposium of your sweetest look's
Sunflower awning by the nurse-faced chrysanthemums childhood
Again represents a summer spent sticking knives into porcelain
    raspberries, when China's
Still a country! Oh, King Edward abdicated years later, that's
Exactly when. If you were seventy thousand years old, and I were a pill,
I know I could cure your headache, like playing baseball in drinking
    water, as baskets
Of towels sweetly touch the bathroom floor! O benches of nothing
Appear and reappear—electricity! I'd love to be how
You are, as if
The world were new, and the selves were blue
Which we don
When it's dawn,
Until evening puts on
The gray hooded selves and the light brown selves of . . .
Water! your tear-colored nail polish
Kisses me! and the lumberyard seems new
As a calm
On the sea, where, like pigeons,
I feel so mutated, sad, so breezed, so revivified, and still so unabdicated—
Not like an edge of land coming over the sea!

West Wind

It's the ocean of western steel
Bugles that makes me want to listen
To the parting of the trees
Like intemperate smiles, in a
Storm coat evangelistically ground
Out of spun glass and silver threads
When stars are in my head, and we
Are apart and together, friend of my youth
Whom I've so recently met—a fragment of the universe
In our coats, a believable doubling
Of the fresh currents of doubt and
Thought! a winter climate
Found in the Southern Hemisphere and where
I am who offers you to wear,
And in this storm, along the tooth of the street,
The intemperate climate of this double frame of the universe.

Spring

Let's take a walk
In the city
Till our shoes get wet
(It's been raining
All night) and when
We see the traffic
Lights and the moon
Let's take a smile
Off the ashcan, let's walk
Into town (I mean
A lemon peel)

Let's make music
(I hear the cats
Purply beautiful
Like hallways in summer
Made of snowing rubber
Valence piccalilli and diamonds)
Oh see the arch ruby
Of this late March sky
Are you less intelligent
Than the pirate of lemons
Let's take a walk

I know you tonight
As I have never known
A book of white stones
Or a bookcase of orange groans
Or symbolism
I think I'm in love
With those imaginary racetracks
Of red traced grey in
The sky and the gimcracks
Of all you know and love
Who once loathed firecrackers

And license plates and
Diamonds but now you love them all

And just for my sake
Let's take a walk
Into the river
(I can even do that
Tonight) where
If I kiss you please
Remember with your shoes off
You're so beautiful like
A lifted umbrella orange
And white we may never
Discover the blue over-
Coat maybe never never O blind
With this (love) let's walk
Into the first
Rivers of morning as you are seen
To be bathed in a light white light
Come on

Aus einer Kindheit

Is the basketball coach a homosexual lemon manufacturer? It is suspected by
   O'Ryan in his submarine.
When I was a child we always cried to be driven for a ride in that submarine.
   Daddy would say Yes!
Mommy would say No! The maid read *Anna Karenina* and told us secrets.
   Some suspected her of a liaison with O'Ryan. Nothing but squirrels
Seemed to be her interest, at the windows, except on holidays, like Easter and
   Thanksgiving, when
She would leave the basement and rave among the leaves, shouting, I am the
   Spirit of Softball! Come to me!
Daddy would always leave town. And a chorus of spiders
Would hang from my bedroom wall. Mommy had a hat made out of pasty
   hooks. She gave a party to limburger cheese.
We all were afraid that O'Ryan would come!
He came, he came! as the fall wind comes, waving and razing and swirling
   the leaves
With his bags, his moustache, his cigar, his golfball, his pencils, his April
   compasses, and over his whole
Body we children saw signs of life beneath the water! Oh!
Will he dance the hornpipe? we wondered, Will he smoke a cigar underneath
   eleven inches of ocean? Will he beat the pavement
Outside our door with his light feet, for being so firm? Is he a lemon
   Memnon?
O'Ryan O'Ryan O'Ryan! The maid came up from the basement, we were all
   astonished. And she said, "Is it Thanksgiving? Christmas? I felt
A force within me stir." And then she saw O'Ryan! The basketball coach
   followed her up from the cellar. He and O'Ryan fight!
No one is homosexual then! happily I swim through the bathtubs with my
   scarlet-haired sister
Z. ("O women I love you!" O'Ryan cried.) And we parked under water.
   Then, looking out the window,
We saw that snow had begun to fall, upon the green grass, and both shyly
   entered the new world of our bleached underwear. Rome! Rome!
Was our maid entertaining that limburger cheese, or my mother? has the
   passageway fallen asleep? and can one's actions for six years be called
   "improper"?

I hope not. I hope the sea. I hope cigars will be smoked. I hope it from New York to California. From Tallahassee to St. Paul.

I hope the orange punching bag will be socked, and that you'll be satisfied, sweet friend. I hope international matrimony, lambent skies, and "Ship, ahoy!"

For we're due to be dawned on, I guess.

Farm's Thoughts

Hay, passion stilled the
Cool and charming disk.
Straw, I know you think I'm rude
And yet it's true: the sun's wrong.
How sweetly the weeks turned
The whole month of September.
Do I believe in you?
Does the rye believe in you?
The sunlight will last all day.
Rye, I think you are mistaken
There. Straw, kiss me. Never, hay.
The sunlight may go wrong
And create a wilderness; a wilderness
Will never create hay. Back me up, then—
The elements create a waterfall.
With vim and vigor, straw,
To avoid being stern I'll
Catapult past the green fruit
Fallen beside honor's mesh. Fresh
Green lives seem to spawn there.
The sun shines down through
Violet-besprinkled fields;
Dawn acts with a club, and we agree on everything
Long beforehand. It's the dew, hay . . .

I am the horse, alive and everything.
On the merry-go-round I made you happy as anything.
In these harvest fields they kick my body like a plaything.

I am the panther, soda fountain of the zoo;
I will represent exoticism here on the farm with you.

I am the elephant, the last laugh of hips.
I land smiling from an Africa of ships.

Near the dirt door, on the road to the farmhouse,
Please pick me up, hold me in your hands, a chicken! not a mouse,

Not a chipmunk, not a lizard, not a cow . . .
Sherbet dreams of me in winter: dairy cow.

Mother farmhouse, residual axis,
Please hear the mushroom phantom sweet
Queer clear voice of the dog-sweets
Left abandoned by a rigorous monster after . . .

Let not civilization enter! Green, draw the curtain.

Morning sweetly shines down on us pigs.
In the afternoon when the rake separates
Diet from dust, the friendly germ will separate some of us
From each other, and heads will be laid in earth.
The best thing a pig can hope for is sun.
When, shyly, in the morning, heads come forth
From the sty, we believe in everything
The air sets forth—mud, green, and trees—if the sun is shining;
If not, then it's a day like any other, a finger stuck in the earth
Like smoke, and the cold breeze of the mud, the deadly hammer
Crashing our skulls for the unreciprocating worm.

In the headlands we heard a murmur. It was the goats! We, the goats,
Wish you, Barbara and Mitchell, a happy stay on the farm.
Drink plenty of goat's milk every morning
And you will grow big and strong
Like the clouds over Mount Sinai, when Moses stood there.
We goats know our Biblical history!
Here is a red-and-blue book in which you can read
About China, and the opera in the Romance countries. Be kind
To goats, and always remember to speak in the morning
Nicely to one another, so as not to ruin the day,
Which might otherwise be spent in cursing and thrashing
As the farmer sometimes does, your Uncle Peter;
Then he kicks tin cans and pulls the beards of us goats.
It is only our love of this environment which helps us to bear
Him. We've never been anyplace else. And we send you a
Kiss.

The horses are real, Mitchell! Oh, what fun we'll have!

Get those goddamn children out of the kitchen, Uncle Lillian,
Or I'll grind them up and feed them to the pigs!

The horror of night
Descends on the cottage,
And only the goat-hair
Is visible, gleaming in the starlight.
The hay is silent. The meadow is overturned,
And the green
Where the children play
Is also the pigs' thatched cottage
Where they roost
In peace and seem
To cry past the straw and the rye to abandoned goodness,
Which is really only another word for
Feathers . . .

    Hi! Kra! Kray! Croak!
Creek! Creek! Fresh water, bleep,
Another day. Haul off and chicken
Every chicken, to chicken chicken, sorrow-pigs!

Filmed in the morning I am
A pond. Dreamed of at night I am a silver
Pond. Who's wading through me? Ugh!

I love you, hay.

I love you, straw.

And so I am the sun.
Don't you wish it about everything?

The pavement that streams past you on the wall.
My laughter is inherited from you all.
The yellow leaves and the green ones know my will.

I am the barefoot hill.

Mitchell, we'll go barefoot.

Hurry into me, the sweet day.
O leaves, can't you find another environment?
Something befriends me and hurts
At the corners of each thing I love.

It looks beautiful out.

Well, to be honest, as the color green,
I can only gather it all in once more and then let it out; this shall be seen
At the end of your stay. Something grows up to become a concert,
And at last the world finds him, the color grey
Accedes to red; and at the lost inn, where many pigs
Have stayed, the doorknobs when they're blue are stones;
In the midst of yellow a word may drop
Which brings it orange.

I am the color blue, on a board in the room.

Bzz, buzz, what beautiful shirt-tails!

Oh how through the air my beloved Master Bee sails!

Geography

In the blue hubbub of the same-through-wealth sky
Amba grew to health and fifteenth year among the jungle scrubbery.
The hate-bird sang on a lower wing of the birch-nut tree
And Amba heard him sing, and in his health he too
Began to sing, but then stopped. Along the lower Congo
There are such high plants of what there is there, when
At morning Amba heard their pink music as gentlemanly
As if he had been in civilization. When morning stank
Over the ridge of coconuts and bald fronds, with agility
Amba climbed the permanent nut trees, and will often sing
To the shining birds, and the pets in their stealth
Are each other among, also, whether it be blue (thhhh) feathers
Or green slumber. Africa in Amba's mind was those white mornings he sang
(thhhh) high trala to the nougat birds, and after
The trenches had all been dug for the day, Amba
Would dream at the edge of some stained and stinking pond
Of the afternight music, as blue pets came to him in his dreams.
From the orange coconuts he would extract some stained milk,
Underneath his feet roots, tangled and filthy green. At night
The moon (zzzzzz) shining down on Amba's sweet mocked sleep.

2

In Chicago Louis walked the morning's rounds with agility.
A boy of seventeen and already recognized as a fast milkman!
The whizz and burr of dead chimes oppressed the
Holocaustic unison of Frank's brain, a young outlaw
Destined to meet dishonor and truth in a same instant,
Crossing Louis' path gently in the street, the great secret unknown.

3

The fur rhubarb did not please Daisy. "Freddie," she called,
"Our fruit's gang mouldy." Daisy, white cheeks with a spot of red
In them, like apples grown in paper bags, smiled
Gently at the fresh new kitchen; and, then, depressed,
She began to cover the rhubarb with her hands.

4

In the crushy green ice and snow Baba ran up and around with
    exuberance!
Today, no doubt, Father and Uncle Dad would come, and together they
    three would chase the whale!
Baba stared down through the green crusty ice at the world of fish
And closed his eyes and began to imagine the sweet trip
Over the musky waters, when Daddy would spear the whale, and the
    wind
Blow "Crad, crad!" through Uncle Dad's fur, and the sweet end
Of the day where they would smile at one another over the smoking
    blubber
And Uncle Dad would tell tales of his adventures past the shadow bar
Chasing the white snow-eagle. Baba ran
Into the perfect igloo screaming with impatience, and Malmal,
His mother, kissed him and dressed him with loving care for the icy
    trip.

5

Ten Ko sprinted over the rice paddies. Slush, slosh, sloosh!
His brother, Wan Kai, would soon be returned from the village
Where he had gone . . . (Blue desire! . . .)

6

Roon startled her parents by appearing perfectly dressed
In a little white collar and gown.
Angebor lifted himself up so he might stare in the window at the pretty girl.
His little hands unclenched and dropped the coins he had saved for the *oona*.
He opened wide his eyes, then blinked at the pretty girl. He had never
    seen anything like that.
That evening, when it whitened in the sky, and a green
Clearness was there, Maggia and Angebor had no *oona*.
But Angebor talked with excitement of what he had seen, and Maggia drank
    zee'th.

7

The little prisoner wept and wailed, telling of his life in the sand
And the burning sun over the desert. And one night it was cool
And dark, and he stole away over the green sand to search for his parents.
And he went to their tent, and they kissed him and covered him with
    loving-kindness.
And the new morning sun shone like a pink rose in the heavens,
And the family prayed, the desert wind scorching their cool skin.

8

Amba arose. Thhhhhhh! went the birds, and clink clank cleck went
The leaves under the monkeys' feet, and Amba went to search for water
Speaking quietly with his fresh voice as he went toward Gorilla Lake
To all the beasts. Wan Kai lifted his body from the rice mat
When his brother Ten Ko came running in. "They have agreed in the
    village,"
He said. Win Tei brought them tea. Outside the rain

Fell. Plop, plop. Daisy felt something stir inside her.
She went to the window and looked out at the snow. Louis came up the stairs
With the milk. "Roon has bronchitis," said the American doctor,
"She will have to stay inside for ten days during this rain." Amba
Sneaked away, and wanted to go there again, but Maggia said he could
       not go again in this rain
And would be sure to lose the money for the *oona*. Baba stared
At the green and black sea. Uncle Dad stood up in the boat, while Baba
Watched Father plunge his harpoon three times in the whale. Daisy turned
Dreamily around, her hand on her cheek. Frank's boot
Kicked in the door. Amba wept; Ahna the deer was dead; she lay amid
       her puzzled young.
The sweet forms of the apple blossoms bent down to Wehtukai.
The boat split. Sun streamed into the apartment. Amba, Amba!
The lake was covered with gloom. Enna plunged into it screaming.

The Circus

We will have to go away, said the girls in the circus
And never come back any more. There is not enough of an audience
In this little town. Waiting against the black, blue sky
The big circus chariots took them into their entrances.
The light rang out over the hill where the circus wagons dimmed away.
Underneath their dresses the circus girls were sweating,
But then, an orange tight sticking to her, one spoke with
Blue eyes, she was young and pretty, blonde
With bright eyes, and she spoke with her mouth open when she sneezed
Lightly against the backs of the other girls waiting in line
To clock the rope, or come spinning down with her teeth on the line,
And she said that the circus might leave—and red posters
Stuck to the outside of the wagon, it was beginning to
Rain—she said might leave but not her heart would ever leave
Not that town but just any one where they had been, risking their lives,
And that each place they were should be celebrated by blue rosemary
In a patch, in the town. But they laughed and said Sentimental
Blonde, and she laughed, and they all, circus girls, clinging
To each other as the circus wagons rushed through the night.

2

In the next wagon, the one forward of theirs, the next wagon
Was the elephants' wagon. A grey trunk dragged on the floor . . .

3

Orville the Midget tramped up and down. Paul the Separated Man
Leaped forward. It rained and rained. Some people in the cities
Where they passed through were sitting behind thick glass
Windows, talking about their brats and drinking chocolate syrup.

4

Minnie the Rabbit fingered her machine gun.
The bright day was golden.
She aimed the immense pine needle at the foxes
Thinking Now they will never hurt my tribe any more.

5

The circus wagons stopped during the night
For eighteen minutes in a little town called Rosebud, Nebraska.
It was after dinner it was after bedtime it was after nausea it was
After lunchroom. The girls came out and touched each other and had fun
And just had time to get a breath of the fresh air of the night in
Before the ungodly procession began once more down the purple
    highway.

6

With what pomp and ceremony the circus arrived orange and red in the
    dawn!
It was exhausted, cars and wagons, and it lay down and leaped
Forward a little bit, like a fox. Minnie the Rabbit shot a little woolen
    bullet at it,
And just then the elephant man came to his doorway in the sunlight and
    stood still.

7

The snoring circus master wakes up, he takes it on himself to arrange the
    circus.
Soon the big tent floats high. Birds sing on the tent.
The parade girls and the living statue girls and the trapeze girls
Cover their sweet young bodies with phosphorescent paint.
Some of the circus girls are older women, but each is beautiful.
They stand, waiting for their cues, at the doorway of the tent.
The sky-blue lion tamer comes in, and the red giraffe manager.

They are very brave and wistful, and they look at the girls.
Some of the circus girls feel a hot sweet longing in their bodies.
But now is it time for the elephants!
Slowly the giant beasts march in. Some of their legs are clothed in blue
    papier-mâché ruffles.
One has a red eye. The elephant man is at the peak of happiness.
He speaks, giddily, to every one of the circus people he passes,
He does not know what he is saying, he does not care—
His elephants are on display! They walk into the sandy ring . . .

8

Suddenly a great scream breaks out in the circus tent!
It is Aileen the trapeze artist, she has fallen into the dust and dirt
From so high! She must be dead! The stretcher bearers rush out,
They see her lovely human form clothed in red and white and orange
    wiry net,
And they see that she does not breathe any more.
The circus doctor leaves his tent, he runs out to care for Aileen.
He traverses the circus grounds and the dusty floor of the circus entrance,
    and he comes
Where she is, now she has begun to move again, she is not dead,
But the doctor tells her he does not know if she will ever be able to
    perform on the trapeze again,
And he sees the beautiful orange and red and white form shaken with sobs,
And he puts his hand on her forehead and tells her she must lie still.

9

The circus girls form a cortege, they stand in file in the yellow and
    white sunlight.
"What is death in the circus? That depends on if it is spring.
Then, if elephants are there, *mon père,* we are not completely lost.
Oh the sweet strong odor of beasts which laughs at decay!
Decay! decay! We are like the elements in a kaleidoscope

But such passions we feel! bigger than beaches and
Rustier than harpoons." After his speech the circus practitioner sat down.

I 0

Minnie the Rabbit felt the blood leaving her little body
As she lay in the snow, orange and red and white,
A beautiful design. The dog laughs, his tongue hangs out, he looks at the sky.
It is white. The master comes. He laughs. He picks up Minnie the Rabbit
And ties her to a pine tree bough, and leaves.

I I

Soon through the forest came the impassioned bumble bee.
He saw the white form on the bough. "Like rosebuds when you are
        thirteen," said Elmer.
Iris noticed that he didn't have any cap on.
"You must be polite when mother comes," she said.
The sky began to get grey, then the snow came.
The two tots pressed together. Elmer opened his mouth and let the snow
        fall in it. Iris felt warm and happy.

I 2

Bang! went the flyswatter. Mr. Watkins, the circus manager, looked
        around the room.
"Damn it, damn these flies!" he said. Mr. Loftus, the circus clerk, stared
        at the fly interior he had just exposed.
The circus doctor stood beside the lake. In his hand he had a black briefcase.
A wind ruffled the surface of the lake and slightly rocked the boats.

Red and green fish swam beneath the surface of the water.
The doctor went into the lunchroom and sat down. No, he said, he
        didn't care for anything to eat.
The soft wind of summer blew in the light green trees.

Collected Poems

BUFFALO DAYS

I was asleep when you waked up the buffalo.

THE ORANGE WIVES

A mountain of funny foam went past.

GREAT HUMAN VOICES

The starlit voices drip.

COLORFUL HOUR

A few green pencils in a born pocket.

EXPRESSION

New little tray.

SLEEP

The bantam hen frayed its passage through the soft clouds.

A MINERAL WICK

Town soda.

SOMEWHERE

Between islands and envy.

CECELIA

Look, a cat.

THE SILVER WORLD

Expands.

JEWELRY SEVENTHS

Minor wonders.

AN ESKIMO COCA COLA

Three-fifths.

THE EXCEPTION PROVES THE RULE

Eight-fifths.
Nine-fifths.
Three-fifths.
Six-fifths.

THE WATER HOSE IS ON FIRE

Grapeline.

THE LINGERING MATADORS

Eskimo City.

EGYPT

Passiveness.

IS THERE A HOUSE INSIDE THAT FUEL ENGINE?

Extra aging will bring your craft over against the rosy skies.

WHY WEREN'T THEY MORE CAREFUL?

Actions.

PEANUT BUTTER CANDY

Ichthious.

THE BRINDLE COWS

Dairy farm, dairy farm,
H-O-T
H-E-A-D.

IN THE MERRY FOAM

Ask them for the blue patience of lovers.

MY MIXUP

The cherries after a shower.

MILKWEED EMBLEMS

The chambered nautilus is weak.

SUPPOSE

Red and white riding hoods.

THE GREEN MEDDLER

Aged in the fire.

A HOUSE IN MISSISSIPPI

Who stole all my new sander supplies?

WICKED OBJECTS

Aeroliths.

FRESH LIMES

A couple's bedroom slippers.

THE WINDOW

The chimney.

PAINTED FOR A ROSE

The exacting pilgrims were delighted with yellow fatigue.

NOONS

Bubbles.

ROOMS

Simplex bumblebees.

IN THE RANCHHOUSE AT DAWN

O corpuscle!
O wax town!

THE OUTSIDES OF THINGS

The sky fold, and then the bus started up.

THE BLACK LION

Never stop revealing yourself.

IN THE COAL MUD

At breakfast we could sob.

THE HAND-PAINTED EARS OF DEATH

Oh look inside me.

ALABAMA

Alabama!

Pregnancy

Inside the pomegranate is the blue sky.

We have been living out the year in Wisconsin.
Sometimes it rains there—tremendous green drops!

We smiled up at the snow—how tremulously! Still . . .

Death is better . . .

The hog leafed through the almanac.

If there is a difference between fortune and misfortune
Which you do not catch immediately, just remember
The house of the orange and yellow squirrels, or the three pigs,
Any house which has easily distinguishable animals in it,
And remember that all animals are unfortunate.
"Yet every animal is fortunate," spoffed the mineral water
From its light green bottle on the Western tea leaves store shelf.
A bossy cow came and stood in the door;
Her hide was mangy. And then we saw the fire extinguisher. Man is unhappy!
A Western boy came and took the bossy cow away.
The Western boy was dressed in leather knickers, and his lean face was
        brown;
A smile played there as he looked at the sissy flowers
And led the bossy cow away to the range. In the cow's mind, pastures of
        green
Were replacing the brown architecture of the store.

Under the archways I could see the yellow pulverization
Of all you had meant to put into Paris—but they were a failure,
Your statues! your stores! and your triumphal arches!
You should have put in mere little shops selling dry goods and trumpets,

With here and there a tree and a necktie, the arch of someone's foot
Who turns out not to be beautiful, but extremely civilized, and a
     showerbath, which turns red
On certain nights, showering the green busses of my favorite city with
     cold blood! Oh ask me again
What you should do, and I will tell you differently! Ask me!

Shall any laundry be put out to dry
With so many yellow and orange sequins falling through the air?

Yes, the donkey has become very corpulent.

Will the blue carpet be sufficiently big to cover the tennis court?

Down the street walked a midget. "She's a good looker, hey?"
He said to a passer-by. O tremulous stomach!

We've been spending the winter in Paris . . .

It rains on the sweater . . .

I've a dog in my stomach!

The dogs moved delicately
On the yellow squares,
And if they sat down to play cards
Weren't they happier than we are?

I am at present owner
Of a great chain of dog-supply stores,
So naturally I hope that your child is a dog . . .

O son! or daughter!
Will you ever forgive
Your maddened daddy
For imagining a doggie
In place of a baby?

Out on the range
The blue sky is changing
To black, and the baby
Cows are rehearsing
Their lives by eating.

Near a blaze of straw
Sit the drooping cowhands;
One has on a red hat,
The other has a blue one.
They look at the babies and mothers.

Do you not think they are thinking
Thoughts like mine? O Paris,
France! with the coffee of your
Cafés, I feel life has arrived
For me! Where are you, city?

It rains on the dachshund
And the collie;
On the beach the red, green, and orange
Crustaceans are moved . . .
Tell me, sons of Atlantis, what will happen next?

Hearing

Hear the beautiful tinny voices of the trumpets
Beside the rushing sound of the great blue waterfall;
See the guns fire, then hear the leaves drop to the ground;
Lie back in your chair—and now there is the clatter of pennies!
The familiar scraping noise of the chair feet on the ground,
As if a worm had grown six feet tall! And here is the worm,
And hear his softly scraping noise at the forest gate.
In the Bourse the diamonds clink and clank against each other,
And the violet airplane speaks to the farmland with its buzz
From high in the air, but you hear the slice
Of shears and watch the happy gardener's face whiten
As he hears the final throbs of his failing heart.
All is not stillness—far from it. The tinny
Trumpets renew their song among the eglantine's
Too speciously gracious brilliance, and a hen drops
An egg, with infinite gentleness, into the straw.

Who is this young man with the tremendous French horn in the garden
With a lady in lilac bending her head to catch each note
That flows, serene and unbidden, from the silvery throat?
I think they are strangers here. Stones fall in the pool.
She smiles, she is very witty, she bends too far, and now we hear
The sound of her lilac dress ripping in the soft summer air.
For it is summer! Hear the cool rush of the stream and the heavy black
Vocalism of leaves in the wind. A note then comes, arises
In the air, it is a glass in which a few warm drops of rain
Make music; there are roars and meows, turkeys and spaniels
Come running to the great piano, which, covered with pearls,
Gives extra, clinking sounds to your delighted ears;
And the dogs bark, and there is the little thrilled silence of snails. . . .
Above all else you hear the daisies being torn apart
By tremendous bumblebees who have come here from another
        Department!
"Wisteria tapping the house, so comes your blood. . . ."

Now rain, now this earth streams with water!
Hear the tooting of Triton among the clouds
And on the earth! See the trumpets of heaven floating toward us
Blaring among the wet masses of citron and vermilion wings!
They play "Put down the cushion on the chair,
Put down the cushion on the chair, put down
The cushion, put it down, put the cushion down on the chair,
Ra ta ta. . . ." The young man's French horn is wet, it makes a different noise,
The girl turns her face toward him and he hears strings (it is another tear in
     her dress!).
In the kitchen the sound of raspberries being mashed in the cream
Reminds you of your childhood and all the fantasies you had then!
In the highest part of an oak tree is a blue bird
Trilling. A drying friend reads *Orlando Furioso*
Sitting on a beach chair; then you hear awnings being stretched out!
A basso sings, and a soprano answers him.
Then there is thunder in a clear blue sky,
And, from the earth, a sigh: "This song is finished."

The Artist

Ah, well, I abandon you, cherrywood smokestack,
Near the entrance to this old green park! . . .

* * *

Cherrywood avalanche, my statue of you
Is still standing in Toledo, Ohio.
O places, summer, boredom, the static of an acrobatic blue!

And I made an amazing zinc airliner
It is standing to this day in the Minneapolis zoo . . .

Old times are not so long ago, plaster of Paris haircut!

* * *

I often think *Play* was my best work.
It is an open field with a few boards in it.

Children are allowed to come and play in *Play*
By permission of the Cleveland Museum.
I look up at the white clouds, I wonder what I shall do, and smile.

Perhaps somebody will grow up having been influenced by *Play*,
I think—but what good will that do?
Meanwhile I am interested in steel cigarettes . . .

* * *

The orders are coming in thick and fast for steel cigarettes, steel cigars.
The Indianapolis Museum has requested six dozen packages.
I wonder if I'd still have the courage to do a thing like *Play?*

I think I may go to Cleveland . . .

* * *

Well, here I am! Pardon me, can you tell me how to get to the Cleveland
Museum's monumental area, *Play?*
"Mister, that was torn down a long time ago. You ought to go and see
the new thing they have now—*Gun.*"
What? *Play* torn down?
"Yes, Mister, and I loved to climb in it too, when I was a kid!" And he
shakes his head
Sadly . . . But I am thrilled beyond expectation!
He liked my work!
And I guess there must be others like that man in Cleveland too . . .

So you see, *Play* has really had its effect!
Now I am on the outskirts of town
And . . . here it is! But it has changed! There are some blue merds lying
in the field
And it's not marked *Play* anymore—and here's a calf!
I'm so happy, I can't tell why!
Was this how I originally imagined *Play,* but lacked the courage?

It would be hard now, though, to sell it to another museum.
I wonder if the man I met's children will come and play in it?
How does one's audience survive?

* * *

Pittsburgh, May 16th. I have abandoned the steel cigarettes. I am
working on *Bee.*
Bee will be a sixty-yards-long covering for the elevator shaft opening in
the foundry sub-basement
Near my home. So far it's white sailcloth with streams of golden paint
evenly spaced out
With a small blue pond at one end, and around it orange and green
flowers. My experience in Cleveland affected me so
That my throat aches whenever I am not working at full speed. I have
never been so happy and inspired and
Play seems to me now like a juvenile experience!

* * *

June 8th. *Bee* is still not finished. I have introduced a huge number of
   red balloons into it. How will it work?
Yesterday X. said, "Are you still working on *Bee?* What's happened to
   your interest in steel cigarettes?"
Y. said, "He hasn't been doing any work at all on them since he went to
   Cleveland." A shrewd guess! But how much can they possibly
   know?

*　*　*

November 19th. Disaster! *Bee* was almost completed, and now the
   immense central piece of sailcloth has torn. Impossible to repair
   it!

December 4th. I've gone back to work on *Bee!* I suddenly thought
   (after weeks of despair!), "I can place the balloons over the tear in
   the canvas!" So that is what I am doing. All promises to be well!

December 6th. The foreman of the foundry wants to look at my work.
   It seems that he too is an "artist"—does sketches and watercolors
   and such . . . What will he think of *Bee?*

*　*　*

Cherrywood! I had left you far from my home
And the foreman came to look at *Bee*
And the zinc airliner flew into *Play!*

The pink balloons aren't heavy, but the yellow ones break.
The foreman says, "It's the greatest thing I ever saw!"
Cleveland heard too and wants me to come back and reinaugurate *Play*

I dream of going to Cleveland but never will
Bee has obsessed my mind.

*　*　*

March 14th. A cold spring day. It is snowing. *Bee* is completed.

*　*　*

O *Bee* I think you are my best work
In the blue snow-filled air
I feel my heart break
I lie down in the snow
They come from the foundry and take *Bee* away
Oh what can I create now, Earth,

Green Earth on which everything blossoms anew?
"A bathroom floor cardboard trolley line
The shape and size of a lemon seed with on the inside
A passenger the size of a pomegranate seed
Who is an invalid and has to lean on the cardboard side
Of the lemon-seed-sized trolley line so that he won't fall off the train."

* * *

I just found these notes written many years ago.
How seriously I always take myself! Let it be a lesson to me.
To bring things up to date: I have just finished *Campaign,* which is a
    tremendous piece of charcoal.
Its shape is difficult to describe; but it is extremely large and would
    reach to the sixth floor of the Empire State Building. I have been
    very successful in the past fourteen or fifteen years.

* * *

Summer Night, shall I never succeed in finishing you? Oh you are the
    absolute end of all my creation! The ethereal beauty of that
    practically infinite number of white stone slabs stretching into
    the blue secrecy of ink! O stabs in my heart!

. . . . Why not a work *Stabs in My Heart?* But *Summer Night?*

January. . . . A troubled sleep. Can I make two things at once? What
    way is there to be sure that the impulse to work on *Stabs in My
    Heart* is serious? It seems occasioned only by my problem about
    finishing *Summer Night . . . ?*

* * *

The *Magician of Cincinnati* is now ready for human use. They are twenty-five tremendous stone staircases, each over six hundred feet high, which will be placed in the Ohio River between Cincinnati and Louisville, Kentucky. All the boats coming down the Ohio River will presumably be smashed up against the immense statues, which are the most recent work of the creator of *Flowers, Bee, Play, Again* and *Human Use.* Five thousand citizens are thronged on the banks of the Ohio waiting to see the installation of the work, and the crowd is expected to be more than fifteen times its present number before morning. There will be a game of water baseball in the early afternoon, before the beginning of the ceremonies, between the Cincinnati Redlegs and the Pittsburgh Pirates. The *Magician of Cincinnati,* incidentally, is said to be absolutely impregnable to destruction of any kind, and will therefore presumably always be a feature of this part of the Ohio. . . .

* * *

May 16th. With what an intense joy I watched the installation of the *Magician of Cincinnati* today, in the Ohio River, where it belongs, and which is so much a part of my original scheme. . . .

May 17th. I feel suddenly freed from life—not so much as if my work were going to change, but as though I had at last seen what I had so long been prevented (perhaps I prevented myself!) from seeing: that there is too much for me to do. Somehow this enables me to relax, to breathe easily. . . .

* * *

There's the *Magician of Cincinnati*
In the distance
Here I am in the green trees of Pennsylvania

How strange I felt when they had installed
The *Magician!* . . . Now a bluebird trills, I am busy making my polished
     stones
For *Dresser.*

The stream the stone the birds the reddish-pink Pennsylvania hills
All go to make up *Dresser*
Why am I camping out?
I am waiting for the thousands of tons of embalming fluid
That have to come and with which I can make these hills.

* * *

GREATEST ARTISTIC EVENT HINTED BY GOVERNOR
Reading, June 4. Greatest artistic event was hinted today by governor.
    Animals converge on meadow where artist working.

CONVERGE ON MEADOW WHERE WORKING

ARTIST HINTED, SAME MAN

. . . *the Magician of Cincinnati*

THREE YEARS

October 14th. I want these hills to be striated! How naive the *Magician of
    Cincinnati* was! Though it makes me happy to think of it. . . . Here, I
    am plunged into such real earth! Striate, hills! What is this deer's head
    of green stone? I can't fabricate anything less than what I think should
    girdle the earth. . . .

PHOTOGRAPH

PHOTOGRAPH

PHOTOGRAPH

Artist who created the *Magician of Cincinnati;* Now at work in Pennsylvania;
The Project—*Dresser*—So Far.

* * *

Ah! . . .

* * *

TONS

SILICON, GRASS AND DEER-HEAD RANGE
Philadelphia. Your voice as well as mine will be appreciated to express the
appreciation of *Dresser,* which makes of Pennsylvania the silicon, grass and
stone-deer-head center of the world. . . . Artist says he may change his mind
about the central bridges. Fountains to give forth real tar-water. Mountain
lake in center. Real chalk cliffs. Also cliffs of clay. Deep declivities nearby.
"Wanted forest atmosphere, yet to be open." Gas . . .

*   *   *

PHOTOGRAPH

SKETCH

DEDICATION CEREMONY

GOES SWIMMING IN OWN STREAM

SHAKING HANDS WITH GOVERNOR

COLOR PICTURE

THE HEAD OF THE ARTIST

THE ARTIST'S HAND

STACK OF ACTUAL BILLS NEEDED TO PAY FOR PROJECT

Story of *Dresser*

PENNSYLVANIA'S PRIDE: *DRESSER*

Creator of *Dresser*

*   *   *

STILL SMILING AT FORGE

Beverly, South Dakota, April 18. Still smiling at forge, artist of *Dresser* says,
"No, of course I haven't forgotten *Dresser.* Though how quickly the years
have gone by since I have been doing *Too!*" We glanced up at the sky and saw
a large white bird, somewhat similar to an immense seagull, which was as if
fixed above our heads. Its eyes were blue sapphires, and its wings were
formed by an ingenious arrangement of whitened daffodil-blossom parts. Its
body seemed mainly charcoal, on the whole, with a good deal of sand mixed
in. As we watched it, the creature actually seemed to move. . . .

August 4th . . . Three four five, and it's finished! I can see it in Beverly . . .

* * *

BEVERLY HONORS ARTIST. CALLED "FOUNDING FATHER"

Beverly, South Dakota, August 14 . . .

MISSISSIPPI CLAIMS BIRTHPLACE

HONORS BIRTHPLACE

BIRTHPLACE HONORS HELD

* * *

INDIANS AND SAVANTS MEET TO PRAISE *WEST WIND*

PAT HONORED

PAT AND *WEST WIND* HONORED

* * *

June 3rd. It doesn't seem possible—the Pacific Ocean! I have ordered sixteen
million tons of blue paint. Waiting anxiously for it to arrive. How would
grass be as a substitute? cement?

* * *

Fresh Air

At the Poem Society a black-haired man stands up to say
"You make me sick with all your talk about restraint and mature talent!
Haven't you ever looked out the window at a painting by Matisse,
Or did you always stay in hotels where there were too many spiders
      crawling on your visages?
Did you ever glance inside a bottle of sparkling pop,
Or see a citizen split in two by the lightning?
I am afraid you have never smiled at the hibernation
Of bear cubs except that you saw in it some deep relation
To human suffering and wishes, oh what a bunch of crackpots!"
The black-haired man sits down, and the others shoot arrows at him.
A blond man stands up and says,
"He is right! Why should we be organized to defend the kingdom
Of dullness? There are so many slimy people connected with poetry,
Too, and people who know nothing about it!
I am not recommending that poets like each other and organize to fight
      them,
But simply that lightning should strike them."
Then the assembled mediocrities shot arrows at the blond-haired man.
The chairman stood up on the platform, oh he was physically ugly!
He was small-limbed and -boned and thought he was quite seductive,
But he was bald with certain hideous black hairs,
And his voice had the sound of water leaving a vaseline bathtub,
And he said, "The subject for this evening's discussion is poetry
On the subject of love between swans." And everyone threw candy hearts
At the disgusting man, and they stuck to his bib and tucker,
And he danced up and down on the platform in terrific glee
And recited the poetry of his little friends—but the blond man stuck his
      head
Out of a cloud and recited poems about the east and thunder,
And the black-haired man moved through the stratosphere chanting
Poems of the relationships between terrific prehistoric charcoal whales,

And the slimy man with candy hearts sticking all over him
Wilted away like a cigarette paper on which the bumblebees have urinated,
And all the professors left the room to go back to their duty,
And all that were left in the room were five or six poets
And together they sang the new poem of the twentieth century
Which, though influenced by Mallarmé, Shelley, Byron, and Whitman,
Plus a million other poets, is still entirely original
And is so exciting that it cannot be here repeated.
You must go to the Poem Society and wait for it to happen.
Once you have heard this poem you will not love any other,
Once you have dreamed this dream you will be inconsolable,
Once you have loved this dream you will be as one dead,
Once you have visited the passages of this time's great art!

2

"Oh to be seventeen years old
Once again," sang the red-haired man, "and not know that poetry
Is ruled with the sceptre of the dumb, the deaf, and the creepy!"
And the shouting persons battered his immortal body with stones
And threw his primitive comedy into the sea
From which it sang forth poems irrevocably blue.

Who are the great poets of our time, and what are their names?
Yeats of the baleful influence, Auden of the baleful influence, Eliot of the
     baleful influence
(Is Eliot a great poet? no one knows), Hardy, Stevens, Williams (is Hardy
     of our time?),
Hopkins (is Hopkins of our time?), Rilke (is Rilke of our time?), Lorca (is
     Lorca of our time?), who is still of our time?
Mallarmé, Valéry, Apollinaire, Éluard, Reverdy, French poets are still of
     our time,
Pasternak and Mayakovsky, is Jouve of our time?

Where are young poets in America, they are trembling in publishing
     houses and universities,
Above all they are trembling in universities, they are bathing the library
     steps with their spit,

They are gargling out innocuous (to whom?) poems about maple trees and
      their children,
Sometimes they brave a subject like the Villa d'Este or a lighthouse in Rhode
      Island,
Oh what worms they are! They wish to perfect their form.

Yet could not these young men, put in another profession,
Succeed admirably, say at sailing a ship? I do not doubt it, Sir, and I wish we
      could try them.
(A plane flies over the ship holding a bomb but perhaps it will not drop the
      bomb,
The young poets from the universities are staring anxiously at the skies,
Oh they are remembering their days on the campus when they looked up to
      watch birds excrete,
They are remembering the days they spent making their elegant poems.)

Is there no voice to cry out from the wind and say what it is like to be the
      wind,
To be roughed up by the trees and to bring music from the scattered houses
And the stones, and to be in such intimate relationship with the sea
That you cannot understand it? Is there no one who feels like a pair of pants?

3

Summer in the trees! "It is time to strangle several bad poets."
The yellow hobbyhorse rocks to and fro, and from the chimney
Drops the Strangler! The white and pink roses are slightly agitated by the
      struggle,
But afterwards beside the dead "poet" they cuddle up comfortingly against
      their vase. They are safer now, no one will compare them to the sea.

Here on the railroad train, one more time, is the Strangler.
He is going to get that one there, who is on his way to a poetry reading.
Agh! Biff! A body falls to the moving floor.

In the football stadium I also see him,
He leaps through the frosty air at the maker of comparisons
Between football and life and silently, silently strangles him!

Here is the Strangler dressed in a cowboy suit
Leaping from his horse to annihilate the students of myth!

The Strangler's ear is alert for the names of Orpheus,
Cuchulain, Gawain, and Odysseus,
And for poems addressed to Jane Austen, F. Scott Fitzgerald,
To Ezra Pound, and to personages no longer living
Even in anyone's thoughts—O Strangler the Strangler!

He lies on his back in the waves of the Pacific Ocean.

4

Supposing that one walks out into the air
On a fresh spring day and has the misfortune
To encounter an article on modern poetry
In *New World Writing,* or has the misfortune
To see some examples of some of the poetry
Written by the men with their eyes on the myth
And the Missus and the midterms, in the *Hudson Review,*
Or, if one is abroad, in *Botteghe Oscure,*
Or indeed in *Encounter,* what is one to do
With the rest of one's day that lies blasted to ruins
All bluely about one, what is one to do?
Oh surely one cannot complain to the President,
Nor even to the deans of Columbia College,
Nor to T. S. Eliot, nor to Ezra Pound,
And supposing one writes to the Princess Caetani,
"Your poets are awful!" what good would it do?
And supposing one goes to the *Hudson Review*
With a package of matches and sets fire to the building?
One ends up in prison with trial subscriptions
To the *Partisan, Sewanee,* and *Kenyon Review!*

5

Sun out! perhaps there is a reason for the lack of poetry
In these ill-contented souls, perhaps they need air!

Blue air, fresh air, come in, I welcome you, you are an art student,
Take off your cap and gown and sit down on the chair.
Together we shall paint the poets—but no, air! perhaps you should go
    to them, quickly,
Give them a little inspiration, they need it, perhaps they are out of
    breath,
Give them a little inhuman company before they freeze the English
    language to death!
(And rust their typewriters a little, be sea air! be noxious! kill them, if
    you must, but stop their poetry!
I remember I saw you dancing on the surf on the Côte d'Azur,
And I stopped, taking my hat off, but you did not remember me,
Then afterwards you came to my room bearing a handful of orange
    flowers
And we were together all through the summer night!)

That we might go away together, it is so beautiful on the sea, there are a
    few white clouds in the sky!

But no, air! you must go . . . Ah, stay!

But she has departed and . . . Ugh! what poisonous fumes and clouds!
    what a suffocating atmosphere!
Cough! whose are these hideous faces I see, what is this rigor
Infecting the mind? where are the green Azores,
Fond memories of childhood, and the pleasant orange trolleys,
A girl's face, red-white, and her breasts and calves, blue eyes, brown
    eyes, green eyes, fahrenheit
Temperatures, dandelions, and trains, O blue?!
Wind, wind, what is happening? Wind! I can't see any bird but the gull,
    and I feel it should symbolize . . .
Oh, pardon me, there's a swan, one two three swans, a great white swan,
    hahaha how pretty they are! Smack!
Oh! stop! help! yes, I see—disrespect for my superiors—forgive me,
    dear Zeus, nice Zeus, parabolic bird, O feathered excellence! white!

There is Achilles too, and there's Ulysses, I've always wanted to see them,
And there is Helen of Troy, I suppose she is Zeus too, she's so terribly
    pretty—hello, Zeus, my you are beautiful, Bang!
One more mistake and I get thrown out of the Modern Poetry
    Association, help! Why aren't there any adjectives around?
Oh there are, there's practically nothing else—look, here's *grey, utter,*
    agonized, total, phenomenal, gracile, invidious, sundered, and *fused,*
Elegant, absolute, pyramidal, and . . . Scream! but what can I describe with
    these words? States!
States symbolized and divided by two, complex states, magic states, states
    of consciousness governed by an aroused sincerity, cockadoodle doo!
Another bird! is it morning? Help! where am I? am I in the barnyard?
    oink oink, scratch, moo! Splash!
My first lesson. "Look around you. What do you think and feel?" *Uhhh*
    . . . "Quickly!" *This Connecticut landscape would have pleased Vermeer.*
    Wham! A-Plus. "Congratulations!" I am promoted.
OOOhhhhh I wish I were dead, what a headache! My second lesson:
    "Rewrite your first lesson line six hundred times. Try to make it into
    a magnetic field." I can do it too. But my poor line! What a
    nightmare! Here comes a tremendous horse.
Trojan, I presume. No, it's my third lesson. "Look, look! Watch him, see
    what he's doing? That's what we want you to do. Of course it won't
    be the same as his at first, but . . ." I demur. Is there no other way to
    fertilize minds?
Bang! I give in . . . Already I see my name in two or three anthologies, a
    serving girl comes into the barn bringing me the anthologies,
She is very pretty and I smile at her a little sadly, perhaps it is my last
    smile! Perhaps she will hit me! But no, she smiles in return, and she
    takes my hand.
My hand, my hand! what is this strange thing I feel in my hand, on my
    arm, on my chest, my face—can it be . . . ? it is! AIR!
Air, air, you've come back! Did you have any success? "What do you
    think?" I don't know, air. You are so strong, air.
And she breaks my chains of straw, and we walk down the road, behind
    us the hideous fumes!
Soon we reach the seaside, she is a young art student who places her
    head on my shoulder,
I kiss her warm red lips, and here is the Strangler, reading the *Kenyon*
    Review! Good luck to you, Strangler!

Goodbye, Helen! goodbye, fumes! goodbye, abstracted dried-up boys!
    goodbye, dead trees! goodbye, skunks!
Goodbye, manure! goodbye, critical manicure! goodbye, you big fat men
    standing on the east coast as well as the west giving poems the
    test! farewell, Valéry's stern dictum!
Until tomorrow, then, scum floating on the surface of poetry! goodbye
    for a moment, refuse that happens to land in poetry's boundaries!
    adieu, stale eggs teaching imbeciles poetry to bolster up your egos!
    adios, boring anomalies of these same stale eggs!
Ah, but the scum is deep! Come, let me help you! and soon we pass
    into the clear blue water. Oh GOODBYE, castrati of poetry!
    farewell, stale pale skunky pentameters (the only honest English
    meter, gloop gloop!)! until tomorrow, horrors! oh, farewell!

Hello, sea! good morning, sea! hello, clarity and excitement, you great
    expanse of green—

O green, beneath which all of them shall drown!

Permanently

One day the Nouns were clustered in the street.
An Adjective walked by, with her dark beauty.
The Nouns were struck, moved, changed.
The next day a Verb drove up, and created the Sentence.

Each Sentence says one thing—for example, "Although it was a dark
    rainy day when the Adjective walked by, I shall remember the pure
    and sweet expression on her face until the day I perish from the
    green, effective earth."
Or, "Will you please close the window, Andrew?"
Or, for example, "Thank you, the pink pot of flowers on the window sill
    has changed color recently to a light yellow, due to the heat from
    the boiler factory which exists nearby."

In the springtime the Sentences and the Nouns lay silently on the grass.
A lonely Conjunction here and there would call, "And! But!"
But the Adjective did not emerge.

As the adjective is lost in the sentence,
So I am lost in your eyes, ears, nose, and throat—
You have enchanted me with a single kiss
Which can never be undone
Until the destruction of language.

Down at the Docks

Down at the docks
Where everything is sweet and inclines
At night
To the sound of canoes
I planted a maple tree
And every night
Beneath it I studied the cosmos
Down at the docks.

Sweet ladies, listen to me.
The dock is made of wood
The maple tree's not made of wood
It is wood
Wood comes from it
As music comes from me
And from this mandolin I've made
Out of the maple tree.

Jealous gentlemen, study how
Wood comes from the maple
Then devise your love
So that it seems
To come from where
All is it yet something more
White spring flowers and leafy bough
Jealous gentlemen.

Arrogant little waves
Knocking at the dock
It's for you I've made this chanson
For you and that big dark blue.

You Were Wearing

You were wearing your Edgar Allan Poe printed cotton blouse.
In each divided up square of the blouse was a picture of Edgar Allan Poe.
Your hair was blonde and you were cute. You asked me, "Do most boys
    think that most girls are bad?"
I smelled the mould of your seaside resort hotel bedroom on your hair
    held in place by a John Greenleaf Whittier clip.
"No," I said, "it's girls who think that boys are bad." Then we read
    Snowbound together
And ran around in an attic, so that a little of the blue enamel was scraped
    off my George Washington, Father of His Country, shoes.

Mother was walking in the living room, her Strauss Waltzes comb in her
    hair.
We waited for a time and then joined her, only to be served tea in cups
    painted with pictures of Herman Melville
As well as with illustrations from his book *Moby Dick* and from his
    novella, *Benito Cereno.*
Father came in wearing his Dick Tracy necktie: "How about a drink,
    everyone?"
I said, "Let's go outside a while." Then we went onto the porch and sat
    on the Abraham Lincoln swing.
You sat on the eyes, mouth, and beard part, and I sat on the knees.
In the yard across the street we saw a snowman holding a garbage can
    lid smashed into a likeness of the mad English king, George the
    Third.

Variations on a Theme by William Carlos Williams

1

I chopped down the house that you had been saving to live in next summer.
I am sorry, but it was morning, and I had nothing to do
and its wooden beams were so inviting.

2

We laughed at the hollyhocks together
and then I sprayed them with lye.
Forgive me. I simply do not know what I am doing.

3

I gave away the money that you had been saving to live on for the next ten
      years.
The man who asked for it was shabby
and the firm March wind on the porch was so juicy and cold.

4

Last evening we went dancing and I broke your leg.
Forgive me. I was clumsy, and
I wanted you here in the wards, where I am the doctor!

From Ko, or, A Season On Earth

Ora non piu: ritorni un' altra volta
chi voluntier la bella istoria ascolta
ORLANDO FURIOSO, end of Canto XVI

CANTO ONE

Meanwhile at the University of Japan
Ko had already begun his studies, which
While making him an educated man
Would also give him as he learned to pitch
And catch—for Ko was more than a mere fan,
But wished as a playing member to do a hitch
With some great team—something to think about
More interesting than merely Safe and Out.

Inyaga, his professor, when he first
Appeared to Ko, seemed fashioned like an ape,
Protruding jaw and tiny eyes that burst
From high strong cheekbones of chimpanzee shape,
But later it was his teaching that Ko cursed,
Of which the body merely was the drape:
Inyaga taught him baseball was a sin.
Ko cried out! Inyaga: "Stop that din

At once, or else you'll suffer!" Ko subsides,
But his resentment every day gets greater.
Meanwhile the Dodgers all had taken brides
As was arranged for them by Mr. Slater,
Their crafty manager, who thus provides
A human interest for the fans, who, later,
When they find out his trick, will make him pay;
But for the moment it is Slater's day.

He drives the players here and there, shouts out
"Champagne!" and wishes all the women well
He's marrying to his players. What about
The women? They're contented. At the bell
They call "the wedding" they respond with shout
And glee, of which there'd be too much to tell;
Instead, I leave this sportive celebration
And go to England, where the Coronation

Of Amaranth the First is taking place.
Here Huddel, with his family gathered round,
Watches the gay procession. Huddel's face
Is twisted and is the color of swampy ground.
His wife, as though much pounded with a mace,
Is crushed and bulky; his daughter's like a mound.
This little group has one malevolent eye
Intent on Amaranth as he passes by.

This latter, radiant with joy, though sad
At his late mother's death, has not a thought
For such as Huddel, but with gestures glad
And strong with youth, proceeding as he ought
In gold and silver, thinks there is no bad
That he can't cure. And then his eye is caught
By jewels shining at a certain distance,
And to the crown he loses all resistance.

Andrews was also at the Coronation,
Dressed in a gray fluff suit which made him bigger
Than usual, but did not see the consummation
Because he was distracted by a chigger
Inside his pants leg. In his consternation
He went to the stationer's to buy a digger
To get it out. Too bad! the place was closed,
As anyone, in truth, might have supposed,

Because of Coronation. On his way
Back to the ceremony Andrews met
An English girl, who, later in that day,
He was quite certain he would not forget,
For various reasons. But of this we may
Speak somewhat later. At the moment let
Us note that Andrews missed the part when Huddel
Got all the Coronation in a muddle.

This latter, mindful of what might have been
If he by nature had but found admission
Into the royal womb, with savage grin
Stared at the glittering blue-white apparition
Of the crown jewels, and past the hats of tin
Padded with blue of the bobbies, into the partition
He clawed his way, where there was no one present
But those of royal blood. "Get out, you peasant!

You imbecile! you nut! you Kerry Blue!
You pig!" all cried. Huddel, though, looked about,
Affirming, "I've as much right here as you.
England is a democracy." "How about
That?" Dukes and Earls exclaimed; "not true:
England, if you had read some you'd find out,
Is a constitutional monarchy, and leans
Mostly on its traditions, kings, and queens.

In a democracy there's no such thing
As royal fam—" But here they were interrupted
By the noises of Huddel's removal, who as if on wings
Was moving from bobby to bobby, by each intercepted
While passing from one to the other, as each of them flings
His burden away from the royal partition, corrupted
By such a foul presence and, finally, dropping it where
There was no Coronation, there was nothing but buildings and air.

Amaranth, since he knew what he had done,
Although convenient, was quite unethical,
Whispered to the Duke of Melbourne to send one
Of his most worthy Cavaliers of Senegal
To seek out Huddel and give him half a ton
Of pence, which might, the King thought, be much
      preferable
To looking at Huddel again, for Huddel was repulsive,
With face of green, and every movement convulsive.

Huddel's family, meanwhile, on the sidewalk lumped
At first, had followed their flying father and now
Approached him in the suburbs. As if humped
From too much weight, the Archbishop of Canterbury's bow
Indicates Coronation's somewhat slumped
To Amaranth and his courtiers. Oh then how
All changes as he raises the crown on high—
Amaranth trembles with joy, and he courses by

The applauding crowds, driven mad by the beautiful sight!
Ko meanwhile had improved himself at bat
And in the field, and in the dim daylight
Of dawn appeared in a fake Dodger hat
In Tampa after forty hours of flight.
He'd flown from dim Japan! and though he'd sat
So long awake, he went without delay
To where the Dodgers in spring training lay.

The Dodgers, each amused by his new mate,
Were not out on the field on time, of course,
And Ko stood swinging at an empty plate
A bat he'd brought along with him. What force
He gets into his swing! Soon at the gate
He heard the Dodgers voicing their remorse
At being up so early. Ko retired
Into a bullpen, which he much admired.

Slater was leader of his merry crew
And brought them on the diamond with a shout,
"If other players slept as much as you,
There'd be no major leagues, I have no doubt!
Fortunately, you're among the happy few
Who really know what baseball is about
And can afford to, wrapped in wifely charms,
Lie fifteen hours a day in Morpheus' arms!"

The players laughed, adopting their positions
Upon the field. They stole and ran and caught
And hit homeruns past where you pay admissions.
Their game, although a practice one, was fought
With ardor and avoidance of omissions—
"My mate is in the stands," each Dodger thought.
When everything was over, they discovered
Ko sleeping on a bench, by tarpaulin covered.

Exhausted by his trip of forty hours,
Ko had, in spite of everything, dropped off
To sleep the minute he sat down. Of flowers
He dreamed, created of some silver stuff
And set upon a screen, not exactly in bowers,
But in formation, as if on a graph.
The background was quite blue, and there appeared
A silver boatman there, who gondoliered

Some ladies dressed in robes of red and purple
Into a little house, shaped like a rectangle
And colored yellow, round which in a circle
Stood little black-limbed trees backed by a fleck-tangle
Of what apparently were leaves. A gurgle
Of water seemed to splash upon the check tangle
Of one of the ladies' gowns as she emerged
To shore, by boatman and companions urged,

85

Apparently, to watch her step. Her silky
Purple checked and splattered gown however
Seemed in the moonlight beautiful and milky
And one could almost quite believe that never
Had water splashed it. All was in a still key.
An enormous yellow hand then pulled a lever,
And Ko saw warriors dressed in red and white
Dancing across some paper, as if in flight.

Each had a black mustache, one stroke of ink
Per warrior, each had long white ink-drawn sleeves
And a red vest, a spear whose tip was pink,
And in the all-white background one perceives
Some bright green tufts of grass. With a great wink
One of the warriors looks at Ko, who leaves
His dream immediately with a cry:
"Oh am I still asleep? Who's passing by?"

"We are the Dodgers," sang that merry band;
"This is our field, our bullpen, our delight,
Our Tampa, our spring training, and our land!
But who are you, who in the dead of night
Of anxious dreams in middle day do stand
And question us? What was it caused your fright?"
The Dodgers then subsided into silence
Like ocean birds returning to their islands.

Ko, then, returning to full consciousness,
Explained to Mr. Slater and his hitters
How baseball had been all his happiness
Since when, a tiny toddler throwing spitters
At paper lanterns, he had made a mess
Of one upon the floor, which was all glitters,
And how, established thus his skill for throwing,
His skill at playing had been ever growing.

"Let's give the kid a chance!" cried Slater, moved
By Ko's intensity, his education,
And by his trans-Pacific flight. "We're grooved
To take another pitcher on. Tarnation!
If this kid's good, the saying will be proved
That there are stranger things in God's creation
Than any of us dreams of. Get a glove,"
He finished; and Ko looked at him with love.

Although their wives were waiting, yet the team
Went willingly out to the field again
To see the stranger pitch. As in a dream,
But not the ones he had, Ko counted ten,
Wound up, and threw the baseball with such steam
That it went through the backstop, lost till when
The field would be torn down, and lazy goats
Would ramble through it gnawing shreds of coats;

It dug into the grandstand, where it stayed.
The crowd went wild—the crowd was mostly team,
Plus several wives. The catcher, with his splayed
Brown weighty glove, first spellbound, with a scream
Fell in the dirt behind the plate and prayed;
And Slater's agitation was extreme.
"Put someone else behind the plate," he cried,
"So that this talent may be verified!"

Another catcher came. Ko raised his torso
In a high arc, then slumped it down again,
Then raised his arm and threw with such a force (Oh
It was beautiful to see) that when
The players' screams died down, they saw that, more so
Than the first, this second ball had pen-
Etrated through the enormous blocks of wood
And made the grandstand shiver where it stood.

Slater had fainted; and the golden sun
Sent down its last warm beams upon his visage
Which lay upon the field like something one
Has splattered golden paint all over (syzyg-
Ies of manager and player that stun
Them both!). With bottled soda, for its fizzage
All shaken up, and then released to spray
The unconscious manager, came shortstop Gray.

Ko meanwhile was preparing a third ball
With glove and gesture, seeing all in ruins
The grandstand, which he thought for sure would fall
With one or two more pitches. But De Bruins,
The first-base coach, ran out and stopped him, all
Emotionally shaken by these doings,
With "You have done enough for now." Ko paused,
Confused by what he'd heard, and as if lost.

But let us see how Andrews, where, in England,
He draws sweet breath of day, is now engaged,
Who, girl-encountering in that queen and king land,
Should by all odds be properly assuaged
By now, outside the window hear a wing land
Or in the corridor a stranger paged.
In fact, it's thus; the girl he lies beside
Has beautiful blonde hair and is blue-eyed.

Her skin is soft, her body white and rounded
Deliciously, her breasts two islands where
Two balneary paradises could be founded
In which all felt a bliss beyond compare;
Her waist is small, as if it had been pounded
By Venus' hammer; and with utmost care
Her legs seem to be sculpted. She's alive!
She touches Andrews. "Take me for a drive

Around the city of London, that I may
See you a bit in some other atmosphere
Than this close-breathing beddy one, that today
I can decide if I really love you, dear,
Or if this has been but a holiday
Enchantment, fleeting as the foam on beer."
Andrews says, "I don't have a car," but Doris
(For that's her name) says, "I've a little Morris.

It's parked outside. You'll recognize it. It's
Red, with a reddish-pink interior. In
The pocket of my coat, with combs and bits
Of paper, are the keys. Hand me that pin,
And you can go down first and get it," sits
In bed, so pretty all from chin to shin
That Andrews, putting on his gray fluff suit,
Rushes to cover her with kisses—the brute!

At last he exits, seeking for the car
In the refreshing air of springtime London;
Remembers, hearing horns blow from afar,
How he the Coronation did abandon;
Starts, but then stops; thinks, "That is how things are—
My abandon-Coronation was not wanton,
But of an accident the glad result,
For which I should not grieve but here exult."

"Oh, thank you, London skies," in exultation
Andrews began to chant, but then decided
It was not really fit that Coronation
Be slighted for a lovely girl who glided
Against him by mistake. With hesitation
He stayed his steps and, doing so, collided
With a fine gentleman propelled by dog
On leash, compelled to leap about like frog.

"Pardon me, Sir," to Andrews said this latter
(The gentleman attired in red), and Andrews
Said "certainly he'd not store up the matter
As source of grief and bitterness, nor hand use
Against a fellow-being for such errata
Of human moving, since it was not a planned ruse
But obviously an accidental bump.
As such, it made in throat appear no lump."

The gentleman, amazed to hear such language
From a common pedestrian, asked the origins
Of gray-fluff-suited Andrews, who with anguish
Said that they were not known: "My father's sins,"
He sadly smiled. "Come, have a fried fish sandwich,"
The gentleman exclaimed, who was on pins
And needles to hear the rest of Andrews' tale;
But for the moment his ruse was destined to fail.

For at this moment Doris, to the door,
Dressed in a light green suit, came, saying, "What!
You haven't yet arrived at my sweet car?"
And then their vessel did another knot,
And Andrews knew he had not known before
That they were on the ocean. "What a spot,"
He sighed, "I'm in, for I'm supposed to be
Reporting to the Station after three."

In fact the boat they rode on was quite large,
So much so it was really understandable
That Andrews did not know it was a barge
On which a little building, which was landable,
Of light materials made, which came from Arg-
Entina, stood. Poor Andrews sighed; his mandible
Fell down a notch: "How could I not have seen,
From where we lay above, the water's sheen?

But, Doris, tell me, when did we put off?
We were attached to land when I came in.
And who's the elegant dog-walking toff
I ran into just now? What was that din
Of horns I heard I naturally enough
Thought Coronation noises? What has been
Your motive in estranging me from shore?
Oh why did you speak of a Morris just before?

How could there be a Morris on the sea?"
Doris began unbuttoning her jacket,
Under which she was naked, hurriedly,
And sighed, "If you would come around in back, it
Would help me to undress more speedily.
I think I really love you. What a racket
My heart is making!" Andrews, with a stare
Of wonder, rushed to her and lost his care.

While their big barge is moving down the Thames,
Let's turn to Indianapolis, where the Speedway
Is filled with customers, who with ahems
And haws are waiting for the sight they need way
Down upon the speedway and with stems
Of pencils write their choices down with greed. Way
Past the starting gate a little car
Is finally admitted 'neath the bar.

It's coming late, but nevertheless may win.
Its driver has a shock of brownish hair
And pretty yellow goggles and smooth chin
And doth a driver's padded garment wear . . .
Boom boom! the axles clash, the gears begin
To grind their way, and who is winning? Where?
A big red car that bears the number Three
Pulls out ahead, or so it seems to me.

No, no—there's one of blue that's shooting out
Ahead of Number Three. What sounds of grinding!
Clashing! crashing! smashing! dashing about!
Then silence . . . then a terrible sound of winding
Followed by an explosion and a shout—
A flash of flame, then smoke, oh smoke so blinding!
Why did we come here anyway? Let's go!
But something . . . something's happened down below.

The little yellow car that we saw enter
The Speedway late now courses all alone
Round and round about the Speedway's center,
While all the others lie in wreckage strown—
Their drivers, half alive, too weak to banter,
Stare at their ruined racing cars and moan.
Who is this driver who has won the race?
There's not a single whisker on his face!

Who is it? "Here is forty thousand dollars
And an invitation to come back next year."
"Show us your face!" a young spectator hollers,
And off the goggles come. . . . With shrieks of fear
The judges scatter, like so many collars
Rustled by winds in May, and there appear
A crowd of blue policemen on the track.
One pulls his pistol out; you hear its crack

And crash of windows in the judges' stand,
Where still the horrid spectacle stands smiling
At all below, above, and with his hand
Makes a large gesture, which, as fans go piling
Out all the gates, sets fire to the grand-
Stands, which burn like tinder. The beguiling
Great theatre of sports goes up in oranger
Flames than rum when lighted in a porringer.

"It's the end of everything," one of the judges said
Who had managed to get outside; "it's the end of the track
And the end of the race, and with so many persons dead
It's the end of the Speedway forever." And he hunched his
    back
And walked through the fallen leaves, where crusts of bread
Lay scattered for Indianapolis' pigeons. "Alack!"
Murmured a schoolboy who had escaped alive,
"Now I shall never be let to learn to drive

In preparation for being a Speedway racer!"
His mother took his hand, and they wandered from sight
Into an ice cream emporium called The Glacier.
Meanwhile, back at the track, what once was bright
Had now turned dark and smouldery like an embrasure,
And all you could see aside from the flames that night
Was the winning yellow car, which stood untouched
In the center of that red chaos, and unsmutched.

The demon, fiend, or hideously maladjusted
Cause of this chaos stood some blocks away
Staring at Indianapolis, which, he trusted,
Would never be the same. "It's a great day
When something burns, explodes, or just is busted!"
He cried, and, looking at the sky, which, gray
With evening, seemed entirely in accord
With what he'd said, flew back to his yellow Ford

And drove it toward St. Paul. In Boston meanwhile
An investigation of the Speedway disaster
Made many a citizen desist from bean while
Reading of its results, which ever faster
Led to the conclusion that in that machine, while
Everyone'd thought there was a driving master,
There really had been some supernatural essence
Who regarded human beings as an excrescence.

The Indianapolis police, in fear
Of horrible reprisals, had done nothing;
They could not forget the horrid demoniac leer
In the judges' stand, that had set their pink hearts pulsing
White Valentine lace immediate as the foam on beer
Which into their chests like a great card still cutting
Would give them, no, no peace, nor any comfort,
But bade them stand stock still in pained discomfort

Or else it would perturb them with its edges.
Though Indianapolis may remember long
Its great disaster, already upon its hedges
Birds sing the very next morning a gay song;
Boys run to school; and carpenters planing wedges
Enjoy the smell of sawdust. Life must go on
Even though what one loves the best's in ruins.
Meanwhile in Tampa Dodger coach De Bruins

Took down his hand from Ko's left arm and said,
"I mean, let's wait till Slater comes to life.
For joy—" "For joy?" said Ko. "—he's almost dead:
Sight of your speedball pierced him like a knife. . . ."
Slater bounced up and interrupted, red
With soda: "We've got to find the kid a wife!"
He wiped some cherry phosphate off his neck.
"He can't be our only bachelor—what the heck!"

"You see—" and Slater then explained to Ko
How all the Dodgers had been married. "Naturally
You wouldn't like to be the exception." "No,"
Ko said, "but I don't know a soul here, actually,
And I'm not sure I'm old enough." "Go, go,"
Laughed Slater, "go and ask the catcher will he
Help you to meet a girl—he knows them all;
He can be seen at every Tampa ball.

His wife, as it turns out, is a Tampa belle,
And thus he's finely suited for the role,
Because he knows the Tampa women well,
Of finding you, as weevil finds a boll,
A wife with whom in company to dwell,
And thus be on the Dodgers, off the dole."
The players all applauded Slater's sally
Into poetry, whose wit was up their alley.

Slater, encouraged, continued, "And if you
Should see a girl whom you would like to wow
So she will be responsive when you woo,
Not scratch your face and answer with meeouw,
And when you speak of moonlight, answer 'oooh,'
Nor drive you from the garden screaming 'ow,'
Just ask   " but here applause him interrupted,
Loud as of Satan's angel band corrupted.

Facing his cheering players, Slater smiled:
"Let me continue, if you will, my friends;
I shall be shortly done;" and with a wild
Gesture of enthusiasm took Ko's hands.
"I think you are right! you are still but a child
And should await the bride that Heaven sends,
Not seek her out because a wily Captain
Thinks it would make the fans somewhat distracted!"

The players sobbed with joy and disbelief,
All standing 'round. What into Slater's heart
Had come, white-wingèd? Never had their chief
Wavered an instant in the sturdy art
Of baseball managing—not love or grief
Had ever made him change in slightest part
What he had decided on as Dodger policy,
Whether it was to play them in the Colise-

Um of Rome, or else in water baseball
To place them on the Grand Canal in Venice
With gondolas for bases. Down each face ball
Of water after ball of water menac-
Ing to flood the field fell. In that place bawl
Forty Dodgers and a girl in tennis
Shorts, the wife of center fielder Hunter,
A so-so hitter but a famous bunter.

They weep at human kindness. Slater's face
Is, in that darkening field, transfixed with light.
To Ko it seemed an ordinary grace
That he was not obliged to choose at sight
A wife so soon; but every Dodger ace
Was well aware that on that breezy night
Something had come to change their dauntless leader,
Who had, till then, been remorseless as a parking meter.

"Play ball!" The spell was broken. It was next day
And they were still all there, surprised and hungry,
In uniforms of red and white, to play
At baseball quite unfit, with wives all angry
Parading in the stands, their faces gray
From waiting up all night, the while a dinghy
Knocked up against a dock, where all would like
To go and sleep, not too far from the dike.

Andrews (upon the Thames, as you recall)
With Doris in a soft and chilly nest
Is now attempting to unravel all
The things that puzzle him—among the rest,
Just who that man was who with light footfall
Had bumped against him when he'd gotten dressed
And gone to get the Morris. "Is it someone
Who owns this boat? His dress was quite uncommon."

"Oh that's my dad," said Doris, "whom you ought
To get to know. He's an important poet."
She leaned against pink pillows. Andrews caught
Her waist as if he were about to throw it,
But only squeezed it. "What's that noise? I thought
I heard a yelp!" "It's Dad—oh wouldn't you know it!
He would come by just now! Well, you and Pater
Should get along, with your poetic nature—"

The cabin door shot open, and a man
(Or was it human?) with a hairy large
Long sloping face, which was all colored tan
Except the blackish nose, came in the Arg-
Entina-purchased cabin with a can
Of worms he used to fish with from the barge
And woofed and barked and quite upset the room
By running 'round. Andrews, alarmed, cried, "Whom . . . ?"

Doris spoke smiling: "Dad's integrity
Makes him, unlike most poets, actualize
In everyday life the poem's unreality.
That dog you saw on deck with steel-gray eyes
Was but a creation of Dad's terrible musical potency.
Then seeing the dog there made him realize
That the dog was himself, since by himself created,
So in this poem it's incorporated!"

"But," Andrews asked, "what poem? where?" and "Ah!"
Breathed Doris, "don't you know that what you're seeing
Is an ACTION POEM?" "You mean he's Joseph Dah,"
Cried Andrews, "the creator of Otherness Being?"
"The very same," sighed Doris. "That's my pa!"
And Joseph, as if by his barks agreeing,
Shook his tan head and frisked back out on deck.
He changed, then smiled: "It's a nice day, by heck!"

And then he dropped a line into the sea
That had a worm on it upon a hook
And was as calm as any man can be
Whose poems do not lie in any book
And so are dead to his posterity.
Back to the cabin he gave not a look;
He stood unmoving as a propped-up log,
And at his feet there was a little dog.

"He's back to human," Doris laughed. "Let's go
Out on the deck and join him," she half-whispered,
Turning about so Andrews could kiss her. "Though
It's likely that it's nicer here." A crisp bird
Call sounded. Doris sighed, "Oh do you know
You make me, Andrews, really want to lisp herd
On herd of fleecy warm and white-lined syllables
To tell my love . . ." Looking for where the pillow was,

Andrews replied, "I also love you, Love."
Just then they heard a huge unpleasant buzz
And felt the flap of wings, while from above
A watermelon head with silver fuzz
Bent down, extending them a horseshoe glove. . . .
"Dad!" Doris screamed. "I am not what I was,"
Dah cried, "Buzz bzzz!" and shut them in a coffin
He threw to the waves, which buffeted it often.

Meanwhile in Kansas there was taking place
A great upheaval. High school girls refused
To wear their clothes to school, and every place
In Kansas male observers were amused
To see the naked girls, who, lacking grace,
Were young, with bodies time had not abused,
And therefore made the wheatfields fresher areas
And streets and barns as well. No matter where he is

A man is cheered to see a naked girl—
Milking a cow or standing in a streetcar,
Opening a filing cabinet, brushing a curl
Back from her eyes while driving in a neat car
Through Wichita in summer—like the pearl
Inside the oyster, she makes it a complete car.
And there were many sermons on the subject,
And autoists, come in to have the hub checked

On their old car, would stand and pass the day
With talking of the various breasts and waists
They'd seen throughout the week, and in what way
They thought the thing, according to their tastes,
Was right or wrong, that these young girls should stray
Through Kansas without even stocking pastes
Upon their legs. Although officially negative,
As for a law, nobody wished to make it if

It were not absolutely necessary—
Unless, that is, the nakedness resulted
In crime and rape and sinking of the ferry
That spanned the Wichita, in youth insulted
And age dishonored, in a broad hysteri-
A, in other words, among the adulthood
Of Kansas caused by the unaccustomed vision
Of these young girls, brought on by the decision

Of the High School Girl Committee of Kansas City,
Kansas, in an attempt for something new
In good old Kansas where the girls are pretty
But life is dry, and there is not the dew
Of new ideas and excitement, witty
Conversation until has grown blue
What once was gray (the window) and one sees
New day resplendent, hears the humming bees,

And, flushed with pleasure, goes into the garden
Out the great concrete door, and sits upon
A bench 'mid red and yellow flowers and arden-
Tly resumes one's colloquy with one
Or two or three friends; but, instead, lifeguardin'
In Kansas City's swimming pools, or done
With supper—mashed potatoes, iced tea, and potroast—
One stands about and looks at a green fencepost

And wishes one were ashes in a jar
Unless there's something doing at the dancehall
Or some new kind of frozen icecream bar
One has a yen to eat. As for romance, all
That one can do is get into one's car
And drive out 'mid the sunflowers, just perchance all
Giving off their pollen, which as a lover
Defeats one who from allergy does suffer

And makes him sneeze instead of kiss. "However,
Economic prosperity has blessed
The State of Kansas," cried the girls—"why never
A corresponding esthetic interest
To make our lives worthwhile?" Then one wild, clever,
Ingenious, terrible girl came to the desk
And said how they, by taking off their clothes,
Could change the dried-out thistle to a rose,

Enchant the atmosphere, and bring to Kansas
A dream! The plan was instantly adopted,
With the results we've seen. From foreign lands as
Far as Tibet and Burma helicopted,
Entrained, en-autoed, or on feet or hands as
Fast as they could move, came hordes who opted
To trade their leisure for a sight so rare—
Girls walking through the Kansas cities bare

Of any vestments, many-colored statues
Which had the gifts of movement and of speech;
Blonde, brown, brunette—like different-colored matches
Their heads; their bodies, almanacs to teach
The riveter his trade, the famous mattress
Tycoon how far and at what points should reach
The springs, the poet how to shape his lines,
The woodsman what is lacking in the pines.

As for the natives, happy Kansans say:
"I wonder what is in East Wichita Hooks
I could have missed when I went there the day
Before yesterday at lunch hour with my books
Still in my briefcase from my office. They
Say where I work the girls with the best looks
Are in South Wichita Turnings. Well, tomorrow
A bike or motorcycle I shall borrow

And ride to see them. Oh what a wonderful Sunday
It's going to be! and after I have stared
My fill (if it's not possible in one day,
Then when I'm tired out), I will, prepared
For the whole weekend, take my lunch, which Monday
I started packing, out to where the Baird
Brothers Wichita Freight and Packing Company flings
Its concrete walls, and past some wooden things

To where, after you pass the first three lampposts,
You see a greenish gully, which, descending,
You find the Little Wichita through damp posts,
Branches, and discarded clothing wending
Its way, and you can eat among the damp hosts
Of weeds and reeds and toads; and then, ascending
To Turnings once again, the girls I'll see
And take a dancing vision home with me

As the bicycle bumps along. Then to North Wichita
On Sunday evening for a glass of soda
(Kansas is 'dry' and if you are not rich at all
You cannot get a drink there) at the Groada
Bowling Alleys, where, without a stitch at all,
From the University which is down the road a
Little, the coeds' bowling team will be playing
The fully-clothed team which from Smith College is straying."

These are the plans of a prince! Yet they are those
Of a plain Kansan, whom to such *bonheur*
The girls' decision brought. O lovely rose
Of girl, where is there any parallel *fleur?* . . .
But now the headlines blaringly expose
(Chiefly the *Times* and *France Observateur*):
AMARANTH PLANS TO VISIT KANSAS TO
SEE IF OLD ENGLAND'S GIRLS SHOULD UNDRESS TOO.

While Amaranth is packing up in state
For his great Kansas visit, and while Ko
And all the other Dodgers lie in great
Exhaustion on the field, and Andrews o–
Vercome by Dah and turned to ocean freight
With Doris moves to westward, and the snow
From the high Himalayas comes unstuck,
Let's pause a moment, like a dairy truck.

The Railway Stationery

The railway stationery lay upon
The desk of the railway clerk, from where he could see
The springtime and the tracks. Engraved upon
Each page was an inch-and-a-half-high T
And after that an H and then an E
And then, slightly below it to the right,
There was COLUMBUS RAILWAY COMPANY
In darker ink as the above was light.
The print was blue. And just beneath it all
There was an etching—not in blue, but black—
Of a real railway engine half-an-inch tall
Which, if you turned the paper on its back,
You could see showing through, as if it ran
To one edge of the sheet then back again.

To one edge of the sheet then back again!
The springtime comes while we're still drenched in snow
And, whistling now, snow-spotted Number Ten
Comes up the track and stops, and we must go
Outside to get its cargo, with our hands
Cold as the steel they touch. Inside once more
Once we have shut the splintery wooden door
Of the railway shack, the stationery demands
Some further notice. For the first time the light,
Reflected from the snow by the bright spring sun,
Shows that the engine wheel upon the right
Is slightly darker than the left-side one
And slightly lighter than the one in the center,
Which may have been an error of the printer.

Shuffling through many sheets of it to establish
Whether this difference is consistent will
Prove that it is not. Probably over-lavish
At the beginning with the ink, he still
(The printer) had the presence of mind to change

His operating process when he noticed
That on the wheels the ink had come out strange.
Because the windows of the shack are latticed
The light that falls upon the stationery
Is often interrupted by straight lines
Which shade the etching. Now the words "Dear Mary"
Appear below the engine on one sheet
Followed by a number of other conventional signs,
Among which are "our love," "one kiss," and "sweet."

The clerk then signs his name—his name is Johnson,
But all he signs is Bill, with a large B
Which overflows its boundaries like a Ronson
With too much fluid in it, which you see
Often, and it can burn you, though the *i*
Was very small and had a tiny dot.
The *l*'s were different—the first was high,
The second fairly low. And there was a spot
Of ink at the end of the signature which served
To emphasize that the letter was complete.
On the whole, one could say his writing swerved
More than the average, although it was neat.
He'd used a blue-black ink, a standing pen,
Which now he stuck back in its stand again.

Smiling and sighing, he opened up a drawer
And took an envelope out, which then he sealed
After he'd read the letter three times more
And folded it and put it in. A field
Covered with snow, untouched by man, is what
The envelope resembled, till he placed
A square with perforated edges that
Pictured a white-haired President, who faced
The viewer, in its corner, where it stuck
After he'd kissed its back and held it hard
Against the envelope. Now came the truck
Of the postman "Hello, Jim." "Hello there, Bill."
"I've got this—can you take it?" "Sure, I will!"

Now the snow fell down gently from the sky.
Strange wonder—snow in spring! Bill walked into
The shack again and wrote the letter *I*
Idly upon a sheet of paper. New
Ideas for writing Mary filled his mind,
But he resisted—there was work to do.
For in the distance he could hear the grind
Of the Seventy-Eight, whose engine was half blue;
So, putting on a cap, he went outside
On the tracks side, to wait for it to come.
It was the Seventy-Eight which now supplied
The city with most of its produce, although some
Came in by truck and some was grown in town.
Now it screams closer, and he flags it down.

Thank You

Oh thank you for giving me the chance
Of being ship's doctor! I am sorry that I shall have to refuse—
But, you see, the most I know of medicine is orange flowers
Tilted in the evening light against a cashmere red
Inside which breasts invent the laws of light
And of night, where cashmere moors itself across the sea.
And thank you for giving me these quintuplets
To rear and make happy . . . My mind was on something else.

Thank you for giving me this battleship to wash,
But I have a rash on my hands and my eyes hurt,
And I know so little about cleaning a ship
That I would rather clean an island.
There one knows what one is about—sponge those palm trees, sweep up
    the sand a little, polish those coconuts;
Then take a rest for a while and it's time to trim the grass as well as
    separate it from each other where gummy substances have made
    individual blades stick together, forming an ugly bunch;
And then take the dead bark off the trees, and perfume these islands a bit
    with a song. . . . That's easy—but a battleship!
Where does one begin and how does one do? to batten the hatches? I
    would rather clean a million palm trees.

Now here comes an offer of a job for setting up a levee
In Mississippi. No thanks. Here it says *Rape or Worse.* I think they must
    want me to publicize this book.
On the jacket it says "Published in Boothbay Harbor, Maine"—what a
    funny place to publish a book!
I suppose it is some provincial publishing house
Whose provincial pages emit the odor of sails
And the freshness of the sea
Breeze. . . . But publicity!

The only thing I could publicize well would be my tooth,
Which I could say came with my mouth and in a most engaging
    manner

With my whole self, my body and including my mind,
Spirits, emotions, spiritual essences, emotional substances, poetry,
    dreams, and lords
Of my life, everything, all embraceleted with my tooth
In a way that makes one wish to open the windows and scream "Hi!" to the
    heavens,
And "Oh, come and take me away before I die in a minute!"

It is possible that the dentist is smiling, that he dreams of extraction
Because he believes that the physical tooth and the spiritual tooth are one.

Here is another letter, this one from a textbook advertiser;
He wants me to advertise a book on chopping down trees.
But how could I? I love trees! and I haven't the slightest sympathy with
    chopping them down, even though I know
We need their products for wood-fires, some houses, and maple syrup—
Still I like trees better
In their standing condition, when they sway at the beginning of evening . . .
And thank you for the pile of driftwood.
Am I wanted at the sea?

And thank you for the chance to run a small hotel
In an elephant stopover in Zambezi,
But I do not know how to take care of guests, certainly they would all leave
    soon
After seeing blue lights out the windows and rust on their iron beds—I'd
    rather own a bird-house in Jamaica:
Those people come in, the birds, they do not care how things are kept up . . .
It's true that Zambezi proprietorship would be exciting, with people getting
    off elephants and coming into my hotel,
But as tempting as it is I cannot agree.
And thank you for this offer of the post of referee
For the Danish wrestling championship—I simply do not feel qualified . . .
But the fresh spring air has been swabbing my mental decks
Until, although prepared for fight, still I sleep on land.
Thank you for the ostriches. I have not yet had time to pluck them,
But I am sure they will be delicious, adorning my plate at sunset,
My tremendous plate, and the plate
Of the offers to all my days. But I cannot fasten my exhilaration to the sun.

And thank you for the evening of the night on which I fell off my horse in
    the shadows. That was really useful.

Lunch

The lanternslides grinding out B-flat minor
Chords to the ears of the deaf youngster who sprays in Hicksville
The sides of a car with the dream-splitting paint
Of pianos (he dreamt of one day cutting the Conservatory
In two with his talent), these lanternslides, I say,
They are—The old woman hesitated. A lifesaver was shoved down her
    throat; then she continued:
They are some very good lanternslides in that bunch. Then she fainted
And we revived her with flowers. She smiled sleepily at the sun.
He is my own boy, she said, with her glass hand falling through the
    sparkling red America of lunch.

That old boilermaker she has in her back yard,
Olaf said, used to be her sweetheart years back.
One day, though, a train passed, and pressed her hard,
And she deserted life and love for liberty.
We carried Olaf softly into the back yard
And laid him down with his head under the steamroller.
Then Jill took the wheel and I tinkered with the engine,
Till we rolled him under, rolled him under the earth.
When people ask us what's in our back yard
Now, we don't like to tell them, Jill says, laying her silver bandannaed
    head on my greened bronze shoulder.
Then we both dazzle ourselves with the red whiteness of lunch.

That old woman named Tessie Runn
Had a tramp boyfriend who toasted a bun.
They went to Florida, but Maxine Schweitzer was hard of
Hearing and the day afterwards the judge adjourned the trial.
When it finally came for judgment to come up
Of delicious courtyards near the Pantheon,
At last we had to let them speak, the children whom flowers had made
    statues
For the rivers of water which came from their funnel;
And we stood there in the middle of existence
Dazzled by the white paraffin of lunch.

Music in Paris and water coming out from the flannel
Of the purist person galloping down the Madeleine
Toward a certain wafer. Hey! just a minute! the sunlight is being rifled
By the green architecture of the flowers. But the boulevard turned a big
    blue deaf ear
Of cinema placards to the detonated traveler. He had forgotten the blue
    defilade of lunch!

Genoa! a stone's throw from Acapulco
If an engine were built strong enough,
And down where the hulls and scungilli,
Glisteningly unconscious, agree,
I throw a game of shoes with Horace Sturnbul
And forget to eat lunch.

O launch, lunch, you dazzling hoary tunnel
To paradise!
Do you see that snowman tackled over there
By summer and the sea? A boardwalk went to Istanbul
And back under his left eye. We saw the Moslems praying
In Rhodes. One had a red fez, another had a black cap.
And in the extended heat of afternoon,
As an ice-cold gradual sweat covered my whole body,
I realized, and the carpet swam like a red world at my feet
In which nothing was green, and the Moslems went on praying,
That we had missed lunch, and a perpetual torrent roared into the sea
Of my understanding. An old woman gave us bread and rolls on the
    street.

The dancing wagon has come! here is the dancing wagon!
Come up and get lessons—here is lemonade and grammar!
Here is drugstore and cowboy—all that is America—plus sex, perfumes,
    and shimmers—all the Old World;
Come and get it—and here is your reading matter
For twenty-nine centuries, and here finally is lunch—
To be served in the green defilade under the roaring tower
Where Portugal meets Spain inside a flowered madeleine.

My ginger dress has nothing on, but yours
Has on a picture of Queen Anne Boleyn

Surrounded by her courtiers eating lunch
And on the back a one of Henry the Eighth
Summoning all his courtiers in for lunch.

And the lunchboat has arrived
From Spain.
Everyone getting sick is on it;
The bold people and the sadists are on it;
I am glad I am not on it,
I am having a big claw of garlic for lunch—
But it plucks me up in the air,
And there, above the ship, on a cloud
I see the angels eating lunch.
One has a beard, another a moustache,
And one has some mustard smeared on his ears.
A couple of them ask me if I want to go to Honolulu,
And I accept—it's all right—
Another time zone: we'll be able to have lunch.
They are very beautiful and transparent,
My two traveling companions,
And they will go very well with Hawaii
I realize as we land there,
That dazzling red whiteness—it is our desire . . .
For whom? The angels of lunch.

On I sat over a glass of red wine
And you came out dressed in a paper cup.
An ant-fly was eating hay-mire in the chair-rafters
And large white birds flew in and dropped edible animals to the ground.
If they had been gulls it would have been garbage
Or fish. We have to be fair to the animal kingdom,
But if I do not wish to be fair, if I wish to eat lunch
Undisturbed—? The light of day shines down. The world continues.

We stood in the little hutment in Biarritz
Waiting for lunch, and your hand clasped mine
And I felt it was sweaty;
And then lunch was served,
Like the bouquet of an enchantress.
Oh the green whites and red yellows
And purple whites of lunch!

The bachelor eats his lunch,
The married man eats his lunch,
And old Uncle Joris belches
The seascape in which a child appears
Eating a watermelon and holding a straw hat.
He moves his lips as if to speak
But only sea air emanates from this childish beak.
It is the moment of sorrows,
And on the shores of history,
Which stretch in both directions, there are no happy tomorrows.
But Uncle Joris holds his apple up and begins to speak
To the child. Red waves fan my universe with the green macaw of
    lunch.

This street is deserted;
I think my eyes are empty;
Let us leave
Quickly.
Day bangs on the door and is gone.

Then they picked him up and carried him away from that company.
When he awoke he was in the fire department, and sleepy but not tired.
They gave him a hoseful of blue Spain to eat for lunch,
And Portugal was waiting for him at the door, like a rainstorm of
    evening raspberries.

It is time to give lunch to my throat and not my chest.
What? either the sting ray has eaten my lunch
Or else—and she searches the sky for something else;
But I am far away, seeming blue-eyed, empirical . . .
Let us give lunch to the lunch—
But how shall we do it?
The headwaiters expand and confer;
Will little pieces of cardboard box do it?
And what about silver and gold pellets?
The headwaiters expand and confer:
And what if the lunch should refuse to eat anything at all?
Why then we'd say be damned to it,
And the red doorway would open on a green railway
And the lunch would be put in a blue car

And it would go away to Whippoorwill Valley
Where it would meet and marry Samuel Dogfoot, and bring forth seven
        offspring,
All of whom would be half human, half lunch;
And when we saw them, sometimes, in the gloaming,
We would take off our mining hats and whistle Tweet twee-oo,
With watering mouths staring at the girls in pink organdy frocks,
Not realizing they really were half edible,
And we would die still without knowing it;
So to prevent anything happening that terrible
Let's give everybody we see and like a good hard bite right now,
To see what they are, because it's time for lunch!

The Departure from Hydra

As I was walking home just now, from seeing
Margaret and Norris off (though Peter,
An Englishman whom Norris had met yesterday,
Went back to change his clothes, and missed the boat)
As I came home along the little street
Without a name on which the only theatre,
The movie theatre, on Hydra is,
Called "The Gardenia" or just plain "Gardenia,"
The street which they today are tearing up
And carrying new stones in to replace
The ones they're tearing up, though it may be
They are the same stones, put in different order
Or in a different way, as I was walking,
With the heat of the day just over, at five-thirty,
I felt quite good, but then felt an awareness
Of something in my legs that might be painful
And then of some slight tension in my jaws
And slight pains in my head; instead of despairing
And giving all thought of pleasure up, I felt
That if I could write down all that I felt
As I came walking there, that that would be
A pleasure also, and with solidity.
I passed a mule—some men were loading up
His fellow-mule with packets—and I stared
At his wide eyes and his long hard flat nose
Or face, at which he turned away his eyes
And stamped his right hoof nervously. I felt
Guilty, a member of a higher species
Deliberately using my power against
A natural inferior because
Really I was afraid that he might kick
When I came past; but when he seemed upset
Then I felt guilty. Then I looked ahead
And saw a view of houses on the hill,
Particularly noticing one red one

And thinking, Yes, that is a part of what
I feel, of the variety of this walk;
Then my mind blurred somewhat, I turned and came
Down this small narrow alley to my home.
As I came in, reviewing the ideas
Which had occurred to me throughout my walk,
It suddenly came to me that maybe Peter
Had missed the Athens boat deliberately;
After all, Margaret was not sure that she
Wanted to accompany him and Norris
On a walking trip on Poros, and Norris had said
He wanted to stay with Margaret, so that Peter
Was disappointed, since he and Norris had planned
That very morning to take such a walking trip,
And he, Peter, had been the most excited
Of all, about it. But now since Margaret and Norris
Were going into Athens, what was there for Peter
To do, why should he take the boat at all,
Even though he'd planned to, to stop at Poros?
Except, of course, to act on some marginal chance
That Norris might get off with him and walk,
Or on the strength of previous expectations,
Emotional impetus lingering. If not,
Perhaps his going to change was just an excuse
To avoid an actual confrontation with Norris
In which he would have to say, "No, I'm not going
Unless you'll come on the walking trip!" but he knew,
Peter, that Norris wanted to stay with Margaret
And that therefore speaking to him would only result
In a little pain and confusion, since both were quite drunk,
Having planned their trip to Poros over beer all morning;
And also, of course, it might result in his getting,
In spite of himself, on the boat, by the talk confused
And not thinking clearly (whereas if he walked away
He had only, really, to wait till the boat had left—
Then he could come back down and think it over,
Surely to find he didn't regret too much
Not getting the boat, because after all the reason
He'd wanted to take the boat had long been gone).
For a human situation often leads

People to do things that they don't desire
At all, but they find that what they did desire
Has somehow led them to this situation
In which not to do that which is proposed
Seems inconsistent, hostile, or insane,
Though much more often very unfriendly; then too
Sometimes it chiefly is a lack of time
To explain how things have changed that leads one, waving
One's hands, aboard a ship that bodes one ill.
To walk away as Peter did is one way
Of avoiding such situations—another way
Is never to deceive or have high hopes
For foolish things; to be straight with oneself,
With one's own body, nature, and society,
To cast off everything that is not clear
And definite, and move toward one desire
After another, with no afterthoughts.
Living in this way one avoids the sudden
Transports of excitement Peter felt
When Norris mentioned a Poros walking tour.
For surely if Peter's natural desires
Had all been satisfied, if his life were running
Smoothly sexually, and if his health
Were excellent and his work going well,
He scarcely would have gotten so excited
At the mere thought of walking around Poros;
This sort of thing, however, often happens
To people from Northern countries, not just Peter,
And perhaps if one is English, Norse, or Swedish,
Danish, Finnish, Swiss, or North American,
One cannot avoid a certain amount of tension,
A certain quavering in the hand which reaches
For a ripe peach or the shoulder of a girl,
One whom, as one walks back from going swimming,
One thinks that one could eat, she's so delicious,
But only thinks it for a little while
(This thought itself is such a Northern one!
A Southerner would think about a place
Where he could go and jump on top of her)—
In any case, then, Northerners find it hard

To avoid such sudden excitements, but the English,
And especially the upper class, are worst of all,
Because besides their climate that's oppressed them
There's also been a restrictive upbringing,
Manners around the house perhaps too severe
For children—I am speaking of those English
Who escape from "class" and become bright or artistic,
The ones one sees on places like this island.
(These sudden outbursts of enthusiasm, of course,
Are often much admired by other people,
Particularly some not very smart ones,
Who think however they're very sensitive
And what they most admire is "vitality"
Which they think things like outbursts are a sign of,
And they can bore you far into the night
With telling you how wonderful some Dane
Or Norsky is, when you could be asleep
Dreaming of satisfying your desires
With persons who are always very warm,
Tender, and exciting—but, awake!
They're talking still, and though your sickly smile
Gets sicklier every moment, they go on:
"Hans suddenly got the idea to
Inundate Denmark. He is wonderful!"
"Oh, marvelous! Where does one go to meet him?"
"I'll give you his address. He has a farm
Where he stays in the summer; he loves animals,
But sometimes when he drinks a lot he beats them
And says that he can understand their language."
"How marvelous!" "And here's his city address:
Beschtungen aber Bass Gehundenweiss
996." "Goodnight." But Peter is
Not an exaggerated case like that,
And not a nagging bore who talks of such
People, but he has "outbursts" all the same.
It is true, in a sense these outbursts are
Difficult to discriminate from real
Vitality, which everyone esteems
These days because of man's oppressed position
In modern society, which saps his strength

And makes him want to do what everyone else does,
Whereas some man who says, "Let's pitch the glasses
Against the lamppost" is likely to be praised
By some low-IQ person who is there
As being really vital, ah he's wonderful.
Vitality, however, usually
Appeals to an answering vital force in others
And brings about making love or great events,
Or it at least gives pleasure—I can't judge
Vitality in any way but the way
It gives me pleasure, for if I do not get
Pleasure from life, of which vitality
Is just the liquid form, then what am I
And who cares what I say? I for one don't.
Therefore I judge vitality that way.)
But Peter, after having this idea
Of a walking trip on Poros, must have felt
That in walking around in the sun all day on an island
About which he knew nothing, there might come
Some insight to him or some relaxation,
Some feeling the way an Italian feels all the time,
Or perhaps not, perhaps he never does;
Peter at any rate was probably not
Conscious of an Italian at the time
He thought with pleasure about the walk on Poros,
But there he was, faced with Norris and Margaret
An hour before the boat came in, and Norris
Was saying "Maybe not." One mistake of Peter,
Or, rather, difficulty, a common one
In such enthusiasms, is that since
One's enthusiasm is motivated by submerged
Feelings and so its object isn't clear
To anyone, it is most likely that
Though they respond excitedly at first,
Partly because excitement is so communicable,
Others, when they think over what you've planned,
Will see it in a greyer light, unless of course
They have the same neuroses that you have,
In which case a whole lifetime might be built
Upon one of these outbursts. Norris, probably,

In drinking with Peter, wanted more than anything
To be agreeable, whereas Peter wanted
To "do" something unusual, not necessarily
Pleasing to Norris, not necessarily displeasing;
Norris, I should imagine, then, once he
Was out of Peter's company, since he'd known him
A very short time, was lacking the chief impulse
That motivated him when he agreed
To take a tour with Peter; therefore Margaret,
Speaking to Norris when he was alone
And saying she did not want to take the trip,
Found he immediately agreed with her,
Expressed some doubts at least, and said all right,
The trip was off then, he'd explain to Peter;
Peter, of course, was very surprised by this,
But still he must have been used to it because
The way that Norris and Margaret acted was based
On laws of human conduct which endure;
And since that outburst surely was not his first,
Peter was probably accustomed to
That sort of outcome of his impulses
And said to himself, "Ah, they don't understand,"
But probably knew inside that there was something
Seriously the matter with him. So when he left
The table and said, "I'm going to get my things,"
It was with a certain tension that he left,
Indicative of the fact he'd not come back,
And of the fact that he knew he would not avoid
Self-doubts because he avoided the useless boat trip;
Of course he wouldn't think he should have gone
But wonder why things had been the way they were.
It was these deeper worries in his mind,
I think, that kept him from leaving even sooner
With the same excuse, rather than a hope that Norris
Would change his mind again. Deep thoughts make helpless
Men for small undertakings. Well, perhaps
The last is speculation, but the rest
Seems surely true. I smiled, and closed the door.

Bertha

Oslo, the ramparts.

NOBLE

    The walls of our castles no longer withstand
    The barbarian attack!

COUNSELOR

                      Seek BERTHA in her haven!

NOBLE

    Bertha! we are at the barbarians' mercy.

BERTHA

    Give the signal for attack!

NOBLE

    Attack? attack? How can we attack?
    We are at the barbarians' mercy, they have surrounded our walls!

BERTHA

    Let me commune with my special gods a little.
    Meanwhile, ATTACK!

NOBLE

                      BERTHA commands attack!

COUNSELOR

                      Oh, the queen is mad!

NOBLE

    Mad, yes—but queen still. Never had Norway fairer or more brave.

OFFICER
To the attack, as commanded by Queen Bertha!

OLD MAN
Unhappy pagans! Soon the wrath of Bertha will be wreaked on them!

(BERTHA *appears, clothed in a ring of white eagles.*)

BARBARIANS
Help, help! Back! We are defeated!

(*They scurry.*)

ALL
Bertha has saved us from the barbarian menace.

(BERTHA *retires.*)

SCENE 2

A study in the castle.

TEACHER
Yes, it's a very interesting tale, that one you tell of the battle.
But why do you think you and your people yourselves are not Barbarians?

BERTHA
Off with my teacher's head!
WHACK!
Let higher learning be disreinstated!

(*Banners are sent up all over the kingdom.*)

SCENE 3

Bertha's summer lodge.

BERTHA

Ah, how sweet it is to take the Norway air
And breathe it in my own lungs, then out again
Where it again mingles with the white clouds and blue Norwegian sky.
For I myself, in a sense, am Norway, and when Bertha breathes
The country breathes, and it breathes itself in,
And so the sky remains perfectly pure Norway.

MESSENGER

Bertha, the land is at peace.

BERTHA

Attack Scotland!

SCENE 4

A little Scotch frontier town, on the battle lines.

SCOTCHMAN

They say Queen Bertha's men rage to win all Scotland as a present for
their mad queen.

SECOND SCOTCHMAN

No one has ever had Scotland defeated for very long; let Queen Bertha
try what she may!

THIRD SCOTCHMAN

Here come the armies of Bertha, Queen of Norway!

BERTHA *(at the head of her army, in a red and blue uniform; plants a banner)*
  Here shall Bertha stay, nor all Scotland conquer!
  Just to this flag's wave shall Bertha of Norway's kingdom reach!
  No greed urges the just Norwegian nation to further spoils.

ALL SCOTCH
  Hurrah for Queen Bertha!

COMMON NORWEGIAN SOLDIER
  She is mad!

  (Trumpets, and dispersal of all troops; the flag alone remains standing on the snowy stage.)

SCENE 5

The Council Chamber.

COUNSELOR
  Queen Bertha, we are tired of useless wars.

BERTHA
  Useless! Do you call it useless to fight off an invader?

COUNSELOR
  I was not speaking of the Barbarian Wars.

BERTHA
  Well, I was! The council is dismissed.

  (Everyone leaves, including BERTHA.*)*

SCENE 6

A rose garden.

GIRL

If Queen Bertha knew we were here!

MAN

She'd chop our two heads off, chip chap chop. There's no doubt about it.

GIRL

Why does she forbid us young lovers to meet in the garden?

MAN

A diseased mind, and the horrid fears of encroaching old age.

(They embrace. Explosion. Both fall dead.)

BERTHA *(from a castle window)*

Let there be no more garden meetings.

SCENE 7

BERTHA *on her throne.*

BERTHA

I am old, I am an old queen. But I still have the power of my childhood
Contained in my office. If I should lose my office, no more power
    would accrue
To my aged and feeble person. But even supposing I keep my power?
What chance is there that anything really nice will happen to me?

(She plays with a flag, musing.)

The flag of Norway! Once its colors drove my young heart wild
With dreams of conquest, first of the Norwegian flag, then of all the other
nations in the world . . .
I haven't gotten very far—yet still Bertha is great! *(Ringing a bell.)*
Call in the High Commissioners!

SCENE 8

The Throne Room.

BERTHA
We must give up the country to the barbarians!
I wish to conquer Norway again!

COUNSELOR *(aside)*
Bertha is mad! (*To* BERTHA:) Yes, your Majesty.

(Clarions are sounded.)

SCENE 9

A public place.

NORWEGIAN CITIZEN
They say Bertha will give us up to the barbarians!

SECOND NORWEGIAN CITIZEN
Impossible!

(The barbarian armies march in, with red and white banners.)

BARBARIAN CHIEFTAIN
On to the Castle! Norway is Barbarian!

(Sounds of cannon.)

SCENE 10

The Throne Room.

MESSENGER

Bertha arrives, at the head of teeming troops!
On her arrival from Scotland all Norway has rallied to her banner!
Millions of Norwegians surround the castle shrieking,
    "Bertha, Queen of Norway!"

BARBARIAN CHIEFTAIN

Let us be gone! We cannot withstand such force.
Quickly, to the tunnel!

(They disappear.)

*(*BERTHA *appears in regal splendor and walks to her throne,
followed by applauding citizens. She ascends the throne.)*

BERTHA

Norway!

(She falls from the throne and lies dead in front of it.)

NOBLE

Bertha is dead!

CITIZEN

She was a great queen!

SECOND CITIZEN

She conquered her own country many times!

THIRD CITIZEN

Norway was happy under her rule!

(Trumpets and sirens.)

Poem

The thing
To do
Is organize
The sea
So boats will
Automatically float
To their destinations.
Ah, the Greeks
Thought of that!
Well, what if
They
Did? We have no
Gods
Of the winds!
And therefore
Must use
Science!

Sleeping with Women

Caruso: a voice.
Naples: sleeping with women.
Women: sleeping in the dark.
Voices: a music.
Pompeii: a ruin.
Pompeii: sleeping with women.
Men sleeping with women, women sleeping with women, sheep sleeping
    with women, everything sleeping with women.
The guard: asking you for a light.
Women: asleep.
Yourself: asleep.
Everything south of Naples: asleep and sleeping with them.
Sleeping with women: as in the poems of Pascoli.
Sleeping with women: as in the rain, as in the snow.
Sleeping with women: by starlight, as if we were angels, sleeping on the train,
On the starry foam, asleep and sleeping with them—sleeping with women.
Mediterranean: a voice.
Mediterranean: a sea. Asleep and sleeping.
Streetcar in Oslo, sleeping with women, Toonerville Trolley
In Stockholm asleep and sleeping with them, in Skansen
Alone, alone with women,
The rain sleeping with women, the brain of the dog-eyed genius
Alone, sleeping with women, all he has wanted,
The dog-eyed fearless man.
Sleeping with them: as in *The Perils of Pauline*
Asleep with them: as in Tosca
Sleeping with women and causing all that trouble
As in Roumania, as in Yugoslavia
Asleep and sleeping with them
Anti-Semitic, and sleeping with women,
Pro-canary, Rashomon, Shakespeare, tonight, sleeping with women
A big guy sleeping with women
A black seacoast's sleeve, asleep with them

And sleeping with women, and sleeping with them
The Greek islands sleeping with women
The muddy sky, asleep and sleeping with them.
Sleeping with women, as in a scholarly design
Sleeping with women, as if green polarity were a line
Into the sea, sleeping with women
As if wolverines, in a street line, as if sheep harbors
Could come alive from sleeping with women, wolverines
Greek islands sleeping with women, Nassos, Naxos, Kos,
Asleep with women, Mykonos, miotis,
And myositis, sleeping with women, blue-eyed
Red-eyed, green-eyed, yellow reputed, white-eyed women
Asleep and sleeping with them, blue, sleeping with women
As in love, as at sea, the rabbi, asleep and sleeping with them
As if that could be, the stones, the restaurant, asleep and sleeping with them,
Sleeping with women, as if they were knee
Arm and thigh asleep and sleeping with them, sleeping with women.
And the iris peg of the sea
Sleeping with women
And the diet pill of the tree
Sleeping with women
And the apology the goon the candlelight
The groan: asking you for the night, sleeping with women
Asleep and sleeping with them, the green tree
The iris, the swan: the building with its mouth open
Asleep with women, awake with man,
The sunlight, asleep and sleeping with them, the moving gong
The abacus, the crab, asleep and sleeping with them
And moving, and the moving van, in London, asleep with women
And intentions, inventions for sleeping with them
Lands sleeping with women, ants sleeping with women, Italo-Greek or
    Anglo-French orchestras
Asleep with women, asleep and sleeping with them,
The foam and the sleet, asleep and sleeping with them,
The schoolboy's poem, the crippled leg
Asleep and sleeping with them, sleeping with women
Sleeping with women, as if you were a purist
Asleep and sleeping with them.
Sleeping with women: there is no known form for the future

Of this undreamed-of view: sleeping with a chorus
Of highly tuned women, asleep and sleeping with them.
Bees, sleeping with women
And tourists, sleeping with them
Soap, sleeping with women; beds, sleeping with women
The universe: a choice
The headline: a voice, sleeping with women
At dawn, sleeping with women, asleep and sleeping with them.
Sleeping with women: a choice, as of a mule
As of an island, asleep or sleeping with them, as of a Russia,
As of an island, as of a drum: a choice of views: asleep and sleeping with
    them, as of high noon, as of a choice, as of variety, as of the sunlight,
    red student, asleep and sleeping with them,
As with an orchid, as with an oriole, at school, sleeping with women, and
    you are the one
The one sleeping with women, in Mexico, sleeping with women
The ghost land, the vectors, sleeping with women
The motel man, the viaduct, the sun
The universe: a question
The moat: a cathexis
What have we done? On Rhodes, man
On Samos, dog
Sleeping with women
In the rain and in the sun
The dog has a red eye, it is November
Asleep and sleeping with them, sleeping with women
This June: a boy
October: sleeping with women
The motto: a sign; the bridge: a definition.
To the goat: destroy; to the rain: be a settee.
O rain of joy: sleeping with women, asleep and sleeping with them.
Volcano, Naples, Caruso, asleep and sleeping, asleep and sleeping with them
The window, the windrow, the hedgerow, irretrievable blue,
Sleeping with women, the haymow, asleep and sleeping with them, the canal
Asleep and sleeping with them, the eagle's feather, the dock's weather, and
    the glue:
Sleeping with you; asleep and sleeping with you: sleeping with women.
Sleeping with women, charming aspirin, as in the rain, as in the snow,

Asleep and sleeping with you: as if the crossbow, as of the moonlight
Sleeping with women: as if the tractate, as if d'Annunzio
Asleep and sleeping with you, asleep with women
Asleep and sleeping with you, asleep with women, asleep and sleeping
     with you, sleeping with women
As if the sun, as of Venice and the Middle Ages' "true
Renaissance had just barely walked by the yucca
Forest" asleep and sleeping with you
In China, on parade, sleeping with women
And in the sun, asleep and sleeping with you, sleeping with women,
Asleep with women, the docks, the alley, and the prude
Sleeping with women, asleep with them.
The dune god: sleeping with women
The dove: asleep and sleeping with them
Dials sleeping with women; cybernetic tiles asleep and sleeping with them
Naples: sleeping with women; the short of breath
Asleep and sleeping with you, sleeping with women
As if I were you—moon idealism
Sleeping with women, pieces of stageboard, sleeping with women
The silent bus ride, sleeping with you.
The chore: sleeping with women
The force of a disaster: sleeping with you
The organ grinder's daughter: asleep with bitumen, sunshine, sleeping
     with women,
Sleeping with women: in Greece, in China, in Italy, sleeping with blue
Red green orange and white women, sleeping with two
Three four and five women, sleeping on the outside
And on the inside of women, a violin, like a vista, women, sleeping with
     women
In the month of May, in June, in July
Sleeping with women, "I watched my life go by" sleeping with women
A door of pine, a stormfilled valentine asleep and sleeping with them
"This Sunday heart of mine" profoundly dormoozed with them
They running and laughing, asleep and sleeping with them
"This idle heart of mine" insanely "shlamoozed" asleep and sleeping with
     them,
They running in laughter
To the nearest time, oh doors of eternity
Oh young women's doors of my own time! sleeping with women

Asleep and sleeping with them, all Naples asleep and sleeping with them,
Venice sleeping with women, Burgos sleeping with women, Lausanne
    sleeping with women, hail depth-divers
Sleeping with women, and there is the bonfire of Crete
Catching divorce in its fingers, purple sleeping with women
And the red lights of dawn, have you ever seen them, green ports sleeping
    with women, acrobats and pawns,
You had not known it ere I told it you asleep with women
The Via Appia Antica asleep with women, asleep and sleeping with them
All beautiful objects, each ugly object, the intelligent world,
The arena of the spirits, the dietetic whisky, the storms
Sleeping with women, asleep and sleeping with them,
Sleeping with women. And the churches in Antigua, sleeping with women
The stone: a vow
The Nereid: a promise—to sleep with women
The cold—a convention: sleeping with women
The carriage: sleeping with women
The time: sometimes
The certainty: now
The soapbox: sleeping with women
The time and again nubile and time, sleeping with women, and the time now
Asleep and sleeping with them, asleep and asleep, sleeping with women,
    asleep and sleeping with them, sleeping with women.

The Pleasures of Peace

Another ribald tale of the good times at Madame Lipsky's.
Giorgio Finogle had come in with an imitation of the latest Russian poet,
The one who wrote the great "Complaint About the Peanut Farm" which I
    read to you last year at Mrs. Riley's,
Do you remember? and then of course Giorgio had written this imitation
So he came in with it. . . . Where was I and what was I saying?
The big beer parlor was filled with barmaids and men named Stuart
Who were all trying to buy a big red pitcher of beer for an artiste named
    Alma Stuart
Whom each claimed as his very own because of the similarity in names—
This in essence was Buddy's parody—Oh Giorgio, you idiot, Marian Stuart
    snapped,
It all has something to do with me! But no, Giorgio replied,
Biting in a melancholy way the edge off a cigar-paper-patterned envelope
In which he had been keeping the Poem for many days
Waiting to show it to his friends. And actually it's not a parody at all,
I just claimed it was, out of embarrassment. It's a poetic present for you all,
All of whom I love! Is it capable to love more than one—I wonder! Alma
    cried,
And we went out onto the bicycle-shaped dock where a malicious swarm of
    mosquitoes
Were parlaying after having invaded the old beer parlor.
The men named Stuart were now involved in a fight to the death
But the nearer islands lay fair in the white night light.
Shall we embark toward them? I said, placing my hand upon one exceedingly
    gentle
And fine. A picture of hairnets is being projected. Here
Comes someone with Alma Stuart! Is it real, this night? Or have we a gentle
    fantasy?
The Russian poet appears. He seems to consider it real, all right. He's
Quite angry. Where's the Capitalist fairy that put me down? he squirts
At our nomadic simplicity. "Complaint About the Peanut Farm" is a terrific
    poem. Yes,
In a way, yes. The Hairdresser of Night engulfs them all in foam.

"I love your work, *The Pleasures of Peace*," the Professor said to me next day;
"I think it adequately encompasses the hysteria of our era
And puts certain people in their rightful place. Chapeau! Bravo!"
"You don't get it," I said. "I like all this. I called this poem
Pleasures of Peace because I'm not sure they will be lasting!
I wanted people to be able to see what these pleasures are
That they may come back to them." "But they are all so hysterical, so—so
    transitory,"
The critic replied. "I mean, how can you—what kind of pleasures are these?
They seem more like pains to me—if I may say what I mean."
"Well, I don't know, Professor," I said; "permanent joys
Have so far been denied this hysterical person. Though I confess
Far other joys I've had and will describe in time.
And then too there's the pleasure of *writing* these—perhaps to experience is
    not the same."
The Professor paused, lightly, upon the temple stair.
"I will mention you among the immortals, Ken," he said,
"Because you have the courage of what you believe.
But there I will never mention those sniveling rats
Who only claim to like these things because they're fashionable."
"Professor!" I cried, "My darling! my dream!" And she stripped, and I saw
    there
Creamy female marble, the waist and thighs of which I had always dreamed.
"Professor! Loved one! why the disguise?" "It was a test," she said,
"Of which you have now only passed the first portion.
You must write More, and More—"
"And be equally persuasive?" I questioned, but She
Had vanished through the Promontory door.

So now I must devote my days to The Pleasures of Peace—
To my contemporaries I'll leave the Horrors of War,
They can do them better than I—each poet shares only a portion
Of the vast Territory of Rhyme. Here in Peace shall I stake out
My temporal and permanent claim. But such silver as I find
I will give to the Universe—the gold I'll put in other poems.
Thus in time there'll be a mountain range of gold
Of considerable interest. Oh may you come back in time
And in my lifetime to see it, most perfect and most delectable reader!
We poets in our youth begin with fantasies,

But then at least we think they may be realities—
The poems we create in our age
Require your hand upon our shoulder, your eye on our page.

Here are listed all the Pleasures of Peace that there could possibly be.
Among them are the pleasures of Memory (which Delmore Schwartz
     celebrated), the pleasures of autonomy,
The pleasures of agoraphobia and the sudden release
Of the agoraphobic person from the identified marketplace, the pleasures of
     roving over you
And rolling over the beach, of being in a complicated car, of sleeping,
Of drawing ropes with you, of planning a deranged comic strip, of shifting
     knees
At the accelerator pump, of blasphemy, of cobra settlement in a dilapidated
     skin country
Without clops, and therefore every pleasure is also included; which, after
     these—

Chapter Thirty Seven.
On the Planisphere everyone was having a nut
When suddenly my Lulu appeared.
She was a big broad about six feet seven
And she had a red stone in her ear
Which was stringent in its beauty.
I demanded at once the removal of people from the lobby
So we could begin to down ABC tablets and start to feel funny
But Mordecai La Schlomp our Leader replied that we did not need any
That a person could feel good without any artificial means.
Oh the Pleasures of Peace are infinite and they cannot be counted—
One single piece of pink mint chewing gum contains more pleasures
Than the whole rude gallery of war! And the moon passes by
In an otherwise undistinguished lesson on the geography of this age
Which has had fifty-seven good lovers and ninety-six wars. By Giorgio
     Finogle.

It turns out that we're competing for the Peace Award,
Giorgio Finogle and I. We go into the hair parlor, the barber—
We get to talking about war and about peace.
The barber feels that we are really good people at heart
Even though his own views turn out to be conservative.

"I've read Finogle's piece, the part of it that was in *Smut*," he
Says, "and I liked it. Yours, Koch, I haven't yet seen,
But Alyne and Francie told me that you were the better poet."
"I don't know," I said. "Giorgio is pretty good." And Giorgio comes back
   from the bathroom
Now, with a grin on his face. "I've got an idea for my
Pleasures of Peace," he says; "I'm going to make it include
Each person in the universe discussing their own bag—
Translation, their main interest, and what they want to be—"
"You'll never finish it, Giorgio," I said. "At least I'll
Get started," he replied, and he ran out of the barbershop.

In the quiet night we take turns riding horseback and falling asleep.
Your breasts are more beautiful than a gold mine.
I think I'll become a professional man.
The reason we are up-to-date is we're some kind of freaks.
I don't know what to tell the old man
But he is concerned with two kinds of phenomena and I am interested in
   neither. What *are* you interested in?
Being some kind of freaks, I think. Let's go to Transylvania.
I don't understand your buddy all the time. Who?
The one with HANDLEBAR written across his head.
He's a good guy, he just doesn't see the difference between a man and a bike.
   If I love you
It's because you belong to and have a sublime tolerance
For such people. Yes, but in later life, I mean—
It is Present Life we've got to keep up on the screen,
Isn't it. Well yes, she said, but—
I am very happy that you are interested in it. The French poodle stopped
   being Irish entirely
And we are all out of the other breeds.
The society woman paused, daintily, upon the hotel stair.
No, I must have a poodle, said she; not an Irish setter
Would satisfy me in my mad passion for the poodle breeds!
As usual, returning to the bed
I find that you are inside it and sound asleep. I smile happily and look at your
   head.
It is regular-size and has beautiful blonde hair all around it.
Some is lying across the pillow. I touch it with my feet
Then leap out the window into the public square,
And I tune my guitar.

"O Mistress Mine, where are you roving?" That's my tune! roars Finogle,
     and he
Comes raging out of the *Beefsteak*—I was going to put that in MY Pleasures
     of Peace.
Oh normal comportment! even you too I shall include in the Pleasures of
     Peace,
And you, relative humidity five hundred and sixty-two degrees!
But what of you, poor sad glorious aqueduct
Of boorish ashes made by cigarettes smoked at the Cupcake
Award—And Sue Ellen Musgrove steps on one of my feet. "Hello!"
She says. "You're that famous COKE, aren't you,
That no one can drink? When are you going to give us your famous Iliad
That everyone's been talking of, I mean your Pleasures of Peace!"

Life changes as the universe changes, but the universe changes
More slowly, as bedevilments increase.
Sunlight comes through a clot for example
Which Zoo Man has thrown on the floor. It is the Night of the Painted
     Pajamas
And the Liberals are weeping for peace. The Conservatives are raging for it.
The Independents are staging a parade. And we are completely naked
Walking through the bedroom for peace. I have this friend who had myopia
So he always had to get very close to people
And girls thought he was trying to make out—
Why didn't he get glasses?—He was a Pacifist! The Moon shall overcome!

Outside in the bar yard the Grecians are screaming for peace
And the Alsatians, the Albanians, the Alesians, the Rubans, the Aleutians,
And the Iranians, all, all are screaming for peace.
They shall win it, their peace, because I am going to help them!
And he leaped out the window for peace!
Headline: GIORGIO FINOGLE,
NOTED POET, LAST NIGHT LEAPED OUT THE WINDOW FOR
     PEACE.
ASIDE FROM HEAD INJURIES HIS CONDITION IS REPORTED
     NORMAL.
But Giorgio never was normal! Oh the horrors of peace,
I mean of peace-fighting! But Giorgio is all right,
He is still completely himself. "I am going to throw this hospital

136

Bed out the window for peace," when we see him, he says.
And, "Well, I guess your poem will be getting way ahead of mine now," he
    says
Sadly, ripping up an envelope for peace and weakly holding out his hand
For my girl, Ellen, to stroke it; "I will no longer be the most famous poet
For peace. You will, and you know it." "But you jumped out the
Window, Finogle," I said, "and your deed shall live longer
In men's imaginations than any verse." But he looked at the sky
Through the window's beautiful eye and he said, "Kenneth, I have not
    written one word
Of my Poem for Peace for three weeks. I've struck a snarl
And that's why (I believe) I jumped out the
Window—pure poetic frustration. Now tell them all that, how
They'll despise me, oh sob sob—" "Giorgio," I said, trying to calm him
    down but laughing
So hard I could barely digest the dinner of imagination
In which your breasts were featured as on a Popeye card
When winter has lighted the lanterns and the falls are asleep
Waiting for next day's shards, "Giorgio," I said, "the pleasures—"
But hysteria transported us all.

When I awoke you were in a star-shaped muffin, I was in a loaf of bread
Shaped like a camera, and Giorgio was still in his hospital bed
But a huge baker loomed over us. One false moof and I die you! he said
In a murderous throaty voice and I believe in the yellow leaves, the
Orange, the red leaves of autumn, the tan leaves, and the promoted ones
Of green, of green and blue. Sometimes walking through an ordinary garden
You will see a bird, and the overcoat will fall from your
Shoulders, slightly, exposing one beautiful curve
On which sunbeams alighting forget to speak a single word
To their parent sun and are thus cut off
Without a heating unit, but need none being on your breast
Which I have re-christened "Loaves" for the beginning of this year
In which I hope the guns won't fire any more, the baker sang
To his baker lady, and then he had totally disappeared.
It looks as though everyone were going to be on our side!

And the flowers came out, and they were on our side,
Even the yellow little ones that grow beside your door
And the huge orange ones were bending to one side

As we walked past them, I looked into your blue eyes
And I said, "If we come out of this door
Any more, let it be to enter only this nervous paradise
Of peaceful living conditions, and if Giorgio is roped down
Let them untie him, so he can throw his hospital bed out the door
For all we need besides peace, which is considerable, but first we need
      that—"

Daredevil, Julian and Maddalo, and John L. Lewis
Are running down the stairways for peace, they are gathering the ice
And throwing it in buckets, they are raising purple parasols for peace
And on top of these old sunlight sings her song, "New lights, old lights
      again, blue lights for peace,
Red lights for the low, insulted parasol, and a few crutches thrown around for
      peace"—
Oh contentment is the key
To continuing exploration of the nations and their feet;
Therefore, andiamo—the footfall is waiting in the car
And peaceful are the markets and the sneaks;
Peaceful are the Garfinkle ping-pong balls
And peaceful are the blooms beneath the sea
Peaceful are the unreserved airplane loops and the popularly guided blips
Also the Robert Herrick stone sings a peaceful song
And the banana factory is getting hip, and the pigs' Easter party too is
      beginning to join in a general celebration
And the women and men of old Peru and young Haifa and ancient Japan and
      beautiful young rippling Lake Tahoe
And hairy old Boston and young Freeport and young Santo Domingo and
      old father Candelabra the Chieftain of Hoboes
Are rolling around the parapets for peace, and now the matadors are
      throwing in
Huge blops of canvas and the postgraduates are filling in
As grocery dates at peanut dances and the sunlight is filling in
Every human world canvas with huge and luminous pleasure gobs of peace—
And the Tintorettos are looking very purple for peace
And the oyster campus is beginning its peaceful song—

Oh let it be concluded, including the medals!
Peace will come thrusting out of the sky
Tomorrow morning, to bomb us into quietude.

For a while we can bid goodbye
To the frenesies of this poem, The Pleasures of Peace.
When there is peace we will not need anything but bread
Stars and plaster with which to begin.
Roaming from one beard to another we shall take the tin
From the mines and give it to roaring Fidel Castro.
Where Mao Tse Tung lies buried in ocean fields of sleeping cars
Our Lorcaesque decisions will clonk him out
And resurrect him to the rosebuddy sky
Of early evening. And the whip-shaped generals of Hanoi
Shall be taken in overcoats to visit the sky
And the earth will be gasping for joy!

"A wonder!" "A rout!" "No need now for any further poems!" "A Banzai for
    peace!" "He can speak to us all!"
And "Great, man!" "Impressive!" "Something new for you, Ken"
    "Astounding!" "A real
Epic!" "The worst poem I have ever read!" "Abominably tasteless!" "Too
    funny!" "Dead, man!
A cop-out! a real white man's poem! a folderol of honky blank spitzenburger
    smugglerout Caucasian gyp
Of phony bourgeois peace poetry, a total shrig!" "Terrific!" "I will
    expect you at six!"
"A lovely starry catalogue for peace!" "Is it Shakespeare or Byron who
    breathes
In the lines of his poem?" "You have given us the Pleasures of Peace,
Now where is the real thing?" "Koch has studied his history!" "Bold!"
    "Stunning!" "It touches us like leaves
Sparkling in April—but is that all there is
To his peace plea?" Well, you be the one
To conclude it, if you think it needs more—I want to end it,
I want to see real Peace again! Oh peace bams!
I need your assistance—and peace drams, distilling through the world! peace
    lamps, be shining! and peace lambs, rumble up the shore!
O Goddess, sweet Muse, I'm stopping—now show us where you are!

And the big boats come sailing into the harbor for peace
And the little apes are running around the jungle for peace
And the day (that is, the star of day, the sun) is shining for peace
Somewhere a moustachioed student is puzzling over the works of Raymond
    Roussel for peace

And the Mediterranean peach trees are fast asleep for peace
With their pink arms akimbo and the blue plums of Switzerland for peace
And the monkeys are climbing for coconuts and peace
The Hawaiian palm
And serpents are writhing for peace—those are snakes—
And the Alps, Mount Vesuvius, all the really big important mountains
Are rising for peace, and they're filled with rocks—surely it won't be long;
And Leonardo da Vinci's *Last Supper* is moving across the monastery wall
A few micrometers for peace, and Paolo Uccello's red horses
Are turning a little redder for peace, and the Anglo-Saxon dining hall
Begins glowing like crazy, and Beowulf, Robert E. Lee, Sir Barbarossa, and
      Baron Jeep
Are sleeping on the railways for peace and darting around the harbor
And leaping into the sailboats and the sailboats will go on
And underneath the sailboats the sea will go on and we will go on
And the birds will go on and the snappy words will go on
And the tea sky and the sloped marine sky
And the hustle of beans will go on and the unserious canoe
It will all be going on in connection with you, peace, and my poem, like a
      Cadillac of wampum
Unredeemed and flying madly, will go exploding through
New cities sweet inflated, planispheres, ingenious hair, a camera smashing
Badinage, cerebral stands of atmospheres, unequaled, dreamed of
Empeacements, candled piers, fumisteries, emphatic moods, terrestrialism's
Crackle, love's flat, sun's sweets, O Peace, to you.

Equal to You

Can you imagine the body being
The really body the being the reality
Body being the body if reality
Is what it is it is, not that reality
Doesn't infer the body, still
The body being the bearer of reality
And the barer of the body
The body being reality
That is reality's reality
Hardly on earth ever seen
But from it we have the word *connubial*
Which means
The body bearing the body in reality
And reality being the body
And body-reality being borne.
I am bearing a burden
Which reminded me of you
Bearing away the swell
Of the sea
But can you imagine the body bearing reality
And being reality
That's where we get the
Word *connubial* which is a word for the body's being
Being in reality and being a body
In reality and bearing the burden
Of the body in reality, by being real
And by being the body of the real.

From The Duplications

FROM PART ONE

One night in Venice, near the Grand Canal,
A lovely girl was sitting by her stoop,
Sixteen years old, Elizabeth Gedall,
When, suddenly, a giant ice-cream scoop
Descended from the clouded blue corral
Of heaven and scooped her skyward with a loop-
The-loopy motion, which the gods of Venice
Saw, and, enraged, they left off cosmic tennis

And plotted their revenge. They thought some outer
Space denizen or monster had decided
To take this child, perhaps who cared about her
And wished to spare her heart a world divided,
Or else who wanted to hug, kiss, and clout her,
And, lust upwelling, the right time had bided,
Or something such—so thought, at least, the gods of
Her native city, famed for bees and matzoh.

Venice, Peru, of course, is where it happened,
A city modeled on the Italian one
Which was all paid for by Commander Papend,
A wealthy Yugoslav who liked his fun.
The Com had sexual urges large as Lapland
And was as set for action as a gun
In madman's hands who hates the world around him—
But Com was filled with love, his heart all pounding!

And so he'd made this North Italian jewel,
Canals and palaces on every side,
An urban re-creation, not renewal,
A daring lust's restatement of life's pride;
Huge bumboats carrying marble, masks, and fuel
Clogged South American streams, till Nature cried
"Some madman's building Venice in Peru!
Abomination beneath the sky's blue!"

In protest of his act, waves shook the earth:
Shock and resentment over this new Venice!
And Central South America gave birth
To hideous monstrous bees, so huge disfenes-
Tration would result when their great girth
Against some building window hurled its menace!
So, windowless new Venice had to be.
But there was one thing that could stop a bee

Of overwhelming size: a matzoh placard
Placed on the shoreside gilding of the house.
It must of course be large, huge as the Packard
Driven for Canada Dry by Mickey Mouse
Attempting to establish the world's record;
Minnie is at his side, and Gabby Grouse,
A brand new character who's been invented
Since Disney's death—they think he'd have consented.

Walt Disney dead! And Salvador Dali lives!
Paul Eluard gone, and Aragon still alive!
How strange the breathing tickets that fate gives—
Bees dance to show, when entering the hive,
Which way best flowers are, but are like sieves
To death's mysterious force. Oh you who drive
The car, stop speeding; breathe a little longer.
Create, and make us gladder now and stronger!

As Papend did by carrying out his plan
"Venice in South America," an almost
Perfectly accurate copy. Yet one can
Discern things here and there I think would gall most
Other Venetians: bees and the whitish tan
Enormous matzoh placards which some tall ghost
Might use for palace walls. O strange piazzas
Of South America, deranged by matzohs!

How was it known, you ask me, that the busy
Bees would stop marauding if confronted
With matzoh placards? Well, it makes bees dizzy
To look at matzoh. If more details are wanted,
See *Matzoh-Loving Bees* by E. McTizzy
Where all's explained: the stinger's slightly stunted
Or blunted, I forget, by the bakery pleating
Of the matzoh, made in this case not for eating

But civil defense. . . .

. . . . Meanwhile in Greece, near lines
Which run from Theseus' temple to Poseidon's
Let's turn our gaze, like Heaven's, which divines
A motor vehicle with an inside ins-
Ide its outside larger than the spines
Of dinosaurs, which men with subtle guidance
From bits of bone and dust have put together
Inside museums to resist the weather

So we can walk around them saying, "Jesus!
What if them fuckers walked around today?"
And now and then a guard comes up and teases
Some little chap with "Did you see that, hey?
It moved! The thing's alive!" which so increases
The pleasure of the people there that they
Laugh to themselves at both the boy and guard—
So huge this automobile was. "Take a card,"

Said Minnie, as they drove, to Gabby Grouse;
"Mickey, how many do you have by now?"
"Dear, I can't play while driving. Here's the house!"
Gabbed Mick. "Look, dear," mouthed Minnie, "Clarabelle Cow
Is cropping grass as evenly as a louse
Creeps through the hair of evening. And a bough
Heavy with honeysuckle hangs above
Our nest of nozzling and our lair of love!"

"Truer were never spoken mousie words!"
Sang Mickey as he drove the gleaming Packard
Into the barn. Above him busy birds
Conduct their songfest, and not one is laggard.
"Clarabelle's milk has been too full of curds!"
Cries Pluto, running to them. Thought a faggot
By some, this dog was said to favor fellas
Of every species when he lived in Hellas.

But Mickey didn't give a damn! He smacked
Pluto between the ears and gave a whistle!
Clarabelle Cow came munching up. Mick whacked
Her on the ass and said, "I picked this thistle
In far-off Zululand, my love. Half-cracked,
I've brought it from that bush like an epistle,
Clarabelle Cow, for you! Now, food and rest!
Tomorrow we must be at our rodent best!

Come on! We've got to get this car unpacked!
No time for fooling now; we have one night
And one night only, one, to be exact,
One twelve-hour span to seek our souls' delight
And then before Greece's hellish dawn has cracked
We must be on the road again in flight,
In glorious flight, world's record speed to try
On all the roads of Greece, for Canada Dry!"

"Oh, Mickey, can't you stay here more?" cried Clara,
Hot for some consummation with the mouse;
"They say upon the shores of the blue Cari-
Bbean Sea is a pagoda house
Where mice love more than Deirdre did in Tara!
Oh, that I there could shed my milky blouse
And be with you a weekend or a year!"
So saying, she rough-tongued his rounded ear.

"Clara, beware!" cried Minnie. "I'll not let you
So carry on with Mick while I'm alive!
Even if you make him now, he'll soon forget you
When we go speeding off upon our drive
Over the million roads of Greece. Upset you?
Too bad! He's mine! You, just when we arrive,
Start making cow eyes at him. Your tough luck!
Alone with him tonight I'll squeak and fuck!"

. . . .

FROM PART TWO

. . . . Well,
I must confess that I don't quite feel ready
To leap back into things just yet and tell
How this and that were—I still feel unsteady:
Sometimes I ring with insights like a bell—
At others I feel close to Zacowitti!
I think I want to stall to tell you more
Of what I've felt, since on Hibernia's shore

I walked each day with Homer Brown and wrote
So many pages leading up to this one.
We'd see green fields so worthy of our note
That I at least was tempted to go kiss one.
But didn't, since I'm neither sheep nor goat,
But tried instead distilling all the bliss one
Feels in such happy times into my eight-line
Poetic sets with a late-sixties dateline—

And which will be resumed, but not this second.
I said I want to say things, and I do,
To catch myself and you up on the fecund,
Or fecund-seeming, life this long-lapsed Jew,
To whom the Talmud Torah had not beckoned
Imperiously since nineteen forty-two,
Lived since that time, but most to tell you of
That Irish time I wrote this, which I love

To think about, but I have never done so
At length at all because of life's fast pace
Which, starting off with waking, makes me run so
That I am short of breath and red of face
By evening, as if Tempus held a gun so
That Fugit could escape. Oh lovely lace
Of memory, that we can hold and contemplate—
How much of you mind's attic does accommodate!

There must be miles of you that are still folded
And stacked away in trunks I'll never get to!
Some people claim that some of theirs have molded—
I must confess mine I have not known yet to:
What I have Lear'd or Tristran-and-Isolde'd
Is with me still, each sit-down and each set-to,
For me to find the temporal space to climb to
And speculate about and find the rhyme to.

I want to do this now with those six weeks
I spent in Kinsale working on this epic
Which of things unattempted boldly speaks
In verse Orlandic, Don-Juanesque, and Beppic:
Of how Alaskan toucans got their beaks,
And why the waters of the vast Pacific
Are blue at dawn and pink by half past seven;
Of how things are on earth, and how in heaven—

A work perhaps I never can conclude.
It's my own fault—I like works to be endless,
So no detail seems ever to intrude
But to be part of something so tremendous,
Bright, clear, complete, and constantly renewed,
It totally obliterates addenda's
Intended use, to later compensate
For what was not known at the earlier date.

So, Memory, back! to those sweet times in Cork, which
Have not yet gotten my complete attention,
And, Muse! help me to find that tuning fork which
Makes anything it touches good to mention.
I'm starting up this work now in New York, which
Is as unlike Kinsale as hypertension
Is unlike pleasant calm and sunny weather—
By verse I hope to get them all together

And most specifically by verse concerning
The days I spent in Kinsale. Well, I've said that
At least two times already and am burning
To carry on this discourse with my head that
The world calls poetry and I call yearning—
If you don't mind, do please forget you read that:
It's far beneath my standards and I worry
You'll think it's me—it's not—I'm in a hurry

To catch my feelings while they pass me fleetingly
And so don't want to stop at every boner
Like scholars who er-umly and indeedingly
Lard everything so much you wish a stone or
A rowboat's oar would batter them obediently
Then magically fly back to its owner
Who thus would not be punished. I like catching
Pure chickens of discourse while they're still hatching

And so, unhushed, rush on. I had a bedroom
In that three-story house which the Browns lived in;
Each day I wrote my poem in the said room
While Betty Brown diced, sliced, and carved, and sieved in
The kitchen which was under it. The red room
Across the hall from mine, designed by Rifkin,
Homer and Betty dwelt in, and the other
Room on that floor was Katherine's, whom her mother

Would sing to sleep two times a day or once,
Depending if she was in a napping period;
When she was, there was one nap after lunch
Or sometimes none, at which time cries were myriad
And I would set my elbow with a crunch
Upon the desk and, like a man much wearièd
By journey long across a perilous waste,
Put head in hand and groan as one disgraced

By having lost all natural zest for living,
All inspiration, talent, luck, and skill.
I've always thought I should be more forgiving
And not be seized by the desire to kill
When someone interrupts me at my knitting
Of words together, but I'm that way still.
I've not, however, murdered anyone,
I swear, as I am Stuart's and Lillian's son.

How moved I am to write their names, how curious
They sound to me, as Kenneth does, my own one,
Which, though I'm no more Scots than Madame Curie is,
I like for the plain clear Highlandsy tone one
(Or I) can hear in it. Some names sound spurious,
Like "Impsie," or Sir Lalla Rookh Ben Lomond.
Some are invented; some we choose by fantasy;
Some hoping to inherit; some, romantically—

If, for example, Dad once loved a lassie
Named Billy Jo, he might call baby Billy,
If baby is a boy, or if the chassis
Of that small creature shows that it is silly
To think she's the same sex as Raymond Massey
And may one day play Lincoln, perhaps Tillie
Might satisfy his crazed nostalgic need
To see his old flame at his wife's breast feed.

In any case, names are a sort of token
Which parents give a child when it sets out
Into life's subway system, which is broken
And filled with people eating sauerkraut;
We pass the turnstile when our name is spoken
But it's the train that hurries us about,
I.e. our brain, brawn, energy, and genius,
Whether we're named Kaluka or Frobenius.

So names begin us, but—On with my story!
If I have interrupted interruptions
Of interrupted interruptions, glory
Will never be my lot, but foul corruptions;
For that which feeds upon itself grows gory—
But there, again, enough! All my productions
Are subject to this peril; let's go on.
Already in the east I see the dawn

Growing more quickly than the flush of red
Upon the back of Lisa who has lain
Four hours naked in the sand instead
Of going to the store at Fifth and Main
To buy some pinking scissors as she said
That she was going to, wherefore her pain;
And out of the vague silence of the night
Come clippery sounds of birds, not yet in flight.

So did the mornings greet me in Kinsale,
Often, when I would read all night, or, oftener,
When I would have some nightmare by the tail
Which crushed the woof of sleep like fabric softener
And brought me naked to the shade, where pale
Aurora seemed, as Joyce said, to be "doffin' 'er
Glarious gowrments to receive the Sun"—
Those garbs were pink and red. O Day begun,

How energizing so to contemplate you
Before the full awareness of the twenty-
Four hours we have to know you makes us hate you,
Sometimes; sometimes one minute of you's plenty
And makes one wish to ante- or post-date you
Just so you go away—but in the denty
Sweet early scuds of dawning, how delicious
You, Day, can be! so that, sometimes, ambitious

Poets have hailed you at your birth with names
Like Monday, Tuesday, Thursday, Friday, Sunday,
Saturday, Wednesday, Pottsday, Day of Flames,
Day of Decision, Pet and Family Fun Day,
All Fools Day, Hallowe'en, Christmas, Henry James
Commemorative Reading Day, Clean Gun Day,
Happy Hog Day, and so on, as if, by calling
You names, one might prevision your befalling

Or something of that kind. Well, at the window
Sometimes I'd stay a while and sometimes hurry
Back into bed whose sheets like very thin dough
Were slightly rough for sleeping (made by Murray)
And doze again, then later would begin to
Get dressed for breakfast, which, in a great flurry
Of soda bread, we three would eat together
With Katherine Brown, in the cold Irish weather.

Then after that quite often I would run
Along a kind of sidewalk that ran upwards
From where the house was, up to where the sun
Would have been closer if in the cloudy cupboards
It did not hang away till day was done.
Then homeward, past proud dames in Mother Hubbards
And former Irish exiles who'd found out
That Budweiser was nothing to the stout

Served at "The Spaniard" on Saint Bernard's Hill.
Sometimes "Good marnin" would emerge from these
I passed, and sometimes not, for they were still
And I was running, it was not with ease
We could converse. My lungs with breath would fill,
My heart with beats, and then my mind would seize
Sometimes a phrase or line that made me race to
Get back in time so I could find a place to

Put it into my poem in time to carry
With it all its inspired associations.
One's words, though, once excited, mate and marry
Incessantly, incestuously, like patients
Gone mad with love, so even sometimes the very
Words I would lose enroute spawned duplications
Stretching as far as sight. Back at my desk
I'd sit then, breathless and Chirrurgeresque

With lacy inspirations and complexities
Made up of breath and heartbeats and confusions,
As one may have of fish as to what sex it is,
As to which of my *trouvailles* were delusions
And which could guide my poem as sheep executives
Ideally guide their flocks, toward such effusions
Of epic lyric life that I would find
The sole true story of man's secret mind.

A large ambition! Strange that words suggest to us
That we can do such things. And strange the feeling
That we have done it sometimes; strange that Aeschylus
Probably felt the same beneath the ceiling
Of the Greek room he wrote in for the festivals
Of le Théâtre Grec. And it is healing,
The thought that one is capable in some way
Of being in control on this huge Stunway

Of our existence. Anyway, I'd sit
Un-Aeschylean, certainly, at that
Table I used for desk, and stretch my wit
In such way as I could. There was a flat
Quality to my living there that fit
The kind of thing that I was working at:
Friendly but not involved with anyone—
Not lonely, but, whenever I wished, alone. . . .

The Circus

I remember when I wrote The Circus
I was living in Paris, or rather we were living in Paris
Janice, Frank was alive, the Whitney Museum
Was still on 8th Street, or was it still something else?
Fernand Léger lived in our building
Well it wasn't really our building it was the building we lived in
Next to a Grand Guignol troupe who made a lot of noise
So that one day I yelled through a hole in the wall
Of our apartment I don't know why there was a hole there
Shut up! And the voice came back to me saying something
I don't know what. Once I saw Léger walk out of the building
I think. Stanley Kunitz came to dinner. I wrote The Circus
In two tries, the first getting most of the first stanza;
That fall I also wrote an opera libretto called Louisa or Matilda.
Jean-Claude came to dinner. He said (about "cocktail sauce")
It should be good on something but not on these (oysters).
By that time I think I had already written The Circus.
Part of the inspiration came while walking to the post office one night
And I wrote a big segment of The Circus
When I came back, having been annoyed to have to go
I forget what I went there about
You were back in the apartment what a dump actually we liked it
I think with your hair and your writing and the pans
Moving strummingly about the kitchen and I wrote The Circus
It was a summer night no it was an autumn one summer when
I remember it but actually no autumn that black dusk toward the post office
And I wrote many other poems then but The Circus was the best
Maybe not by far the best there was also Geography
And the Airplane Betty poems (inspired by you) but The Circus was the best.

Sometimes I feel I actually am the person
Who did this, who wrote that, including that poem The Circus
But sometimes on the other hand I don't.
There are so many factors engaging our attention!
At every moment the happiness of others, the health of those we know and
      our own!

And the millions upon millions of people we don't know and their well-being
    to think about
So it seems strange I found time to write The Circus
And even spent two evenings on it, and that I have also the time
To remember that I did it, and remember you and me then, and write this
    poem about it.
At the beginning of The Circus
The Circus girls are rushing through the night
In the circus wagons and tulips and other flowers will be picked
A long time from now this poem wants to get off on its own
Someplace like a painting not held to a depiction of composing The Circus.

Noel Lee was in Paris then but usually out of it
In Germany or Denmark giving a concert
As part of an endless activity
Which was either his career or his happiness or a combination of both
Or neither I remember his dark eyes looking he was nervous
With me perhaps because of our days at Harvard.

It is understandable enough to be nervous with anybody!

How softly and easily one feels when alone
Love of one's friends when one is commanding the time and space syndrome
If that's the right word which I doubt but together how come one is so nervous?
One is not always but what was I then and what am I now attempting to create
If create is the right word
Out of this combination of experience and aloneness
And who are you telling me it is or is not a poem (not you)? Go back with me
    though
To those nights I was writing The Circus.
Do you like that poem? have you read it? It is in my book Thank You
Which Grove just reprinted. I wonder how long I am going to live
And what the rest will be like I mean the rest of my life.

John Cage said to me the other night How old are you? and I told him forty-six
(Since then I've become forty-seven) he said
Oh that's a great age I remember.
John Cage once told me he didn't charge much for his mushroom
    identification course (at the New School)
Because he didn't want to make a profit from nature.

He was ahead of his time I was behind my time we were both in time
Brilliant go to the head of the class and "time is a river"
It doesn't seem like a river to me it seems like an unformed plan
Days go by and still nothing is decided about
What to do until you know it never will be and then you say "time"
But you really don't care much about it any more
Time means something when you have the major part of yours ahead of you
As I did in Aix-en-Provence that was three years before I wrote The Circus
That year I wrote Bricks and The Great Atlantic Rainway
I felt time surround me like a blanket endless and soft
I could go to sleep endlessly and wake up and still be in it
But I treasured secretly the part of me that was individually changing
Like Noel Lee I was interested in my career
And still am but now it is like a town I don't want to leave
Not a tower I am climbing opposed by ferocious enemies.

I never mentioned my friends in my poems at the time I wrote The Circus
Although they meant almost more than anything to me
Of this now for some time I've felt an attenuation
So I'm mentioning them maybe this will bring them back to me
Not them perhaps but what I felt about them
John Ashbery Jane Freilicher Larry Rivers Frank O'Hara
Their names alone bring tears to my eyes
As seeing Polly did last night.
It is beautiful at any time but the paradox is leaving it
In order to feel it when you've come back the sun has declined
And the people are merrier or else they've gone home altogether
And you are left alone well you put up with that your sureness is like the sun
While you have it but when you don't its lack's a black and icy night. I came
    home

And wrote The Circus that night, Janice. I didn't come and speak to you
And put my arm around you and ask you if you'd like to take a walk
Or go to the Cirque Medrano though that's what I wrote poems about
And am writing about that now, and now I'm alone

And this is not as good a poem as The Circus
And I wonder if any good will come of either of them all the same.

The Magic of Numbers

THE MAGIC OF NUMBERS — 1

How strange it was to hear the furniture being moved around in the
　　apartment upstairs!
I was twenty-six, and you were twenty-two.

THE MAGIC OF NUMBERS — 2

You asked me if I wanted to run, but I said no and walked on.
I was nineteen, and you were seven.

THE MAGIC OF NUMBERS — 3

Yes, but does X really like us?
We were both twenty-seven.

THE MAGIC OF NUMBERS — 4

You look like Jerry Lewis (1950).

THE MAGIC OF NUMBERS — 5

Grandfather and grandmother want you to go over to their house for dinner.
They were sixty-nine, and I was two and a half.

THE MAGIC OF NUMBERS — 6

One day when I was twenty-nine years old I met you and nothing happened.

THE MAGIC OF NUMBERS — 7

No, of course it wasn't I who came to the library!
Brown eyes, flushed cheeks, brown hair. I was twenty-nine, and you were
　　sixteen.

THE MAGIC OF NUMBERS—8

After we made love one night in Rockport I went outside and kissed the road
I felt so carried away. I was twenty-three, and you were nineteen.

THE MAGIC OF NUMBERS—9

I was twenty-nine, and so were you. We had a very passionate time.
Everything I read turned into a story about you and me, and everything I did
    was turned into a poem.

Alive for an Instant

I have a bird in my head and a pig in my stomach
And a flower in my genitals and a tiger in my genitals
And a lion in my genitals and I am after you but I have a song in my heart
And my song is a dove
I have a man in my hands I have a woman in my shoes
I have a landmark decision in my reason
I have a death rattle I have summer in my brain water
This is the matter with me and the hammer of my mother and father
Who created me with everything
But I lack calm I lack rose
Though I do not lack extreme delicacy of rose petal
Who is it that I wish to astonish?
In the birdcall I found a reminder of you
But it was thin and brittle and gone in an instant
Has nature set out to be a great entertainer?
Obviously not A great reproducer? A great Nothing?
Well I will leave that up to you
I have a knocking woodpecker in my heart and I think I have three souls
One for love one for poetry and one for acting out my insane self
Not insane but boring but perpendicular but untrue but true
The three rarely sing together take my hand it's active
The active ingredient in it is a touch
I am Lord Byron I am Percy Shelley I am Ariosto
I eat the bacon I went down the slide I have a thunderstorm in my inside I
        will never hate you
But how can this maelstrom be appealing? do you like menageries? my god
Most people want a man! So here I am
I have a pheasant in my reminders I have a goshawk in my clouds
Whatever is it which has led all these animals to you?
A resurrection? or maybe an insurrection? an inspiration?
I have a baby in my landscape and I have a wild rat in my secrets from you.

Some General Instructions

Do not bake bread in an oven that is not made of stone
Or you risk having imperfect bread. Byron wrote,
"The greatest pleasure in life is drinking hock
And soda water the morning after, when one has
A hangover," or words to that effect. It is a
Pleasure, for me, of the past. I do not drink so much
Any more. And when I do, I am not in sufficiently good
Shape to enjoy the hock and seltzer in the morning.
I am envious of this pleasure as I think of it. Do not
You be envious. In fact I cannot tell envy
From wish and desire and sharing imperfectly
What others have got and not got. But *envy* is a good word
To use, as *hate* is, and *lust,* because they make their point
In the worst and most direct way, so that as a
Result one is able to deal with them and go on one's way.
I read *Don Juan* twenty years ago, and six years later
I wrote a poem in emulation of it. I began
Searching for another stanza but gave in
To the ottava rima after a while, after I'd tried
Some practice stanzas in it; it worked so well
It was too late to stop, it seemed to me. Do not
Be in too much of a hurry to emulate what
You admire. Sometimes it may take a number of years
Before you are ready, but there it is, building
Inside you, a constructing egg. Low-slung
Buildings are sometimes dangerous to walk in and
Out of. A building should be at least one foot and a half
Above one's height, so that if one leaps
In surprise or joy or fear, one's head will not be injured.
Very high ceilings such as those in Gothic
Churches are excellent for giving a spiritual feeling.
Low roofs make one feel like a mole in general. But
Smallish rooms can be cozy. Many tiny people
In a little room make an amusing sight. Large
Persons, both male and female, are best seen out of doors.

Ships sided against a canal's side may be touched and
Patted, but sleeping animals should not be, for
They may bite, in anger and surprise. Of all animals
The duck is seventeenth lowliest, the eagle not as high
On the list as one would imagine, rating
Only ninety-fifth. The elephant is either two or four
Depending on the author of the list, and the tiger
Is seven. The lion is three or six. Blue is the
Favorite color of many people because the sky
Is blue and the sea is blue and many people's eyes
Are blue, but blue is not popular in those countries
Where it is the color of mold. In Spain blue
Symbolizes cowardice. In America it symbolizes "Americanness."
The racial mixture in North America should
Not be misunderstood. The English came here first,
And the Irish and the Germans and the Dutch. There were
Some French here also. The Russians, the Jews, and
The Blacks came afterwards. The women are only coming now
To a new kind of prominence in America, where Liberation
Is their byword. Giraffes, which people ordinarily
Associate with Africa, can be seen in many urban zoos
All over the world. They are an adaptable animal,
As Greek culture was an adaptable culture. Rome
Spread it all over the world. You should know,
Before it did, Alexander spread it as well. Read
As many books as you can without reading interfering
With your time for living. Boxing was formerly illegal
In England, and also, I believe, in America. If
You feel a law is unjust, you may work to change it.
It is not true, as many people say, that
That is just the way things are. Or, Those are the rules,
Immutably. The rules can be changed, although
It may be a slow process. When decorating a window, you
Should try to catch the eye of the passer-by, then
Hold it; he or she should become constantly more
Absorbed in what is being seen. Stuffed animal toys should be
Fluffy and a pleasure to hold in the hands. They
Should not be too resistant, nor should they be made
With any poisonous materials. Be careful not to set fire
To a friend's house. When covering over

A gas stove with paper or inflammable plastic
So you can paint the kitchen without injuring the stove,
Be sure there is no pilot light, or that it is out.
Do not take pills too quickly when you think you have a cold
Or other minor ailment, but wait and see if it
Goes away by itself, as many processes do
Which are really part of something else, not
What we suspected. Raphael's art is no longer as popular
As it was fifty years ago, but an aura
Still hangs about it, partly from its former renown.
The numbers seven and eleven are important to remember in dice
As are the expressions "hard eight," "Little Joe," and "fever,"
Which means *five*. Girls in short skirts when they
Kneel to play dice are beautiful, and even if they
Are not very rich or good rollers, may be
Pleasant as a part of the game. Saint Ursula
And her eleven thousand virgins has
Recently been discovered to be a printer's mistake;
There were only eleven virgins, not eleven thousand.
This makes it necessary to append a brief explanation
When speaking of Apollinaire's parody *Les*
Onze Mille Verges, which means eleven thousand
Male sexual organs—or sticks, for beating. It is a pornographic book.
Sexual information should be obtained while one is young
Enough to enjoy it. To learn of cunnilingus at fifty
Argues a wasted life. One may be tempted to
Rush out into the streets of Hong Kong or
Wherever one is and try to do too much all in one day.
Birds should never be chased out of a nature sanctuary
And shot. Do not believe the beauty of people's faces
Is a sure indication of virtue. The days of
Allegory are over. The Days of Irony are here.
Irony and Deception. But do not harden your heart. Remain
Kind and flexible. Travel a lot. By all means
Go to Greece. Meet persons of various social
Orders. Morocco should be visited by foot,
Siberia by plane. Do not be put off by
Thinking of mortality. You live long enough. There
Would, if you lived longer, never be any new
People. Enjoy the new people you see. Put your hand out

And touch that girl's arm. If you are
Able to, have children. When taking pills, be sure
You know what they are. Avoid cholesterol. In conversation
Be understanding and witty, in order that you may give
Comfort and excitement at the same time. This is the high road to popularity
And social success, but it is also good
For your soul and for your sense of yourself. Be supportive of others
At the expense of your wit, not otherwise. No
Joke is worth hurting someone deeply. Avoid contagious diseases.
If you do not have money, you must probably earn some
But do it in a way that is pleasant and does
Not take too much time. Painting ridiculous pictures
Is one good way, and giving lectures about yourself is another.
I once had the idea of importing tropical birds
From Africa to America, but the test cage of birds
All died on the ship, so I was unable to become
Rich that way. Another scheme I had was
To translate some songs from French into English, but
No one wanted to sing them. Living outside Florence
In February, March, and April was an excellent idea
For me, and may be for you, although I recently revisited
The place where I lived, and it is now more "built up";
Still, a little bit further out, it is not, and the fruit trees
There seem the most beautiful in the world. Every day
A new flower would appear in the garden, or every other day,
And I was able to put all this in what I wrote. I let
The weather and the landscape be narrative in me. To make money
By writing, though, was difficult. So I taught
English in a university in spite of my fear that
I knew nothing. Do not let your fear of ignorance keep you
From teaching, if that would be good for you, nor
Should you let your need for success interfere with what you love,
In fact, to do. Things have a way of working out
Which is nonsensical, and one should try to see
How that process works. If you can understand chance,
You will be lucky, for luck is what chance is about
To become, in a human context, either
Good luck or bad. You should visit places that
Have a lot of savor for you. You should be glad

To be alive. You must try to be as good as you can.
I do not know what virtue is in an absolute way,
But in the particular it is excellence which does not harm
The material but ennobles and refines it. So, honesty
Ennobles the heart and harms not the person or the coins
He remembers to give back. So, courage ennobles the heart
And the bearer's body; and tenderness refines the touch.
The problem of being good and also doing what one wishes
Is not as difficult as it seems. It is, however,
Best to get embarked early on one's dearest desires.
Be attentive to your dreams. They are usually about sex,
But they deal with other things as well in an indirect fashion
And contain information that you should have.
You should also read poetry. Do not eat too many bananas.
In the springtime, plant. In the autumn, harvest.
In the summer and winter, exercise. Do not put
Your finger inside a clam shell or
It may be snapped off by the living clam. Do not wear a shirt
More than two times without sending it to the laundry.
Be a bee fancier only if you have a face net. Avoid flies,
Hornets, and wasps. Clasp other people's hands firmly
When you are introduced to them. Say "I am glad to meet you!"
Be able to make a mouth and cheeks like a fish. It
Is entertaining. Speaking in accents
Can also entertain people. But do not think
Mainly of being entertaining. Think of your death.
Think of the death of the fish you just imitated. Be artistic, and be unfamiliar.
Think of the blue sky, how artists have
Imitated it. Think of your secretest thoughts,
How poets have imitated them. Think of what you feel
Secretly, and how music has imitated that. Make a moue.
Get faucets for every water outlet in your
House. You may like to spend some summers on
An island. Buy woolen material in Scotland and have
The cloth cut in London, lapels made in France.
Become religious when you are tired of everything
Else. As a little old man or woman, die
In a fine and original spirit that is yours alone.
When you are dead, waste, and make room for the future.

Do not make tea from water which is already boiling.
Use the water just as it starts to boil. Otherwise
It will not successfully "draw" the tea, or
The tea will not successfully "draw" it. Byron
Wrote that no man under thirty should ever see
An ugly woman, suggesting desire should be so strong
It affected the princeliest of senses; and Schopenhauer
Suggested the elimination of the human species
As the way to escape from the Will, which he saw as a monstrous
Demon-like force which destroys us. When
Pleasure is mild, you should enjoy it, and
When it is violent, permit it, as far as
You can, to enjoy you. Pain should be
Dealt with as efficiently as possible. To "cure" a dead octopus
You hold it by one leg and bang it against a rock.
This makes a noise heard all around the harbor,
But it is necessary, for otherwise the meat would be too tough.
Fowl are best plucked by humans, but machines
Are more humanitarian, since extended chicken
Plucking is an unpleasant job. Do not eat unwashed beets
Or rare pork, nor should you gobble uncooked dough.
Fruits, vegetables, and cheese make an excellent diet.
You should understand some science. Electricity
Is fascinating. Do not be defeated by the
Feeling that there is too much for you to know. That
Is a myth of the oppressor. You are
Capable of understanding life. And it is yours alone
And only this time. Someone who excites you
Should be told so, and loved, if you can, but no one
Should be able to shake you so much that you wish to
Give up. The sensations you feel are caused by outside
Phenomena and inside impulses. Whatever you
Experience is both "a person out there" and a dream
As well as unwashed electrons. It is your task to see this through
To a conclusion that makes sense to all concerned.
Now go. You cannot come back until these lessons are learned
And you can show that you have learned them for yourself.

The Art of Poetry

To write a poem, perfect physical condition
Is desirable but not necessary. Keats wrote
In poor health, as did D. H. Lawrence. A combination
Of disease and old age is an impediment to writing, but
Neither is, alone, unless there is arteriosclerosis—that is,
Hardening of the arteries—but that we shall count as a disease
Accompanying old age and therefore a negative condition.
Mental health is certainly not a necessity for the
Creation of poetic beauty, but a degree of it
Would seem to be, except in rare cases. Schizophrenic poetry
Tends to be loose, disjointed, uncritical of itself, in some ways
Like what is best in our modern practice of the poetic art
But unlike it in others, in its lack of concern
For intensity and nuance. A few great poems
By poets supposed to be "mad" are of course known to us all,
Such as those of Christopher Smart, but I wonder how crazy they were,
These poets who wrote such contraptions of exigent art?
As for Blake's being "crazy," that seems to me very unlikely.

But what about Wordsworth? Not crazy, I mean, but what about his later
     work, boring
To the point of inanity, almost, and the destructive "corrections" he made
To his *Prelude*, as it nosed along, through the shallows of art?
He was really terrible after he wrote the "Ode:
Intimations of Immortality from Recollections of Early Childhood," for the
     most part,
Or so it seems to me. Walt Whitman's "corrections," too, of the *Leaves of
     Grass*,
And especially "Song of Myself," are almost always terrible.

Is there some way to ride to old age and to fame and acceptance
And pride in oneself and the knowledge society approves one
Without getting lousier and lousier and depleted of talent? Yes,
Yeats shows it could be. And Sophocles wrote poetry until he was a hundred
     and one,
Or a hundred, anyway, and drank wine and danced all night.

But he was an Ancient Greek and so may not help us here. On
The other hand, he may. There is, it would seem, a sense
In which one must grow and develop, and yet stay young—
Not peroxide, not stupid, not transplanting hair to look peppy,
But young in one's heart. And for this it is a good idea to have some
Friends who write as well as you do, who know what you are doing,
And know when you are doing something wrong.
They should have qualities that you can never have,
To keep you continually striving up an impossible hill.
These friends should supply such competition as will make you, at times,
    very uncomfortable.
And you should take care of your physical body as well
As of your poetic heart, since consecutive hours of advanced concentration
Will be precious to your writing and may not be possible
If you are exhausted and ill. Sometimes an abnormal or sick state
Will be inspiring, and one can allow oneself a certain number,
But they should not be the rule. Drinking alcohol is all right
If not in excess, and I would doubt that it would be beneficial
During composition itself. As for marijuana, there are those who
Claim to be able to write well under its influence
But I have yet to see the first evidence for such claims.
Stronger drugs are ludicrously inappropriate, since they destroy judgment
And taste, and make one either like or dislike everything one does,
Or else turn life into a dream. One does not write well in one's sleep.

As for following fashionable literary movements,
It is almost irresistible, and for a while I can see no harm in it,
But the sooner you find your own style the better off you will be.
Then all "movements" fit into it. You have an "exercycle" of your own.
Trying out all kinds of styles and imitating poets you like
And incorporating anything valuable you may find there,
These are sound procedures, and in fact I think even essential
To the perfection of an original style which is yours alone.
An original style may not last more than four years,
Or even three or even two, sometimes on rare occasions one,
And then you must find another. It is conceivable even that a style
For a very exigent poet would be for one work only,
After which it would be exhausted, limping, unable to sustain any wrong or
    right.
By "exigent" I mean extremely careful, wanting each poem to be a
    conclusion

Of everything he senses, feels, and knows.
The exigent poet has his satisfactions, which are relatively special
But that is not the only kind of poet you can be. There is a pleasure in being
     Venus,
In sending love to everyone, in being Zeus,
In sending thunder to everyone, in being Apollo
And every day sending out light. It is a pleasure to write continually
And well, and that is a special poetic dream
Which you may have or you may not. Not all writers have it.
Browning once wrote a poem every day of one year
And found it "didn't work out well." But who knows?
He went on for a year—something must have been working out.
And why only one poem a day? Why not several? Why not one every hour for
     eight to ten hours a day?
There seems no reason not to try it if you have the inclination.

Some poets like "saving up" for poems, others like to spend incessantly what
     they have.
In spending, of course, you get more, there is a "bottomless pocket"
Principle involved, since your feelings are changing every instant
And the language has millions of words, and the number of combinations is
     infinite.
True, one may feel, perhaps Puritanically, that
One person can only have so much to say, and, besides, ten thousand poems
     per annum
Per person would flood the earth and perhaps eventually the universe,
And one would not want so many poems—so there is a "quota system"
Secretly, or not so secretly, at work. "If I can write one good poem a year,
I am grateful," the noted Poet says, or "six" or "three." Well, maybe for that
     Poet,
But for you, fellow paddler, and for me, perhaps not. Besides, I think poems
Are esthetecologically harmless and psychodegradable
And never would they choke the spirits of the world. For a poem only
     affects us
And "exists," really, if it is worth it, and there can't be too many of those.
Writing constantly, in any case, is the poetic dream
Diametrically opposed to the "ultimate distillation"
Dream, which is that of the exigent poet. Just how good a poem should be
Before one releases it, into one's own work and then into the purview of others,

May be decided by applying the following rules: ask 1) Is it astonishing?
Am I pleased each time I read it? Does it say something I was unaware of
Before I sat down to write it? and 2) Do I stand up from it a better man
Or a wiser, or both? or can the two not be separated? 3) Is it really by me
Or have I stolen it from somewhere else? (This sometimes happens,
Though it is comparatively rare.) 4) Does it reveal something about me
I never want anyone to know? 5) Is it sufficiently "modern"?
(More about this a little later) 6) Is it in my own "voice"?
Along with, of course, the more obvious questions, such as
7) Is there any unwanted awkwardness, cheap effects, asking illegitimately for
      attention,
Show-offiness, cuteness, pseudo-profundity, old hat checks,
Unassimilated dream fragments, or other "literary," "kiss-me-I'm-poetical"
      junk?
Is my poem free of this? 8) Does it move smoothly and swiftly
From excitement to dream and then come flooding reason
With purity and soundness and joy? 9) Is this the kind of poem
I would envy in another if he could write? 10)
Would I be happy to go to Heaven with this pinned on to my
Angelic jacket as an entrance show? Oh, would I? And if you can answer to
      all these Yes
Except for the 4th one, to which the answer should be No,
Then you can release it, at least for the time being.
I would look at it again, though, perhaps in two hours, then after one or two
      weeks,
And then a month later, at which time you can probably be sure.

To look at a poem again of course causes anxiety
In many cases, but that pain a writer must learn to endure,
For without it he will be like a chicken which never knows what it is doing
And goes feathering and fluttering through life. When one finds the poem
Inadequate, then one must revise, and this can be very hard going
Indeed. For the original "inspiration" is not there. Some poets never
      master the
Art of doing this, and remain "minor" or almost nothing at all.
Such have my sympathy but not my praise. My sympathy because
Such work is difficult, and some persons accomplish nothing whatsoever
In the course of their lives; at least these poets are writing
"First versions," but they can never win the praise
Of a discerning reader until they take large-hearted Revision to bed

And win her to their cause and create through her "second-time-around"
        poems
Or even "third-time-around" ones. There are several ways to gain
The favors of this lady. One is unstinting labor, but be careful
You do not ruin what is already there by unfeeling rewriting
That makes it more "logical" but cuts out its heart.
Sometimes neglecting a poem for several weeks is best,
As if you had forgotten you wrote it, and changing it then
As swiftly as you can—in that way, you will avoid at least dry "re-detailing"
Which is fatal to any art. Sometimes the confidence you have from a
        successful poem
Can help you to find for another one the changes you want.
Actually, a night's sleep and a new day filled with confidence are very
        desirable,
And, once you get used to the ordinary pains that go with revising,
You may grow to like it very much. It gives one the strange feeling
That one is "working on" something, as an engineer does, or a pilot
When something goes wrong with the plane; whereas the inspired first
        version of a poem
Is more like simply a lightning flash to the heart.
Revising gives one the feeling of being a builder. And if it brings pain? Well,
It sometimes does, and women have pain giving birth to children
Yet often wish to do so again, and perhaps the grizzly bear has pain
Burrowing down into the ground to sleep all winter. In writing
The pain is relatively minor. We need not speak of it again
Except in the case of the fear that one has "lost one's talent,"
Which I will go into immediately. This fear
Is a perfectly logical fear for poets to have,
And all of them, from time to time, have it. It is very rare
For what one does best and that on which one's happiness depends
To so large an extent, to be itself dependent on factors
Seemingly beyond one's control. For whence cometh Inspiration?
Will she stay in her Bower of Bliss or come to me this evening?
Have I gotten too old for her kisses? Will she like that boy there rather than
        me?
Am I a dried-up old hog? Is this then the end of it? Haven't I
Lost that sweet easy knack I had last week,
Last month, last year, last decade, which pleased everyone
And especially pleased me? I no longer can feel the warmth of it—
Oh, I have indeed lost it! Etcetera. And when you write a new poem

You like, you forget this anguish, and so on till your death,
Which you'll be remembered beyond, not for "keeping your talent,"
But for what you wrote, in spite of your worries and fears.

The truth is, I think, that one does not lose one's talent,
Although one can misplace it—in attempts to remain in the past,
In profitless ventures intended to please those whom
Could one see them clearly one would not wish to please,
In opera librettos, or even in one's life
Somewhere. But you can almost always find it, perhaps in trying new forms
Or not in form at all but in the (seeming) lack of it—
Write "stream of consciousness." Or, differently again, do some translations.
Renounce repeating the successes of the years before. Seek
A success of a type undreamed of. Write a poetic fishing manual. Try an Art
    of Love.
Whatever, be on the lookout for what you feared you had lost,
The talent you misplaced. The only ways really to lose it
Are serious damage to the brain or being so attracted
To something else (such as money, sex, repairing expensive engines)
That you forget it completely. In that case, how care that it is lost?
In spite of the truth of all this, however, I am aware
That fear of lost talent is a natural part of a poet's existence.
So be prepared for it, and do not let it get you down.

Just how much experience a poet should have
To be sure he has enough to be sure he is an adequate knower
And feeler and thinker of experience as it exists in our time
Is a tough one to answer, and the only sure rule I can think of
Is experience as much as you can and write as much as you can.
These two can be contradictory. A great many experiences are worthless
At least as far as poetry is concerned. Whereas the least promising,
Seemingly, will throw a whole epic in one's lap. However, that is Sarajevo
And not cause. Probably. I do not know what to tell you
That would apply to all cases. I would suggest travel
And learning at least one other language (five or six
Could be a distraction). As for sexuality and other
Sensual pleasures, you must work that out for yourself.
You should know the world, men, women, space, wind, islands, governments,
The history of art, news of the lost continents, plants, evenings,
Mornings, days. But you must also have time to write.

You need environments for your poems and also people,
But you also need life, you need to care about these things
And these persons, and that is the difficulty, that
What you will find best to write about cannot be experienced
Merely as "material." There are some arts one picks up
Of "living sideways," and forwards and backwards at the same time,
But they often do not work—or do, to one's disadvantage:
You feel, "I did not experience that. That cow did
More than I. Or that 'Blue Man' without a thought in the world
Beyond existing. He is the one who really exists.
That is true poetry. I am nothing." I suggest waiting a few hours
Before coming to such a rash decision and going off
Riding on a camel yourself. For you cannot escape your mind
And your strange interest in writing poetry, which will make you,
Necessarily, an experiencer and un-experiencer
Of life at the same time, but you should realize that what you do
Is immensely valuable, and difficult, too, in a way riding a camel is not,
Though that is valuable too—you two will amaze each other,
The Blue Man and you, and that is also a part of life
Which you must catch in your poem. As for how much one's poetry
Should "reflect one's experience," I do not think it can avoid
Doing that. The naïve version of such a concern
Of course is stupid, but if you feel the need to "confront"
Something, try it, and see how it goes. To "really find your emotions,"
Write, and keep working at it. Success in the literary world
Is mostly irrelevant but may please you. It is good to have a friend
To help you past the monsters on the way. Becoming famous will not hurt
     you
Unless you are foolishly overcaptivated and forget
That this too is merely a part of your "experience." For those who make
     poets famous
In general know nothing about poetry. Remember your obligation is to write,
And, in writing, to be serious without being solemn, fresh without being cold,
To be inclusive without being asinine, particular
Without being picky, feminine without being effeminate,
Masculine without being brutish, human while keeping all the animal graces
You had inside the womb, and beast-like without being inhuman.
Let your language be delectable always, and fresh and true.
Don't be conceited. Let your compassion guide you
And your excitement. And always bring your endeavors to their end.

One thing a poem needs is to be complete
In itself and not need others to complement it.
Therefore this poem about writing should be complete
With information about everything concerned in the act
Of creating a poem. A work also should not be too long.
Each line should give a gathered new sensation
Of "Oh, now I know that, and want to go on!"
"Measure," which decides how long a poem should be,
Is difficult, because possible elaboration is endless,
As endless as the desire to write, so the decision to end
A poem is generally arbitrary yet must be made
Except in the following two cases: when one embarks on an epic
Confident that it will last all one's life,
Or when one deliberately continues it past hope of concluding—
Edmund Spenser and Ezra Pound seem examples
Of one of these cases or the other. And no one knows how
The Faerie Queene continued (if it did, as one writer said,
The last parts destroyed in the sacking of Spenser's house
By the crazed but justified Irish, or was it by his servants?).
It may be that Spenser never went beyond Book Six
In any serious way, because the thought of ending was unpleasant,
Yet his plan for the book, if he wrote on, would oblige him to end it. This
    unlike Pound
Who had no set determined place to cease. Coming to a stop
And giving determined form is easiest in drama,
It may be, or in short songs, like "We'll Go
No More a-Roving," one of Byron's most
Touching poems, an absolute success, the best
Short one, I believe, that Byron wrote. In all these
Cases, then, except for "lifetime" poems, there is a point one reaches
When one knows that one must come to an end,
And that is the point that must be reached. To reach it, however,
One may have to cut out much of what one has written along the way,
For the end does not necessarily come of itself
But must be coaxed forth from the material, like a blossom.

Anyone who would like to write an epic poem
May wish to have a plot in mind, or at least a mood—the
Minimum requirement is a form. Sometimes a stanza,

Like Spenser's, or Ariosto's ottava rima, will set the poem going
Downhill and uphill and all around experience
And the world in the maddest way imaginable. Enough,
In this case, to begin, and to let oneself be carried
By the wind of eight (or, in the case of Spenser, nine) loud rhymes.
Sometimes blank verse will tempt the amateur
Of endless writing; sometimes a couplet; sometimes "free verse."
"Skeltonics" are hard to sustain over an extended period
As are, in English, and in Greek for all I know, "Sapphics."
The epic has a clear advantage over any sort of lyric
Poem in being there when you go back to it to continue. The
Lyric is fleeting, usually caught in one
Breath or not at all (though see what has been said before
About revision—it can be done). The epic one is writing, however,
Like a great sheep dog is always there
Wagging and waiting to welcome one into the corner
To be petted and sent forth to fetch a narrative bone.
O writing an epic! what a pleasure you are
And what an agony! But the pleasure is greater than the agony,
And the achievement is the sweetest thing of all. Men raise the problem,
"How can one write an epic in the modern world?" One can answer,
"Look around you—tell me how one cannot!" Which is more or less what
Juvenal said about Satire, but epic is a form
Our international time-space plan cries out for—or so it seems
To one observer. The lyric is a necessity too,
And those you may write either alone
Or in the interstices of your epic poem, like flowers
Crannied in the Great Wall of China as it sweeps across the earth.
To write only lyrics is to be sad, perhaps,
Or fidgety, or overexcited, too dependent on circumstance—
But there is a way out of that. The lyric must be bent
Into a more operative form, so that
Fragments of being reflect absolutes (see for example the verse of
William Carlos Williams or Frank O'Hara), and you can go on
Without saying it all every time. If you can master the knack of it,
You are a fortunate poet, and a skilled one. You should read
A great deal, and be thinking of writing poetry all the time.
Total absorption in poetry is one of the finest things in existence—
It should not make you feel guilty. Everyone is absorbed in something.
The sailor is absorbed in the sea. Poetry is the mediation of life.

The epic is particularly appropriate to our contemporary world
Because we are so uncertain of everything and also know too much,
A curious and seemingly contradictory condition, which the epic salves
By giving us our knowledge and our grasp, with all our lack of control as
    well.
The lyric adjusts to us like a butterfly, then epically eludes our grasp.
Poetic drama in our time seems impossible but actually exists as
A fabulous possibility just within our reach. To write drama
One must conceive of an answerer to what one says, as I am now conceiving
    of you.

As to whether or not you use rhyme and how "modern" you are
It is something your genius can decide on every morning
When you get out of bed. What a clear day! Good luck at it!
Though meter is probably, and rhyme too, probably, dead
For a while, except in narrative stanzas. You try it out.
The pleasure of the easy inflection between meter and these easy vocable
    lines
Is a pleasure, if you are able to have it, you are unlikely to renounce.
As for "surrealistic" methods and techniques, they have become a
Natural part of writing. Your poetry, if possible, should be extended
Somewhat beyond your experience, while still remaining true to it;
Unconscious material should play a luscious part
In what you write, since without the unconscious part
You know very little; and your plainest statements should be
Even better than plain. A reader should put your work down puzzled,
Distressed, and illuminated, ready to believe
It is curious to be alive. As for your sense of what good you
Do by writing, compared to what good statesmen, doctors,
Flower salesmen, and missionaries do, perhaps you do less
And perhaps more. If you would like to try one of these
Other occupations for a while, try it. I imagine you will find
That poetry does something they do not do, whether it is
More important or not, and if you like poetry, you will like doing that
    yourself.

Poetry need not be an exclusive occupation.
Some think it should, some think it should not. But you should
Have years for poetry, or at least if not years months
At certain points in your life. Weeks, days, and hours may not suffice.

Almost any amount of time suffices to be a "minor poet"
Once you have mastered a certain amount of the craft
For writing a poem, but I do not see the good of minor poetry,
Like going to the Tour d'Argent to get dinner for your dog,
Or "almost" being friends with someone, or hanging around but not
    attending a school,
Or being a nurse's aide for the rest of your life after getting a degree in
    medicine,
What is the point of it? And some may wish to write songs
And use their talent that way. Others may even end up writing ads.
To those of you who are left, when these others have departed,
And you are a strange bunch, I alone address these words.

It is true that good poetry is difficult to write.
Poetry is an escape from anxiety and a source of it as well.
On the whole, it seems to me worthwhile. At the end of a poem
One may be tempted to grow too universal, philosophical, and vague
Or to bring in History, or the Sea, but one should not do that
If one can possibly help it, since it makes
Each thing one writes sound like everything else,
And poetry and life are not like that. Now I have said enough.

From The Art of Love

From 1

To win the love of women one should first discover
What sort of thing is likely to move them, what feelings
They are most delighted with their lives to have; then
One should find these things and cause these feelings. Now
A story illustrates: of course the difficulty
Is how to talk about winning the love
Of women and not also speak of loving—a new
Problem? an old problem? Whatever—it is a something secret
To no one who has finally experienced it. Presbyopic. And so,
Little parks in Paris, proceed, pronounce
On these contributing factors to the "mental psyche
Of an airplane." Renumerate
The forces which gloss our tongues! And then Betty,
The youngest rabbit, ran, startled, out into the driveway,
Fear that Terry will run over her now calmed. Back
To the Alps, back to the love of women, the sunset
Over "four evenly distributed band lots in
Which you held my hand," mysterious companion
With opal eyes and oval face without whom I
Could never have sustained the Frogonian evening—
Wait a minute! if this is to be a manual of love, isn't it
Just about time we began? Well . . . yes. Begin.

Tie your girl's hands behind her back and encourage her
To attempt to get loose. This will make her breasts look
Especially pretty, like the Parthenon at night. Sometimes those illuminations
Are very beautiful, though sometimes the words
Are too expected, too French, too banal. Ain't youse a cracker,
Though? And other poems. Or Freemasonry Revisited. Anway,
Tie her up. In this fashion, she will be like Minnie Mouse, will look
Like starlight over the sensuous Aegean. She will be the greatest thing you
    ever saw.

However, a word of advice, for cold September evenings,
And in spring, summer, winter too, and later in the fall:
Be sure she likes it. Otherwise
You are liable to lose your chances for other kinds of experiments,
Like the Theseion, for example. Or the two-part song. Yes! this
Is Athens, king of the cities, and land of the
Countries of the Fall. Where *atoma* means person, and where was
A lovely epoch once though we however must go on
With contemporary problems in ecstasy. Let's see. Your
Girl's now a little tied up. Her hands stretched behind her at
An angle of about 40 degrees to her back, no say, seventeen
And Z—sending his first roses at seventeen (roses also work
As well as hand tying but in a different less fractured
Framework) and she receiving them writing "I have never
Received roses before from a man. Meet me at the fountain
At nine o'clock and I will do anything you want." He was
Panicky! and didn't know what to do. What had he wanted
That now seemed so impossible? he didn't exactly know
How to do it. So he wrote to her that night amid the capitals
Of an arboring civilization, "Fanny I can't come. The maid is shocked. The
Butter factory is in an endzone of private feelings. So
The chocolate wasp stands on the Venetian steps. So
The cloudbursts are weeping, full of feeling
And stones, so the flying boats are loving and the tea
Is full of quotients. So—" That's enough cries Fanny she tears
It up then she reads it again.

. . . .

To lack a woman, to not have one, and to be longing for one
As the grass grows around the Perrier family home,
That is the worst thing in life, but nowhere near the best is to have one
And not know what to do. So we continue these instructions.

. . . .

Oh the animals moving in the stockyards have no idea of these joys
Nor do the birds flying high in the clouds. Think: tenderness cannot be all
Although everyone loves tenderness. Nor violence, which gives the sense of
    life
With its dramas and its actions as it is. Making love must be everything—
A city, not a street; a country, not a city; the universe, the world—

178

Make yours so, make it even a galaxy, and be conscious and unconscious of it
all. That is the art of love.

From 4

. . . .

What is Love's Ideal City? what strange combination
Of Paris and Venice, of Split for the beauty of its inhabitants,
Of Waco for its byways, of Vladivostok for its bars?
What, precisely, is meant by the "love of God"? or the "love of humanity"?
How can women best be conquered in different cities?
What places, or bits of landscape, most speak of love?
How to make your girlfriend into an airplane, or a living kite;
How to convert success in business or art into success in love;
Keeping one's libidinous impulses at a peak all the time;
How to explain, and how to prosper with having two loves, or three, or four,
    or five;
Meeting women, disguised, in museums, and walking with them, naked, in
    the country;
How to speak of love when you do not know the language; how to master
    resentment;
How to cause all the women eating in a given restaurant to fall in love
    with you at the same time;
Greek aphrodisiac foods, how to eat them and how to prepare them;
One secret way to make any woman happy she is with you;
Apollo: woman-chaser, homosexual, or both? Zeus: godlike ways of seducing
    women;
How to judge the accuracy of what you remember about past love;
Building a house ideally suited to love; how to reassure virgins;
How to avoid being interested in the wrong woman; seven sure signs of
    someone you don't want to love;
Three fairly reliable signs of someone you do;
Use of the car—making love under the car; in the car; on the car roof;
Traveling with women; what to do when suddenly you know that the whole
    relationship is no longer right;
How to pump fresh air into the lungs of a drowned woman; the "kiss of
    death"; how to appear totally confident and totally available for love at
    the same time;

Maintaining good looks under exhausting conditions; forty-one things to
    think about in bed;
How to win the love of a girl who is half your age; how to win the love of one
    who is one fifth your age;
Bracelets women like to have slipped onto them; places in which women are
    likely to slip and thus fall into your arms;
The bridge of ships: how to make love there in twenty-five different positions
So as to have a happy and rosy complexion later, at the "Captain's Table";
Love in different cultures: how to verify what you are feeling in relation to
    the different civilizations of the world—
Room for doubt: would the Greeks have called this "love"? Do such feelings
    exist in China?
Did they exist in Ming China? And so on. The Birthday of Love—
On what day is Eros's birthday correctly celebrated? Was love born only
    once?
Is there actually a historical date? Presents to give on such a day.
What memorable thing did Spinoza say about love? How to deal with the
    sweethearts of your friends
When they want to go to bed with you; how to make love while asleep;
The Book of Records, and what it says; how to end a quarrel;
How to plan a "day of love"—what food and drink to have by your
    side, what newspapers and books;
How to propose the subject so that your girlfriend will go away with you
On a "voyage to the moon," i.e., lie under the bed while you
Create a great hole in the mattress and springs with your hatchet
And then leap on her, covered with feathers and shiny metal spring
Fragments, screaming, as you at last make love, "We are on the moon!" How
    to dress
Warmly for love in the winter, and coolly in the sun;
Mazes to construct in which you can hide naked women and chase them;
Dreams of love, and how they are to be interpreted;
How "love affairs" usually get started; when to think of marriage; how to
    prevent your girl from marrying someone else;
"Magical feelings"—how to sustain them during a love affair; traveling with
    a doctor
As a way to meet sick girls; traveling with a police officer as a way to meet
    criminal girls;
What is "Zombie-itis"? do many women suffer from it? how can it be enjoyed
Without actually dying? where are most adherents to it found?
What ten things must an older man never say to a young woman?

What about loving outdoors? what good can we get there from trees, stones,
and rivers?

Are there, in fact, any deities or gods of any kind to Love?

And if so, can they be prayed to? Do the prayers do any good?

What can be done to cure the "inability to love"? senseless promiscuity?
twenty-four-hour-a-day masturbatory desires?

What nine things will immediately give anyone the power to make love?

What three things must usually be forgotten in order to make love?

Ways of leaving your initials on women; other "personalizing insignia";

How to turn your girl into a duck, turkey, or chicken, for fifteen minutes;

What to do when she comes back to herself, so she will not be angry or
frightened;

How to make love while standing in the sea; cures for "frozen legs"; Love's
icebox;

Love Curses to blight those who interfere with you, and Love Charms to win
those who resist you;

Traveling while flat on your back; Women from Sixteen Countries; what to
do with a Communist or other Iron-Curtain-Country Girl

So that politics will not come into it, or will make your pleasure even greater;

How to identify yourself, as you make love, with sunlight, trees, and clouds;

What to do during a Sex Emergency: shortage of women, lack of desire,
absence of space in which to sit or lie down;

How to really love a woman or girl for the rest of your life; what to do if she
leaves you;

Seventeen tried and tested cures for the agonies of lost love;

Telling a "true" emotion from an in some way "untrue" one;

How to compensate for being too "romantic"; can enjoyed love ever come up
to romantic expectations?

Ways of locating women who love you in a crowd; giving in totally to love;

How to transform a woman into a "Human Letter"

By covering her with inscriptions, which you then ship to yourself

In another bedroom, unwrap it, read it, and make love;

Making love through a piece of canvas; making love through walls;

What to do when one lover is in a second-floor apartment, the other in the
first-floor one;

Openings in the ceiling, and how to make them; how to answer the question

"What are you doing up there on the ceiling?" if someone accidentally comes
home;

Ways to conceal the fact that you have just made love or

Are about to make love; how to explain pink cheeks, sleepiness.

Is love all part of a "Great Plan," and, if so, what is the Plan?
If it is to keep the earth populated, then what is the reason behind that?
Throwing your girl into the ocean and jumping in after her, aphrodisiac
　　effects of; genius,
Its advantages and disadvantages in love; political antagonism in love:
She is a Muslim, you are a Republican; or she is a Maoist, and you are for
　　improving the system;
How to keep passion alive while beset by anxiety and doubt;
What is the best way to make love in a rocket? what is the second-best way?
How to make sure one's feeling is "genuine"; how to use gags; when to wear
　　a hat;
At what moment does drunkenness become an impediment to love?
What is the role of sex in love? Is fidelity normal? Are all women, in one
　　sense, the same woman?
How can this best be explained to particular women? Drawing one's portrait
　　on a woman's back—
Materials and methods; is growing older detrimental to love?
Use of the aviary; use of the kitchen garden; what are eighteen totally
　　unsuspected enemies of love?
Does lack of love "dry people up"? how can one be sure one's love will be
　　lasting?
What reasonable substitute, in love's absence, could be found for love?

The best authors to consult about love (aside from the author of this
Volume) are Ovid, Ariosto, Byron, and Stendhal. Places or bits of landscape
Which most speak of love: Piazzale Michelangelo, looking down at the Arno,
　　above Florence;
The candy factory in Biarritz, specializing in ruby-red hearts;
Gus's Place, in Indonesia, a small cart-wheel store full of white paper; the
　　Rotterdam Harbor on an April evening.
The Ideal City of Love should be a combination
Of Naples, for its byways and its silences and its Bay; Paris,
For the temerity and the lovification of its inhabitants;
Rome, for its amazement, not for its traffic; Split, for its absence of the
　　Baroque;
Austin, Texas, for having so many girls there; Hangkow for its evenings.
This ideal city of love will not be as spread out
As London is, nor as over-towering as New York, but it will be a city.
　　Suburbs are inimical to love,
Imposing the city's restrictions without its stimulation and variety.

The city must include numerous young women. Therefore city planners
Will include as many colleges as they can and encourage
Such professions as will draw young women to the city from outside.

To make your girl into an airplane, ask her to lie down on a large piece of
    canvas
Which you have stretched out and nailed to a thin sheet of aluminum, or, if
    you are economizing, of balsa wood.
When she has lain down, wrap the stuff she is lying on around her
And ask her to stretch out her arms, for these will be the wings
Of the plane (she should be lying on her stomach), with her neck stretched
    taut, her chin
Resting on the canvas (her head should be the "nose" of the plane); her legs
    and feet should be
Close together (tied or strapped, if you like). Now, once she is in airplane
    position,
Wrap the aluminum or balsa-coated canvas more closely around her and
    fasten it at the edges
With staples, glue, or rivets. Carry her to the airport, or to any convenient
    field,
And put her on the ground. Ask her to "take off!" If she does, you have lost
    a good mistress. If not
(And it is much more likely to be "if not"), you will enjoy making love there
    on the field—
You, both pilot and crew, and passengers, and she your loving plane!

Perhaps you would also like to turn your girl into a shoe or into a shoebox
Or a plaster cherry tree or any one of a million other things. A booklet is
    coming out
Specifically and entirely on that, called *The Shop of Love.*

The best way to conquer women in different cities is to know the mayor or
    ruler of the particular city
And have him introduce you to the women (perhaps while they are under the
    influence of a strong love-making drug).
To revive an old love affair, write the woman concerned, or call her up.
    Suggest converting her into a plane.
If she loves you still, she'll hesitate or say yes. If she says no, propose
    converting her into the summer dawn.

To cause all the women in a given restaurant to wish to make love to you,
Bring in the model of an airplane and stare at it attentively and refuse to eat.

You can tell a woman's character by looking in her shoe, if you have the
    special glasses described in *The Shop of Love.*
Otherwise, the eyes, mouth, and breasts are better indications.
If the breasts are round, she may be foolish; if the eyes are green, she may be
    Jewish;
If the mouth is full, she may be pettish. But everything she is will be for you.

The wrong woman can be identified by the following characteristics:
She eats at least twice as much as you do; her shoes or clothing are
    unbuttoned or untied; she dislikes cold water;
Her face is the shape of a donkey's; she fears evening
For evening draws one closer to bed. She contradicts herself
And is stubborn about each thing she said. She is perpetually unhappy
And would hate you bitterly for changing her condition. Immediately leave
    her! This person is not for you!

Two signs of love-worthiness in a woman are climbing to the roof
Without fear and with a smile on her face; turning around to look at you
    after she turns away from you.

Use of the car is now located in *The Shop of Love.*

When you know the relationship is not right, think of it all again.
Try again the next day. If you still think the same thing, end it.

The kiss of death is currently prohibited by law. Look for it in later editions.

To maintain good looks under exhausting conditions, think about an eskimo
Riding a white horse through a valley filled with falling other eskimos
So that he always has to be attentive, so that no eskimo falls on his head.
This will give you an alert look, which is half of beauty.

One thing to think about in bed is the full extent of this poem.
Another is the city of Rome. Another is the Byzantine stained-glass window
    showing Jesus as a human wine-press.
Do not think of cancellation of air trips, botched tennis racquets, or slightly
    torn postage stamps.

Think of the seasons. Think of evening. Think of the stone duck
Carved by the cement company in Beirut, to advertise
Their product. Think of October. Do not think of sleep.

To win the love of a girl half your age, add your age and hers together
And divide by two; act as if you were the age represented by that number
And as if she were too; the same with girls one fourth or one fifth your age.
This is called "Age Averaging," and will work in all those cases
In which age difference is a problem. Often it is not.

Love between living beings was unknown in Ming China. All passion was
     centered on material things.
This accounts for the vases. In Ancient Greece there was no time for love. In
     Somaliland only little children love each other.

Spinoza's remark was "Love is the idea of happiness attached to an external
     cause."

Friends' sweethearts should be put off until the next day.

To make love while asleep, try reading this book. It has been known to cause
     Somnamoria.

The Book of Records says the record number of times a man made love in a
     twenty-four-hour period was 576 times.
The record number of times a woman made love was 972 times.
The man died, and the woman went to sleep and could not be awakened
     for two years.
She later became the director of a large publishing house and then later in
     life became a nun.
The most persons anyone ever made love to in rapid succession (without a
     pause of any kind) was seventy-one.

Dreams about love should be acted on as quickly as possible
So as to be able to fully enjoy their atmosphere. If you dream about a woman,
     phone her at once and tell her what you have dreamed.

Zombie-itis is love of the living dead. It is comparatively rare.
If a woman likes it, you can probably find other things she likes that you will
     like even more.

Ten things an older man must never say to a younger woman:
1) I'm dying! 2) I can't hear what you're saying! 3) How many fingers are you
    holding up?
4) Listen to my heart. 5) Take my pulse. 6) What's your name?
7) Is it cold in here? 8) Is it hot in here? 9) Are you in here?
10) What wings are those beating at the window?
Not that a man should stress his youth in a dishonest way
But that he should not unduly emphasize his age.

The inability to love is almost incurable. A long sea voyage
Is recommended, in the company of an irresistible woman.

To turn a woman into a duck, etc., hypnotize her and dress her in costume.
To make love standing in water, see "Elephant Congress" in the *Kama Sutra*
    (chap. iv).
During a shortage of women, visit numerous places; give public lectures;
    carry this volume.

Lost love is cured only by new love, which it usually makes impossible.
Finding a woman who resembles the lost woman may offer temporary relief.

One test for love is whether at the beginning you are or are not able to think
    about anything else.

To locate unknown-about love for you in a woman in a crowd,
Look intently at everyone you find attractive, then fall to the ground.
She will probably come up to you and show her concern.

Railway Express will not handle human letters, but Bud's Bus and Truck
    Service will.

Sleepiness may be explained by drugs; pink cheeks, by the allergy that caused
    you to take them.

Love's being part of a Great Plan is an attractive idea
But has never been validated to anyone's complete satisfaction.

Throwing your girl in the ocean makes her feel sexy when she gets out.
    Genius is not a disadvantage.

186

Hats should never be worn when making love. All women are not the same woman
Though they may sometimes seem so. The aviary is best used on summer nights. There is no
Substitute for or parallel to love, which gives to the body
What religion gives to the soul, and philosophy to the brain,
Then shares it among them all. It is a serious matter. Without it, we seem only half alive.

May good fortune go with you, then, dear reader, and with the women you love.

The Boiling Water

A serious moment for the water is when it boils
And though one usually regards it merely as a convenience
To have the boiling water available for bath or table
Occasionally there is someone around who understands
The importance of this moment for the water—maybe a saint,
Maybe a poet, maybe a crazy man, or just someone temporarily disturbed
With his mind "floating," in a sense, away from his deepest
Personal concerns to more "unreal" things. A lot of poetry
Can come from perceptions of this kind, as well as a lot of insane
    conversations.
Intense people can sometimes get stuck on topics like these
And keep you far into the night with them. Still, it is true
That the water has just started to boil. How important
For the water! And now I see that the tree is waving in the wind
(I assume it is the wind)—at least, its branches are. In order to see
Hidden meanings, one may have to ignore
The most exciting ones, those that are most directly appealing
And yet it is only these appealing ones that, often, one can trust
To make one's art solid and true, just as it is sexual attraction
One has to trust, often, in love. So the boiling water's seriousness
Is likely to go unobserved until the exact strange moment
(And what a temptation it is to end the poem here
With some secret thrust) when it involuntarily comes into the mind
And then one can write of it. A serious moment for this poem will be
    when it ends,
It will be like the water's boiling, that for which we've waited
Without trying to think of it too much, since "a watched pot never boils,"
And a poem with its ending figured out is difficult to write.

Once the water is boiling, the heater has a choice: to look at it
And let it boil and go on seeing what it does, or to take it off and use the
    water for tea,
Chocolate, or coffee, or beef consommé. You don't drink the product then
Until the water has ceased to boil, for otherwise
It would burn your tongue. Even hot water is dangerous and has a thorn

Like the rose, or a horn like the baby ram. Modest hot water, and the tree
Blowing in the wind. The connection here is how serious is it for the tree
To have its arms wave (its branches)? How did it ever get such flexibility
In the first place? and who put the boiling potentiality into water?
A tree will not boil, nor will the wind. Think of the dinners
We could have, and the dreams, if only they did.
But that is not to think of what things are really about. For the tree
I don't know how serious it is to be waving, though water's boiling
Is more dramatic, is more like a storm, high tide
And the ship goes down, but it comes back up as coffee, chocolate, or tea.

How many people I have drunk tea or coffee with
And thought about the boiling water hardly at all, just waiting for it to boil
So there could be coffee or chocolate or tea. And then what?
The body stimulated, the brain alarmed, grounds in the pot,
The tree, waving, out the window, perhaps with a little more élan
Because we saw it that way, because the water boiled, because we drank tea.

The water boils almost every time the same old way
And still it is serious, because it is boiling. That is what,
I think, one should see. From this may come compassion,
Compassion and a knowledge of nature, although most of the time
I know I am not going to think about it. It would be crazy
To give such things precedence over such affairs of one's life
As involve more fundamental satisfactions. But is going to the beach
More fundamental than seeing the water boil? Saving of money,
It's well known, can result from an aesthetic attitude, since a rock
Picked up in the street contains all the shape and hardness of the world.
One sidewalk leads everywhere. You don't have to be in Estapan.
A serious moment for the island is when its trees
Begin to give it shade, and another is when the ocean washes
Big heavy things against its side. One walks around and looks at the island
But not really at it, at what is on it, and one thinks,
It must be serious, even, to be this island, at all, here,
Since it is lying here exposed to the whole sea. All its
Moments might be serious. It is serious, in such windy weather, to be a sail
Or an open window, or a feather flying in the street.

Seriousness, how often I have thought of seriousness
And how little I have understood it, except this: serious is urgent
And it has to do with change. You say to the water,
It's not necessary to boil now, and you turn it off. It stops
Fidgeting. And starts to cool. You put your hand in it
And say, The water isn't serious any more. It has the potential,
However—that urgency to give off bubbles, to
Change itself to steam. And the wind,
When it becomes part of a hurricane, blowing up the beach
And the sand dunes can't keep it away.
Fainting is one sign of seriousness, crying is another.
Shuddering all over is another one.

A serious moment for the telephone is when it rings,
And a person answers, it is Angelica, or is it you
And finally, at last, who answer, my wing, my past, my
Angel, my flume, and my de-control, my orange and my good-bye kiss,
My extravagance, and my weight at fifteen years old
And at the height of my intelligence, oh Cordillera two
And sandals one, C'est toi à l'appareil? Is that you at
The telephone, and when it snows, a serious moment for the bus is when
        it snows
For then it has to slow down for sliding, and every moment is a trust.

A serious moment for the fly is when its wings
Are moving, and a serious moment for the duck
Is when it swims, when it first touches water, then spreads
Its smile upon the water, its feet begin to paddle, it is in
And above the water, pushing itself forward, a duck.
And a serious moment for the sky is when, completely blue,
It feels some clouds coming; another when it turns dark.
A serious moment for the match is when it bursts into flame
And is all alone, living, in that instant, that beautiful second for which it
        was made.
So much went into it! The men at the match factory, the mood of
The public, the sand covering the barn
So it was hard to find the phosphorus, and now this flame,
This pink white ecstatic light blue! For the telephone when it rings,
For the wind when it blows, and for the match when it bursts into flame.

Serious, all our life is serious, and we see around us
Seriousness for other things, that touches us and seems as if it might
be giving clues.
The seriousness of the house when it is being built
And is almost completed, and then the moment when it is completed.
The seriousness of the bee when it stings. We say, He has taken his
life,
Merely to sting. Why would he do that? And we feel
We aren't concentrated enough, not pure, not deep
As the buzzing bee. The bee flies into the house
And lights on a chair arm and sits there, waiting for something to be
Other than it is, so he can fly again. He is boiling, waiting. Soon he is
forgotten
And everyone is speaking again.

Seriousness, everyone speaks of seriousness
Certain he knows or seeking to know what it is. A child is bitten by an
animal
And that is serious. The doctor has a serious life. He is somewhat, in
that, like the bee.
And water! water—how it is needed! and it is always going down
Seeking its own level, evaporating, boiling, now changing into ice
And snow, now making up our bodies. We drink the coffee
And somewhere in this moment is the chance
We will never see each other again. It is serious for the tree
To be moving, the flexibility of its moving
Being the sign of its continuing life. And now there are its blossoms
And the fact that it is blossoming again, it is filling up with
Pink and whitish blossoms, it is full of them, the wind blows, it is
Warm, though, so much is happening, it is spring, the people step out
And doors swing in, and billions of insects are born. You call me and
tell me
You feel your life isn't worth living. I say that I'm coming to see you.
I put the key in
And the car begins to clatter, and now it starts.

Serious for me that I met you, and serious for you
That you met me, and that we do not know
If we will ever be close to anyone again. Serious the recognition of the
probability

That we will, although time stretches terribly in between. It is serious
          not to know
And to know and to try to figure things out. One's legs
Cross, foot swings, and a cigarette is blooming, a gray bouquet, and
The water is boiling. Serious the birth (what a phenomenon!) of anything and
The movements of the trees, and for the lovers
Everything they do and see. Serious intermittently for consciousness
The sign that something may be happening, always, today,
That is enough. For the germ when it enters or leaves a body. For the fly
          when it lifts its little wings.

Our Hearts

1

All hearts should beat when Cho Fu's orchestra plays "Love"
And then all feet should start to move in the dance.
The dancing should be very quick and all step lightly.
Everyone should be moving around, all hearts beating—
Tip tap tip tap. The heart is actually beating all the time
And with almost the same intensity. The difference is not in our hearing
Which is also almost always the same. The difference must be really,
Then, in our consciousness, which, they say, is variegated.
Black-and-white shoes, red dress, an eye of flame,
A teeth of pearl, a hose of true, a life of seethings. Would
You like to dance? The excitement, it is there all the time.
Is human genius there all the time? With the analogy of dreams,
Which supposedly we have every night, one is tempted
To say, The seething is always there, and with it the possibility for great art.

2

The government is there all the time, or actually the people
Struggle first so the government will be there then so it will not
Be overpowering. When does the art come, and the seething,
And when is the best point for justice, in all these I would like to be living.
The houses come and then the industry and then the people
And the government must control the industry. No smoke in the houses.
And there are people who study this all the time,
Economists, government people, they sit down and talk about
And study these things. And some otherwise indistinguishable boys
And girls become scientists, and complicate these things,
Make them better and worse, and some pale insecure others
Come along and do poems and paintings, and all die
And new ones are born, and there gets to be history and culture
And civilization and the death of civilization and the life of it and in it.

3

We, who are born in it, walk around in it, and look at these things
And think of these things. Some things are first and some are second.
No one has yet completely figured out our brain
But some are trying. One of the first things is we try to be "all right,"
To do well and to succeed. Whether this is in all human brains
(We think not) or only in our civilization's, we don't know
For sure, or much care, but we act by it anyway, just as we act
By the morality we happen to be born with (i.e., not eating our
    grandparents
As Herodotus said the Egyptians thought it proper to do).
And in the dim, dazzling adolescent ballrooms we start on our way.
Later, much later perhaps, we try to figure it out—
Or sometimes just start working mechanically on one aspect.
Finding ourselves "in love," we may attach supreme value to that
Or to some crazy religion, finding ourselves in a church at sunset.

4

What do you think it is really all explainable by, this
Mystery that has been built up by a natural process
And how much of it do we need? The foot of everyone is advancing
And the knees of everyone should be flexing, legs dancing
And lips moving gaily up over the teeth
For the speaking, and hands driven into the pockets, eyes shining, stub-
bed toes forgotten as we walk down the somewhere else saying God Damn
It's good to see you. But what shall we do? The greatest plan
Is participate, aid, and understand. Every dog should be at the foot
Of every man. What evidence this past give us! Examples
With which we impregnate today. But the shirt should fit
Over the chest, the light silk panties over the rear.
The sky is shining. The sun is a basket of wash
Let down for our skin, and germs are all around us like cash.

5

In nature is no explanation. In city is no
Explanation. In language is no
Explanation. Explanation is a dog, is a languishing lad
Lanky with lurid binoculars, dilapidated-looking. I am
Sitting and you are standing. We have a knowledge of good and bad.
We are exploding with doubts and with talents. We look everywhere.
We are glad when we find something simple.
Breathing is simple, walking is simple, and dancing, sometimes, moving
    one's feet.
A simple way to say that things are simple
Is immensely enjoyable but it is not explanation.
The people should be rushing along. There is in that way no problem
Except there is this problem How to participate aid and understand
Simultaneously. It seems there is too much. Participating in the wall
You forget to understand the tax reform. And aid no one.

6

So what is the ecstasy we are allowed to have in this one life
As everybody says that we are getting on with living here?
Should you devote your life to reform? or to understanding your life?
Are different kinds of people born, some for aiding,
Some for participating in, some for understanding life?
Which one are you and how do you know? You are crazy
And don't know it, one person says, and another says, You are asleep.
To myself I seem sane and awake, and I go on.
Maybe a fundamental-type solution, "loss in nature," "mystical religion"
Or "sexual explosiveness" is what we need. But dear civilization—
Who would like to give up theater for climbing up a tree? No one wants
    you to.
Remember where this meditation began (with Cho Fu's orchestra).
It is the problem of living and not being the first one
And yet wanting to do as much as that first one, and, because there is all
    that train behind one, more.

7

The people look at all the people they are walking around
One being peaceful or horrid or lonely or bored
Or pleasant and contented the right kind
Of civilization could be good for all these people
And certainly food would be good for the hungry people
And limitations must be placed on the greedy people
And guns must be taken away from the aggressive people
And medicine must be given to the ailing people
And so on and each individual one of the people
Who dreams every night (it is supposed) may be supposed
To have the seething and the golden curiosity. How to organize the thing
So that each of these people
Is happy with it, happy with him, with her, and me
And we also are, and it, and all, with them? That would be the day—
How can it be with everyone feeling he is the main one and the germs
        there every day?

8

Different civilizations simultaneously existing,
Indian in the throes of one, samurai in the waning of another,
Heck-saying businessman in mine, and little civilizations suggesting
        something
Like farmyard civilization, fishingman and net and boat civilization,
And then back to your own and to my own, all the
Efficiency the good will the weakness and the snobbery
The uncertainty the recovery the rather long life the bursts
Of helpless enthusiasm the sweet reformers in the streets
Today as I just looked out the window and here come the riot police
And the sitting inside and not knowing if I should be outside, in the
        midst of this.
The orchestra plays and everyone is growing up and being
One of who are a various number of beings
Simultaneously dreaming of existing
As the civilizations say they are when we speak.

9

To be a back, that doesn't break, and to hate what is mysterious
That doesn't need to be, grant me O Athena
Of the roses and the gamma globulin—however, prayer
Is nothing I can ever be serious about (I think).
The answer is elusive and the work about it goes on
A long time and so we want our lives to go on
Among other things in hope to find an answer. Though we know
That the answer of eighty will not be the answer of eighteen.
En route we give titles to things, we further
Complicate our own situation and that of other persons
And we get wiser, sometimes, and kinder, and probably less exciting
(Certainly so), and grow out of our illusions (sometimes) and so
Can look around and say, Oh! So! but usually without the time
Or power to change anything (sometimes—maybe a fraction—if so, it's
    amazing!)—then off we go.

To Marina

So many convolutions and not enough simplicity!
When I had you to write to it
Was different. The quiet, dry Z
Leaped up to the front of the alphabet.
You sit, stilling your spoons
With one hand; you move them with the other.
Radio says, "God is a postmaster."
You said, Ziss is lawflee. And in the heat
Of writing to you I wrote simply. I thought
These are the best things I shall ever write
And have ever written. I thought of nothing but touching you.
Thought of seeing you and, in a separate thought, of looking at you.
You were concentrated feeling and thought.
You were like the ocean
In which my poems were the swimming. I brought you
Earrings. You said, These are lawflee. We went
To some beach, where the sand was dirty. Just going in
To the bathing house with you drove me "out of my mind."

It is wise to be witty. The shirt collar's far away.
Men tramp up and down the city on this windy day.
I am feeling a-political as a shell
Brought off some fish. Twenty-one years
Ago I saw you and loved you still.
Still! It wasn't plenty
Of time. Read Anatole France. Bored, a little. Read
Tolstoy, replaced and overcome. You read Stendhal.
I told you to. Where was replacement
Then? I don't know. He shushed us back into ourselves.
I used to understand
The highest excitement. Someone died
And you were distant. I went away
And made you distant. Where are you now? I see the chair
And hang onto it for sustenance. Good God how you kissed me
And I held you. You screamed

And I wasn't bothered by anything. Was nearest you.
And you were so realistic
Preferring the Soviet Bookstore
To my literary dreams.
"You don't like war," you said
After reading a poem
In which I'd simply said I hated war
In a whole list of things. To you
It seemed a position, to me
It was all a flux, especially then.
I was in an
Unexpected situation.
Let's take a walk
I wrote. And I love you as a sheriff
Searches for a walnut. And And so unless
I'm going to see your face
Bien soon, and you said
You must take me away, and
Oh Kenneth
You like everything
To be pleasant. I was burning
Like an arch
Made out of trees.

I'm not sure we ever actually took a walk.
We were so damned nervous. I was heading somewhere. And you had to be
At an appointment, or else be found out! Illicit love!
It's not a thing to think of. Nor is it when it's licit!
It is too much! And it wasn't enough. The achievement
I thought I saw possible when I loved you
Was that really achievement? Were you my
Last chance to feel that I had lost my chance?
I grew faint at your voice on the telephone
Electricity and all colors were mine, and the tops of hills
And everything that breathes. That was a feeling. Certain
Artistic careers had not even started. And I
Could have surpassed them. I could have I think put the
Whole world under our feet. You were in the restaurant. It
Was Chinese. We have walked three blocks. Or four blocks. It is New York

In nineteen fifty-three. Nothing has as yet happened
That will ever happen and will mean as much to me. You smile, and
        turn your head.

What rocketing there was in my face and in my head
And bombing everywhere in my body
I loved you I knew suddenly
That nothing had meant anything like you
I must have hoped (crazily) that something would
As if thinking you were the person I had become.

My sleep is beginning to be begun. And the sheets were on the bed.
A clock rang a bird's song rattled into my typewriter.
I had been thinking about songs which were very abstract.
Language was the champion. The papers lay piled on my desk
It was really a table. Now, the telephone. Hello, what?
What is my life like now? Engaged, studying and looking around
The library, teaching—I took it rather easy
A little too easy—we went to the ballet
Then dark becomes the light (blinding) of the next eighty days.
Orchestra cup became As beautiful as an orchestra or a cup, and
Locked climbs becomes If we were locked, well not quite, rather
Oh penniless could I really die, and I understood everything
Which before was running this way and that in my head
I saw titles, volumes, and suns I felt the hot
Pressure of your hands in that restaurant
To which, along with glasses, plates, lamps, lusters,
Tablecloths, napkins, and all the other junk
You added my life for it was entirely in your hands then—
My life
Yours, My Sister Life of Pasternak's beautiful title
My life without a life, my life in a life, my life impure
And my life pure, life seen as an entity
One death and a variety of days
And only one life.

I wasn't ready
For you.

I understood nothing
Seemingly except my feelings
You were whirling
In your life
I was keeping
Everything in my head
An artist friend's apartment
Five flights up the
Lower East Side nineteen
Fifty-something I don't know
What we made love the first time I
Almost died I had never felt
That way it was like being stamped on in Hell
It was roses of Heaven
My friends seemed turned to me to empty shell

On the railroad train's red velvet back
You put your hand in mine and said
"I told him"
Or was it the time after that?
I said Why did you
Do that you said I thought
It was over. Why? Because you were so
Nervous of my being there it was something I thought

I read
Tolstoy. You said
I don't like the way it turns out (*Anna
Karenina*) I had just liked the strength
Of the feeling you thought
About the end. I wanted
To I don't know what never leave you
Five flights up the June
Street emptied of fans, cups, kites, cops, eats, nights, no
The night was there
And something like air I love you Marina
Eighty-five days
Four thousand three hundred and sixty-
Two minutes all poetry was changed
For me what did I do in exchange

I am selfish, afraid you are
Overwhelmingly parade, back, sunshine, dreams
Later thousands of dreams

You said
You make me feel nawble (noble). I said
Yes. I said
To nothingness, This is all poems. Another one said (later)
That is so American. You were Russian.
You thought of your feelings, one said, not of her,
Not of the real situation. But my feelings were a part,
They were the force of the real situation. Truer to say I thought
Not of the whole situation
For your husband was also a part
And your feelings about your child were a part
And all my other feelings were a part. We
Turned this way and that, up-
Stairs then down
Into the streets.
Did I die because I didn't stay with you?
Or what did I lose of my life? I lost
You. I put you
In everything I wrote.

I used that precious material I put it in forms
Also I wanted to break down the forms
Poetry was a real occupation
To hell with the norms, with what is already written
Twenty-nine in love finds pure expression
Twenty-nine years you my whole life's digression
Not taken and Oh Kenneth
Everything afterwards seemed nowhere near
What I could do then in several minutes—
I wrote,
"I want to look at you all day long
Because you are mine."

I am twenty-nine, pocket flap folded
And I am smiling I am looking out at a world that
I significantly re-created from inside

Out of contradictory actions and emotions. I look like a silly child that
Photograph that year—big glasses, unthought-of clothes,
A suit, slight mess in general, cropped hair. And someone liked me,
Loved me a lot, I think. And someone else had, you had, too. I was
Undrenched by the tears I'd shed later about this whole thing when
I'd telephone you I'd be all nerves, though in fact
All life was a factor and all my nerves were in my head. I feel
Peculiar. Or I feel nothing. I am thinking about this poem. I am
     thinking about your raincoat,
I am worried about the tactfulness,
About the truth of what I say.
I am thinking about my standards for my actions
About what they were
You raised my standards for harmony and for happiness so much
And, too, the sense of a center
Which did amazing things for my taste
But my taste for action? for honesty, for directness in behavior?
I believe I simply never felt that anything could go wrong
This was abject stupidity
I also was careless in how I drove then and in what I ate
And drank it was easier to feel that nothing could go wrong
I had those feelings. I
Did not those things. I was involved in such and such
A situation, artistically and socially. We never spent a night
Together it is the New York of
Aquamarine sunshine and the Loew's Theater's blazing swing of light
In the middle of the day

Let's take a walk
Into the world
Where if our shoes get white
With snow, is it snow, Marina,
Is it snow or light?
Let's take a walk

Every detail is everything in its place (Aristotle). Literature is a cup
And we are the malted. The time is a glass. A June bug comes
And a carpenter spits on a plane, the flowers ruffle ear rings.
I am so dumb-looking. And you are so beautiful.

Sitting in the Hudson Tube
Walking up the fusky street
Always waiting to see you
You the original creation of all my You, you the you
In every poem the hidden one whom I am talking to
Worked at Bamberger's once I went with you to Cerutti's
Bar—on Madison Avenue? I held your hand and you said
Kenneth you are playing with fire. I said
Something witty in reply.
It was the time of the McCarthy trial
Hot sunlight on lunches. You squirted
Red wine into my mouth.
My feelings were like a fire my words became very clear
My psyche or whatever it is that puts together motions and
        emotions
Was unprepared. There was a good part
And an alarmingly bad part which didn't correspond—
No letters! no seeming connection! your slim pale hand
It actually was, your blondness and your turning-around-to-me look.
        Good-bye Kenneth.

No, Marina, don't go
And what had been before would come after
Not to be mysterious we'd be together make love again
It was the wildest thing I've done
I can hardly remember it
It has gotten by now
So mixed up with losing you
The two almost seem in some way the same. You
Wore something soft—angora? cashmere?
I remember that it was black. You turned around
And on such a spring day which went on and on and on
I actually think I felt that I could keep
The strongest of all feelings contained inside me
Producing endless emotional designs.

With the incomparable feeling of rising and of being like a banner
Twenty seconds worth twenty-five years
With feeling noble extremely mobile and very free
With Taking a Walk With You, West Wind, In Love With You, and
        Yellow Roses

With pleasure I felt my leg muscles and my brain couldn't hold
With the Empire State Building the restaurant your wrist bones with
     Greenwich Avenue
In nineteen fifty-one with heat humidity a dog pissing with neon
With the feeling that at last
My body had something to do and so did my mind

You sit
At the window. You call
Me, across Paris,
Amsterdam, New
York. Kenneth!
My Soviet
Girlhood. My
Spring, summer
And fall. Do you
Know you have
Missed some of them?
Almost all. I am
Waiting and I
Am fading I
Am fainting I'm
In a degrading state
Of inactivity. A ball
Rolls in the gutter. I have
Two hands to
Stop it. I am
A flower I pick
The vendor his
Clothes getting up
Too early and
What is it makes this rose
Into what is more fragrant than what is not?

I am stunned I am feeling tortured
By "A man of words and not a man of deeds"

I was waiting in a taxicab
It was white letters in white paints it was you
Spring comes, summer, then fall

And winter. We really have missed
All of that, whatever else there was
In those years so sanded by our absence.
I never saw you for as long as half a day.

You were crying outside the bus station
And I was crying—
I knew that this really was my life—
I kept thinking of how we were crying
Later, when I was speaking, driving, walking,
Looking at doorways and colors, mysterious entrances
Sometimes I'd be pierced as by a needle
Sometimes be feverish as from a word
Books closed and I'd think
I can't read this book, I threw away my life
These held on to their lives. I was
Excited by praise from anyone, startled by criticism, always hating it
Traveling around Europe and being excited
It was all in reference to you
And feeling I was not gradually forgetting
What your temples and cheekbones looked like
And always with this secret.

Later I thought
That what I had done was reasonable
It may have been reasonable
I also thought that I saw what had appealed to me
So much about you, the way you responded
To everything your excitement about
Me, I had never seen that. And the fact
That you were Russian, very mysterious, all that I didn't know
About you—and you didn't know
Me, for I was as strange to you as you were to me.
You were like my first trip to France you had
Made no assumptions. I could be
Clearly and passionately and
Nobly (as you'd said) who I was—at the outer limits of my life
Of my life as my life could be
Ideally. But what about the dark part all this lifted
Me out of? Would my bad moods, my uncertainties, my

Distrust of people I was close to, the
Twisty parts of my ambition, my
Envy, all have gone away? And if
They hadn't gone, what? For didn't I need
All the strength you made me feel I had, to deal
With the difficulties of really having you?
Where could we have been? But I saw so many new possibilities
That it made me rather hate reality
Or I think perhaps I already did
I didn't care about the consequences
Because they weren't "poetic" weren't "ideal"
And oh well you said we walk along
Your white dress your blue dress your green
Blouse with sleeves then one without
Sleeves and we are speaking
Of things but not of very much because underneath it
I am raving I am boiling I am afraid
You ask me Kenneth what are you thinking
If I could say
It all then I thought if I could say
Exactly everything and have it still be as beautiful
Billowing over, riding over both our doubts
Some kind of perfection and what did I actually
Say? Marina it's late. Marina
It's early. I love you. Or else, What's this street?
You were the perfection of my life
And I couldn't have you. That is, I didn't.
I couldn't think. I wrote, instead. I would have had
To think hard, to figure everything out
About how I could be with you,
Really, which I couldn't do
In those moments of permanence we had
As we walked along.

We walk through the park in the sun. It is the end.
You phone me. I send you a telegram. It
Is the end. I keep
Thinking about you, grieving about you. It is the end. I write
Poems about you, to you. They
Are no longer simple. No longer

Are you there to see every day or
Every other or every third or fourth warm day
And now it has been twenty-five years
But those feelings kept orchestrating I mean rehearsing
Rehearsing in me and tuning up
While I was doing a thousand other things, the band
Is ready, I am over fifty years old and there's no you—
And no me, either, not as I was then,
When it was the Renaissance
Filtered through my nerves and weakness
Of nineteen fifty-four or fifty-three,
When I had you to write to, when I could see you
And it could change.

The Burning Mystery of Anna in 1951

1. THE BURNING MYSTERY OF ANNA

"I don't know how to kiss."
Won't you come in?

To have bent her back half across the bed.
To be so bending her.

Not yet having said Won't you come in.
Never yet having said it.

Planning to say, Can we
Would you like to come up to my room?

The bedroom stairway
And then thought about it.

My name is you.
I am not interested him the first place.

I come from Corsica.
The scene is very confusing.

She is dancing and I
Think she is pretty. That's one part of it.

2. WHY NOT?

It is satisfying to have a nose
Right in the middle of my face.

You asked me the question and I replied
With as much imagination as I could.

Then one foggy morning we met.
We sat in a cold café and compared viruses.

Oh, sure, I'd heard of you a thousand times
From E and L and X and A and Y.

What was I trying to hide? Something monstrous?
Is there really anything to hide?

I hate all these guiltmongers. God damn it,
I said to myself one day. I'll let fly!

The story of my existence as I reconstruct it
Now is about one sixth part reconstruction.

Suggested to me by plastic instead of cork
In the bottleneck I said, Well listen, now, well, well, to hell with it!
    Why not?

3. WITH DAD

The fly I cast was red.
Dad said Push it!

We went out in the boat.
Marble-like was the sea.

Down to the sand we went
And to the dock next.

Let's go fishing said Dad.
I pulled on red sweater.

I was sitting on the porch
Peacefully when Dad marched out.

This is one of my experiences
Which I think is fairly typical.

You've asked me to tell you
A little bit about my life.

Hello. How are you? I'm fine,
Thanks. Today there is something new.

4. STARTING

The oranges subdued the attack
Or rather we endured it.

I am tired of being attacked, she said.
Then the rain fell.

It was a sunny morning.
Sunny sunny sunny sunny sunny.

The night was dark. The dogs
Howled till it got sunny.

The young man is living with the French
Family near the entrance to the trough.

Actual cash value nineteen dollars.
He puts it on but then she takes it off.

What was it I remembered of L. at school?
A keen bursitis lit the window.

Simple simple simple, simply to start,
To be so easy when one is at the start.

5. A CRITICAL POINT

She: Weren't you curious about our conversation?
I said: I have been watching you all from here.

Then I went up to her and started to speak.
I felt shy but I had to confront the beautiful.

Talking to another stranger, I think a guy
In the distance I saw her, the checked-print-dressed girl I had seen.

Wandering along through the twisting streets of the city
One day as I was, as is my habit.

Perfectly true, but on this day it was different.
You always do the same things every day.

Get up, brush your teeth, eat breakfast, then wander.
I really don't see how you can stand the boredom.

I hope you don't mind if I'm a little critical
I'm afraid that you won't like what I'm going to say.

I had something to say she had never heard.
A bird woke me this morning with the usual.

6. TWO BICYCLE RIDERS

It is the summer of genius! And also of genes!
You replied, as I gulped over the hill-Alps.

What is the nature of things, I replied,
As we tortured the hill-Alps.

This answers all questions, you described,
As we biked over the hill-Alps.

Then tell me more, I think I squeaked,
As we broke the chains of the hill-Alps.

And so that's the truth, you indicted,
As we tore down the mounts of the hill-Alps.

The mention is cotton to the street
Which in turn encapsules drifted attention.

Finally, with courage mounting, I asked you,
What are we doing on these hill-Alps?

O beautiful person silent and serene
Invited by me to pedal on these mountains.

7. ABSTRACT

Unavoidable and inescapable.
What is your nature? I said.

Quiet, but how to make them,
Also, grabbing of the spirit?

Admirable, I said.
They presented a problem.

When I first saw them
They felt complete.

Come, said my mind,
I will show them to you.

Where are these new
Unities? I said.

Then something rainbowed
And a new thing promised.

I was living. I said,
I can do all that I wish.

8. WHAT I WAS THINKING OF

The reeds were very sunny. "Yes, he
Lived here—Cézanne," you said.

Retiring from the bicycles and remarking
How painful it was to bike, pleasanter to walk.

Was it the day a man with a moustache, a girl
Anne, three law students and I went?

Come on, let's go for a walk!
Bring not the bicycle.

Je crois qu'il éxagère, says Marguérite.
Then, twoo–twoo, outside hear a bell.

Up to lunch from the wall about which I wrote
The poem "Bricks."

Standing in the sunlight and thinking
Or doing something like that.

First getting up and down the hill
Walking, until I smelled the fields, on two legs.

From The Red Robins

FROM ACT II, SCENE 3

BOB *(in his plane)*

In the sky, and this is something that has been noticed before, everything seems to be all right. Coming back to land, though, can often be a trial. Balzac wanted everything—fame, money, love, power, acceptance—and he was able to get them all. Yet he was tormented. Byron was born an aristocrat; he was wealthy, handsome—and a great genius. Yet Byron led a miserable life. Tennyson, too, was an unhappy man, in love with his landlady's son.

The most remarkable thing about the sky is that there seems to be nothing there, and this probably has something to do with the feeling of happiness (or perhaps it is only euphoria) which is produced in a person by being there. When Jill and I have our planes close together up high, that is a moment I love. Conversation is often impossible to hear but sometimes seems to have a celestial quality when one is flying.

I wonder if Napoleon was happy—and Homer. Nobody even knows where Homer was born. There are three "Homeric birthplaces" in Greece. Nobody is even sure that Homer wrote the *Odyssey*. Apparently, he was blind. Like us, he was a sailor, though not a sailor of the sky.

Jesus Christ, perhaps the most influential man who ever lived, was almost certainly extremely unhappy. Socrates was unhappy. I guess you think Mao Tse-tung was a happy man. He was suffering from gastric ulcers and could scarcely ascend the ancient speaking mound. The fact that we are betrothed to old age and death is enough to make all people unhappy.

In the air, I feel occupied. There is the steering, there are the controls, there is that sense of being "above it all" yet participating in it in the most lively and exhilarating way. I wonder if "escape" is the right word, as someone once suggested when I talked of these things, for something which so wholly absorbs the being and which requires so much skill, and which brings so much of life into one small span. The countries that float by down beneath me are like chapters in a book; and

I feel them, and what is in the air above them, in my face, and in my
heart, and in my mind. . . .

ACT III, SCENE 8

The sky above Asia. It is late afternoon, changing to dark, and with
BOB's entrance, dawn. The characters appear in the sky one by one—
first, SANTA CLAUS.

SANTA CLAUS
  I am Night. I am Death.
  I am the place where no one can follow.
  They cannot know it.
  My face and form do not show it.
  I am Crime. I am Death.
  I am Night. I am what never can be found.

    (*Enter* JILL)

JILL
  I am Life.
  I cut the Christmas cake with a keen-bladed knife
  And give it out unequally to the casual guests.
  I am involved in everything that is best
  And worst. I set standards for what I try
  But my only negative judgment is to die.
  Neither good nor evil am I,
  In Boston or in Shanghai,
  For I am Life.

    (*Enter* LYN)

LYN
  I am Desire. I am Enchantment and Desire.
  Whenever, wherever I go there, there is fire.
  I burn and will consume. I startle the President in his living room,
  The hawk, and the acrobat on his high wire. I am Desire.

    (*Enter* JIM)

216

JIM

> When will I find the peace of great experience?
> Where is the star I can follow
> That is not hollow, that brings me home again?
> I am Intellectual Desire, Aspiring Mind.
> I fly, criss-crossing earth and humankind.

> (*Enter* EASTER BUNNY)

EASTER BUNNY

> I have infested these airplanes
> With a kind of dream gas
> So that no one will ever clearly know
> Exactly what things mean.
> By this, I expect to prevent
> Them from reaching their destinations!

> (*Enter* BUD)

BUD

> Foolish as usual, our enemy miscalculates
> The nature of our mission—to mediate, to communicate
> To bridge the state between earth and the sky!
> Oh tell me, Apollo-Buddha,
> In what week are you fixing to linger
> In the white bony church of our feet?

> (*Enter* LOUIS)

LOUIS:

> In the peace of the night
> I am the thought of the day
> That is there, but cannot be seen.

> (*Enter* BILL)

BILL

> I am the missing page of the magazine
> That prefigures light.
> I am the body, when it is strong as a stone.

217

(*Enter the* PRESIDENT, *walking slowly, holding a letter.*)

PRESIDENT

Forever, alone . . . Well, maybe not . . . I'll find her with this letter.

(PRESIDENT *walks off. Enter the* STARS.)

STARS

We are the Stars, and we are not known.
Only at midnight is our power shown
And then it is misunderstood.
We do no evil, no good. We stay here to show
As the Ocean stays below to show
That what is not known
Shows many ways to be, although it seems,
Sometimes, that there is but one way alone.

(STARS *leave. It begins to grow light. Enter* BOB)

BOB

Why do you seek me, god of the sickly wail
And uneuphonious song? Is it that I and my kind
Have offended you in the temples of hillocks?
Of pillows? In the sky, everything is the controls
And the whispering of sashes, like the way a bright eye flashes
Or airplane crashes, which is the wind against the plane.

Girl and Baby Florist Sidewalk Pram
Nineteen Seventy Something

Sweeping past the florist's came the baby and the girl
I am the girl! I am the baby!
I am the florist who is filled with mood!
I am the mood. I am the girl who is inside the baby
For it is a baby girl. I am old style of life. I am the new
Everything as well. I am the evening in which you docked your first kiss.
And it came to the baby. And I am the boyhood of the girl
Which she never has. I am the florist's unknown baby
He hasn't had one yet. The florist is in a whirl
So much excitement, section, outside his shop
Or hers. Who is he? Where goes the baby? She
Is immensely going to grow up. How much
Does this rent for? It's more than a penny. It's more
Than a million cents. My dear, it is life itself. Roses?
Chrysanthemums? If you can't buy them I'll give
Them for nothing. Oh no, I can't.
Maybe my baby is allergic to their spores.
So then the girl and her baby go away. Florist stands whistling
Neither inside nor outside thinking about the mountains of Peru.

The Simplicity of the Unknown Past

Out the window, the cow out the window
The steel frame out the window, the rusted candlestand;
Out the window the horse, the handle-less pan,
Real things. Inside the window my heart
That only beats for you—a verse of Verlaine.
Inside the window of my heart is a style
And a showplace of onion-like construction.
Inside the window is a picture of a cat
And outside the window is the cat indeed
Jumping up now to the top of the
Roof of the garage; its paws help take it there.
Inside this window is a range
Of things which outside the window are like stars
Arranged but huge in fashion.
Outside the window is a car, is the rusted wheel of a bicycle.
Inside it are words and paints; outside, smooth hair
Of a rabbit, just barely seen. Inside the glass
Of this window is a notebook, with little marks,
They are words. Outside this window is a wall
With little parts—they are stones. Inside this window
Is the start, and outside is the beginning. A heart
Beats. The cat leaps. The room is light, the sun is almost blinding.
Inside this body is a woman, inside whom is a star
Of some kind or other, which is like a uterus; and
Outside the window a farm machine starts.

From The Green Step

The green step was near the two girls, five-year-olds, in white rather stiff dresses cut out of lace the way valentines sometimes used to be, and they gesticulated toward it, little fingers pointing this way and that. A bird landed twenty feet away from it. The green step was cold and alone. This step had green carpeting on it which had once been mold, a sort of wet tough tissue of mashed-down grass, stems and leaves—"step mulch." At some time this had changed to a carpet. This carpet was much the same color as the mold of green, though less cold to touch, and with a different smell, not dank and brackish but slightly musty, with a suggestion of chalk or of glue. Underneath this covering, the step was gray-white stone. The step led to the front door of a house. It also led to a small auditorium's stage. It led, once, to a place where a throne began. It led to a place where there is a statue surrounded—on all sides, at a distance of five feet—by columns. The statue is of Diana, the goddess of the chase and of the moon. The white columns around this goddess who so affected the inside and the outside of the woods are not much like trees, although they are tall, straight up, and sometimes cold, and one could hide behind them, hide behind one of them if one were small and slim enough. And this, one of the little girls once did. That was before the step led to a concert stage or into a house. The place with the columns seemed, though no one knew why, to have been the first place to which the step went.

Standing on the step one felt between one place and another. Those who went to see the statue of Diana, those who went to the concert or into the house, had never met the man who made the step. The step was originally a random step in the woods. It led a wild life, not wild in itself but lying amidst nature, and being part of it, in random arrangements. A very long time ago the arrangement had been changed by an earthquake; more recently, by a man. That was the man who made the step. He took pleasure in finding the stone, in carrying it away with him. The next day he made the step. The bird flew some distance away.

That was only one time the step was made. At other times it was changed and became different steps. What happened to the step at one time or another did not very much affect the main characteristic, for most of those who used it or even those who saw it, of the step. Its main quality was that it was solid, it could be relied on, it would take you from one place to the next. Oh, people had fallen off the step, but that was never due to any fault of the step. They fell because they were ill, suddenly, or because they had drunk too much alcohol, or even, sometimes, because they were pushed. Not everyone who came up on the step was welcome at all times to whoever happened to be at the top of the step, or rather where the step led to. However the step is not very high, and no one has been seriously hurt from falling when he was standing on it.

The step had no consciousness of the change in its existence from being amidst wild nature to being a part of something that an animate and mobile species had turned into an object which served one of its manifold purposes. The step had, in fact, no consciousness of a world at all. Children would look at the step, sometimes, and think it felt something, but there is no evidence that it did. The step was there, and one day someone stepped on it who killed the bird.

The house the step leads to is a large house with bedrooms upstairs, and a large living room and dining room downstairs and a modern kitchen. It was built a long time ago but the family who own it live somewhere else and the house is rented to a father, a mother, and a son. The son is a hunter. The father spends his days placing cards in a long rectangular cardboard box. The mother goes into different rooms of the house and her clothing almost always has pleats. The member of the family who spends the most time on the step is the son. He will stand there leaning and looking out at the life of man and nature beyond the house. A domestic servant will sometimes stand there, too, replacing the boy.

The stone that forms the basis of the step, under the green carpeting, is slightly veined with grayish white in a way that suggests distances. The lines move outward and suggest a beyond that no one in the story is able to get to. The stone is thought to be made up of rapidly moving electrons, though this is not part of the common experience of anyone who sees it.

The step in the concert hall is the step that goes to the house and that goes to the throne. The throne is made of majolica, silver, and amber. No one is sitting on the throne. No one is playing in the concert hall. The house is rotting, empty, and is being destroyed. The sound of bulldozers, the noise of drilling things fills the street. There is dust everywhere around, making one passer-by think "I would like to get out of all this; I'll go to a concert." The man with a blue hat says, "It is foolish to waste this step." The step is taken to, and sold for a very small sum to the man who arranges performances in the concert hall. Before, leading to the stage, he had only a rotting wooden step. It's a strange thing to buy, he thinks, a step, but yes, I guess I can use it. Now there is an irregular noise—tuning up of instruments. When the concert is over, the people go out into the street. In the air, for a moment, are their comments on what they have heard.

Now night invests the street, and the step leads to a throne. High above the buildings and the trees, azure-, blood- and sulphur-colored formations move about the sky. On her head appear three stars for a crown. Her feet, like clouds, are white. Thundering over the universe, the rainstorm washes this away. Washes her away.

When someone speaks of the step, which had once been part of the house, another says that then there was no green carpet on the step. That would only have been when the step was inside a building. Now in the concert hall, yes, there is green carpeting covering the step, but not before. It is even possible to argue, lightly, as to whether or not it is the same step.

Ideally the step would be part of the procurement of some sort of final fulfillment for everyone, and perhaps it is. The woman knows she will have to sell the piano. She sits down to play it, and once again the child starts to cry. The old man looks at the step and remembers the bird. Every day, for a week, as a child, he had seen it. The concert hall seems to become for him a sort of temple with yellow and white mists beyond, and green and vermilion stripes among its columns, and where one who is a statue, in a final wash of violets and whites, leans over to him and plants a stony kiss on his trembling face. Ah! he screams aloud and everyone turns to look at him. They do not see what is the matter. He walks in the woods. Every day is like a light kiss given by the country, by its air, by its sun, by its trees. There still seems to be no reason to think of a king or a god. Feet tread on the step and the trigger is released. Birds fly in a dance of blood-splatters all over the wall—a painting much later than Cézanne. In the morning the step is nothing and no one in anyone's thoughts. Contracts are made at the Bourse and on the real estate tables. Flies buzz hopelessly against the windows. Men in shirtsleeves, in billows of cigarette smoke, say, "We must take the first step." A dog jumps up, its paws against a little girl's white dress. Her mother is miles away, in a car. The old man is here. A servant comes down the step and picks the child up.

With Janice

The leaves were already on the trees, the fruit blossoms
White and not ruined and pink and not ruined and we
Were riding in a boat over the water in which there was a sea
Hiding the meanings of all our salty words. A duck
Or a goose and a boat and a stone and a stone cliff. The
Hardnesses—and, with a little smile—of life. Sitting
Earlier or later and forgotten the words and the bees
At supper they were about in how you almost gestured but stopped
Knowing there were only one or two things, and that the rest
Were merely complications. But one in a trenchcoat said
It's reversible. And, It's as out-of-date as a reversible coat. And
Magna Bear and Minor Orse were sleeping. The soap
Was climbing in its dish but relaxed and came down when cold water stopped
Rushing in and the bathroom was flooded. I said, It is not about
Things but with things I'd like to go and, too, Will it last
Or will all become uniform again? Even as she goes
Pottering around the island's peripheries she thinks
Of the obligations. And the sympathies, far stronger than bears.
I was a bush there, a hat on a clothes dummy's head. Receiving letters
Sat down. I avoided being punished. I said,
It's cutting the limbs off a tree but there was no
Tree and I had no saw. I was planning to have infinite egress
While keeping some factory on the surface exceedingly cold. It was
A good source of evening. Sweating, asleep in the after-
Noons, later the morning of thumps, unwhittled questions, the freezing
    head. At night
Drinking whiskey, the fishermen were, everyone said, away.
A chrysanthemum though still full of splashes it
Has lost some little of its odor for my nostrils and a girl
In a chalk-pink-and-white dress is handing on the cliff
A glass of emerald water to a pin, or is it a chicken, as you get
Closer you can see it is a mirror made of the brawn
Of water muscles splashing that which has been.
My self, like the connections of an engine—rabbits and the new year—
Having puzzled out something in common, a blue stone duck

As if Homer Hesiod and Shakespeare had never lived at all
And we weren't the deposit. Weinstein puts on his hat
And the women go crazy. Some falter toward the sea. Wein-
Stein come back! But he is leaving. He says Leonard! Good-bye!
So Leonard invites us
To come and to see, where the white water bucket is a dashboard
Of this place to that. You will want to go swimming, and you will
      want to meet
These snobbish absurd Americans who inhabit
The gesso incalcations on the cliff. And we went like a nose
To a neighbor face. Sometimes tilting the grappa
Or in this case the ouzo it spills on my clothes or on yours, the world
      without us, the world outside
As when one of us was sick, which also brought the out world in.
And the art world meanwhile
Was strumming along. Individual struggles
Will long be remembered, of XXX's doing this,
Of YYYY's doing that.
Soap which will start lazily up from those types. Then
We remember to leave and also to stay. Janice said
It may not be hooked on right. Weinstein has been walking
Down a flowery way. Good-bye, nature lovers! he crescendoed.
A locked sail. The bullet of this button isn't right. And the train laughed
And pulled out pulling half of the station with it. The dust
Was indifferent to Americans as to Greeks. What simply was happening
Was beyond the rustication of ideas into the elements but essentially the
      same. Meanwhile, grasses matted,
The leaves winced, ideas one had had in earliest childhood days
Were surprisingly becoming succinct, maybe just before vanishing
Or turning into something you would feel like a belt,
Circling but not in hand. I would find these and set them down
On the sizzling white paper that was slipperier than the knees
That made me feel guilty, and sometimes heavier than the overcoats
      which there we never had
For someone's chest's attention. It was always distraction
But it was also a chair. And a chair is merely a civilized distraction. If
Character wasn't everything, it was something else I didn't
Know less than geography, which is to say, Surprise, Wonder,
Delight. You stood there and the stones
Of Old Greece and our lives, those collegiate stones,

Harvard, Emory, and Marymount, with the blue exegesis of the tide
Against which to fall was a headline—Don't stand.
You give this wish to me—Apollo, in some manner of time, lives on.
    Inside your mind
Things are being washed. Everything was docking
And we went down to see it. Memories of women made exactly the same
Kneeling down in the hot raft of daisies
It also got ragged for my walks. When are we going
To really have the time to have time? I make love to you
Like a rope swinging across a stone wall and you
Are lilacs reflected in a mirror or seen through a window.
Going out. You said I like this one. A pale pink dress
The suds were driving through the water. Moving fairly fast against the
Just plain oxygen we ended up looking
A little bit overcome. But I got up
You got up. We went around
Spilling things and putting a few of them on racks.
Those were the important things we never got done
Because they were behind us or
Surpassing us, otherwise unavailable—cherry
Blossoms, clavicles of girls which I can't touch
In the innocuousness, beetles, burring and scampering around a rose
I see is no longer there. Blossoms on the walk we were here, were there
As much as the heat was. I dried my ear at the sink
Then dried the other and quieted my lips and my nose
With a briny dry towel and you slid upon your shoes
And Katherine jumped up, ran around. Soon she will be
Out as usual, down the roadway formally unopened
For my approach, as if not to be drunk
Were a confidence vote from the leaves for the turmoil inside
The ouzo-fed engines of ourselves, when, seated on slabs of wood
As roses on tough ground as eggs were on the morning, deciding to leave,
We oversleep the boat, a shirt, a white shirt gleaming
On the photographic exception of the tide. An airlane of styles.
If it was said, It's hopeless
And you said, The gardens are going over
The edge of the overside sidewalk. Well,
Maybe and maybe not. A foot, I thought (not very intelligently)
In a shoe of newspapers, even ice unstacked about by process—
I loved the texture of your talk, and another woman's

Breast had a texture of a late summer day, while your
Eyes were walking both inside your head and in me, in each of my activities
While you both found the cat and he was seated, alive,
Beyond ants, on some anthill pebbles and or gravel. The bar wasn't closed
Or open, it was daylight-surprised. Plate glass was nowhere around.
I looked up. I put on my glasses. There were all these artists
Hot with the prayers of nineteen sixty-one—
Let us be potters, or skunks, but not
Business men! I sat down on a stone
And looked around, my last chance
To never be a doctor, as if it meant something, and a father of four—
In these minutes, of fatal decisions. Decisions! Fatal! Lazy,
Air comes in. What could it have been
To be so exciting? And the Scotch tape jumped into the air
With Leonardo out in a boat, and, miles later, acropoles of bones the dead
Dinosaurs and cities, tied to subjects
All of us present have forgotten—women, failing the Weinstein
Of the season. Rather inform
P.M. while you are re-estimating buttons'
Life by leaving them long-ungone-for in the midst
Of the very short walks we take down the long
Bite narrow street—At night electricity is kissing
The emasculated stars—The new things we had done, in pencil at the side
     of the napkin.
It was hot. Ce qui veut dire we, a cat sitting
On a balcony a plant was wilting. What dialect are you speaking,
You, wearing the loafers of the sea? I couldn't care
For everything simultaneously. A mat was exciting enough. The bath came
     separately
From the dawn. You walk around
Simply looking for strawberries, sun, our baby, oxygen—
"Always not quite unbeginning to be or have been begun."
Leonardo erat other. Ira haec perturbat. Let that be. Another was
Absent in a habit fidget. I was
In a rush. Someone said, hush!
Calm down in this—knife—patterns of things—
Where is the music that's fitting for such an occasion
In those miles of hotel
Corridor followed by Weinstein's weeping at the beach
Girls who followed that for love of him

And why is there not more peaceful melting here
Into the wide wood story of the wall
How I loved those made of stone. And yet poetry has
Messages, interrogations of musics that have been used
In the various islands of acts, staying genuinely still,
And seeing—a piece of life and seeing—
It's a wall inside me
Why dancers were always coming out in a pageant
Wrecking the place animals were in there too
As now, so for music fit?
The pink spot you trotted me out to see with under the sigh which
Something and the great writers were all still alive
Much of the worst had happened, the envelope was still unpeeled.
I am stamping on the path. Alone. Nothing is so essential as this—
Moment. And a red fan wings past—flower? Transatlantic systems
    ourselves
The door unopened, the mail came every day. The grass is soft,
Matted, and then there was an enclosure, tar on my leg, on yours
The culture all around us was in fragments, in some chests sure
In others fragments, in some no grasp at all, which I couldn't
Easily perceive, thus making everybody equal,
Almost at least enough to be a rival—perception,
Inspiration—too cloud to care. Voices
I heard on rooftops and cul-de-sacs of meditative sex
Scurried beyond the invisible barrier of you washing
The blouse. Brilliant. In fact, having more meaning
Because of all impulsions. You were
A blue coat—it wasn't
Exactly yours or mine or that place's
But a stinginess of life in packet flying through
Eventually, signing away like papers
A moment of the beach, when the tide dried the invincible
By elbows in comparison to the nude inside—
Look at—it's finished—this rock
Will come with me! Weinstein, walking in his sleep
The first afternoon when I arrived cooling bees they have a hive
Against the cliff, who've kept things in—the art
School, slacks. Normal the Mediterranean
Flows onward and on, boat,
I wore Leonard's jacket and my clothes, then shoes

Meet yours, advancing, so walk about the best
Final of beach, to not notice numbers
Except when they are speaking, as we stopped less
When all this was around.

Days and Nights

1 . THE INVENTION OF POETRY

It came to me that all this time
There had been no real poetry and that it needed to be invented.
Some recommended discovering
What was already there. Others,
Taking a view from further up the hill (remnant
Of old poetry), said just go and start wherever you are.

It was not the kind of line
I wanted so I crossed it out
"Today I don't think I'm very inspired"—
What an existence! How hard to concentrate
On what is the best kind of existence!
What's sure is having only one existence
And its already having a shape.

Extase de mes vingt ans—
French girl with pure gold eyes
In which shine internal rhyme and new kinds of stanzas

When I said to F, Why do you write poems?
He said, Look at most of the poems
That have already been written!

All alone writing
And lacking self-confidence
And in another way filled with self-confidence
And in another way devoted to the brick wall
As a flower is when hummed on by a bee

I thought This is the one I am supposed to like best
The totally indifferent one
Who simply loves and identifies himself with something
Or someone and cares not what others think nor of time
The one who identifies himself with a wall.

I didn't think I was crazy
I thought Orpheus chasms trireme hunch coats melody
And then No that isn't good enough

I wrote poems on the edges of the thistles
Which my walking companions couldn't understand
But that's when I was a baby compared to now

"That is so much like you and your poetry."
This puts me in a self-congratulatory mood
Which I want to "feel out," so we sit together and talk
All through the winter afternoon.

I smoked
After writing five or ten lines
To enjoy what I had already written
And to not have to write any more

I stop smoking
Until after lunch
It is morning
It is spring
The day is breaking
Ten—eleven—noon
I am not smoking
I am asleep

Sense of what primitive man is, in cave and with primitive life
Comes over me one bright morning as I lie in bed
Whoosh! to the typewriter. Lunch! And I go down.

What have I lost?
The Coleridge joke, as W would say.

William Carlos Williams I wrote
As the end word of a sestina. And *grass*
Sleepy, hog snout, breath, and *dream.*
I never finished it.

I come down the hill—cloud
I like living on a hill—head
You are so lucky to be alive—jokes
It chimes at every moment—stung

So much of it was beyond me
The winding of the national highway
The fragments of glass in the convent wall
To say nothing of the habits of the bourgeoisie
And all those pleasures, the neat coat,
The bought wine, and the enabling of the pronouncements.

For Christ's sake you're missing the whole day
Cried someone and I said Shut up
I want to sleep and what he accomplished in the hours I slept
I do not know and what I accomplished in my sleep
Was absolutely nothing.

How much is in the poet and how much in the poem?
You can't get to the one but he gives you the other.
Is he holding back? No, but his experience is like a bubble.
When he gives it to you, it breaks. Those left-over soap dots are the
     work.

Oh you've done plenty I said when he was feeling despondent
Look at R and L and M. But they don't do anything, he replied.

At the window I could see
What never could be inside me
Since I was twelve: pure being
Without desire for the other, not even for the necktie or the dog.

2 . THE STONES OF TIME

The bathtub is white and full of strips
And stripes of red and blue and green and white
Where the painter has taken a bath! Now comes the poet
Wrapped in a huge white towel, with his head full of imagery.

Try being really attentive to your life
Instead of to your writing for a change once in a while
Sometimes one day one hour one minute oh I've done that
What happened? I got married and was in a good mood.

We wrote so much that we thought it couldn't be any good
Till we read it over and then thought how amazing it was!

Athena gave Popeye a Butterfinger filled with stars
Is the kind of poetry Z and I used to stuff in jars

When we took a walk he was afraid
Of the dogs who came in parade
To sniffle at the feet
Of two of the greatest poets of the age.

The stars came out
And I was still writing
My God where's dinner
Here's dinner
My wife! I love you
Do you remember in Paris
When I was thinner
And the sun came through the shutters like a knife?

I said to so many people once, "I write poetry."
They said, "Oh, so you are a poet." Or they said,
"What kind of poetry do you write? modern poetry?"
Or "My brother-in-law is a poet also."
Now if I say, "I am the poet Kenneth Koch," they say, "I think I've
       heard of you"
Or "I'm sorry but that doesn't ring a bell" or
"Would you please move out of the way? You're blocking my view
Of that enormous piece of meat that they are lowering into the Bay
Of Pigs." What? Or "What kind of poetry do you write?"

"Taste," I said to J and he said
"What else is there?" but he was looking around.

"All the same, she isn't made like that,"
Marguerite said, upon meeting Janice,
To her husband Eddie, and since
Janice was pregnant this had a clear meaning
Like the poetry of Robert Burns.

You must learn to write in form first, said the dumb poet.
After several years of that you can write in free verse.
But of course no verse is really "free," said the dumb poet.
Thank you, I said. It's been great talking to you!

Sweet are the uses of adversity
Became Sweetheart cabooses of diversity
And Sweet art cow papooses at the university
And Sea bar Calpurnia flower havens' re-noosed knees

A book came out, and then another book
Which was unlike the first,
Which was unlike the love
And the nightmares and the fisticuffs that inspired it
And the other poets, with their egos and their works,
Which I sometimes read reluctantly and sometimes with great delight
When I was writing so much myself
I wasn't afraid that what they wrote would bother me
And might even give me ideas.

I walked through the spring fountain of spring
Air fountain knowing finally that poetry was everything:
Sleep, silence, darkness, cool white air, and language.

3 . THE SECRET

Flaming
They seem
To come, sometimes,
Flaming
Despite all the old
Familiar effects
And despite my knowing

That, well, really they're not flaming
And these flaming words
Are sometimes the best ones I write
And sometimes not.

The doctor told X don't write poetry
It will kill you, which is a very late example
Of the idea of the immortal killing the man
(Not since Hector or one of those people practically)
X either wrote or didn't I don't remember—
I was writing (what made me think of it)
And my heart beat so fast
I actually thought I would die.

Our idea is something we talked about, our idea
Our idea is to write poetry that is better than poetry
To be as good as or better than the best old poetry
To evade, avoid all the mistakes of bad modern poets
Our idea is to do something with language
That has never been done before
Obviously—otherwise it wouldn't be creation
We stick to it and now I am a little nostalgic
For our idea, we never speak of it any more, it's been
Absorbed into our work, and even our friendship
Is an old, rather fragile-looking thing.
Maybe poetry took the life out of both of them,
Idea and friendship.

I like the new stuff you're doing
She wrote and then she quoted some lines
And made some funny references to the poems
And he said have you forgotten how to write the other kind of poems
Or, rather, she said it I forget which
I was as inspired as I have ever been
Writing half-conscious and half-unconscious every day
After taking a walk or looking at the garden
Or making love to you (as we used to say)

Unconscious meant "grace"
It meant No matter who I am
I am greater than I am
And this is greater
And this, since I am merely the vessel of it,
May be the truth

Then I read Ariosto
I fell to my knees
And started looking for the pins
I had dropped when I decided to be unconscious
I wanted to fasten everything together
As he did and make an enormous poetry Rose
Which included everything
And which couldn't be composed by the "unconscious"
(At least not by the "unconscious" alone)

This rose became a bandanna, which became a house
Which became infused with all passion, which became a hideaway
Which became yes I would like to have dinner, which became hands
Which became lands, shores, beaches, natives on the stones
Staring and wild beasts in the trees, chasing the hats of
Lost hunters, and all this deserves a tone
That I try to give it by writing as fast as I can
And as steadily, pausing only to eat, to sleep,
And to take long walks, where I would sometimes encounter a sheep
Which gave me rhyming material and often a flowering fruit tree,
Pear apple cherry blossom thing and see long paths winding
Up hills and then down to somewhere invisible again
Which I would imagine was a town, in which another scene of the poem
        could take place.

4 . OUT AND IN

City of eternal flowers
And A said Why not make it paternal flowers
And Z said Or sempiternal There were bananas
Lying on the closet shelf by the couch
Forty feet from where your miscarriage began

236

And we were talking about this nonsense
Which meant so much to us, meant so much to us at the time.

Ponte Vecchio going over the Arno
What an image you are this morning
In the eye of almighty God!
I am the old bridge he said she said
I forget if it was a man or a woman
A sexless thing in my life
Like sidewalks couches and lunch

Walking around nervously then going in the house
The entire problem is to sit down
And start writing. Solved! Now the problem
Is to get up. Solved! Now the problem
Is to find something equally worthwhile to do. Solved!
Thank you for coming to see me. But
Thank you for living with me. And
Thank you for marrying me. While
Thank you for the arguments and the fights
And the deadly interpellations about the meanings of things!

Your blue eyes are filled with storms
To alter and mildly disarrange an image of someone's, he said it about
      the eyelid
But you are crying. I have a pain in my side.

The idea of Mallarmé
That
Well that it was so
Vital
Poetry, whatever it was
Is inspiring
Is I find even more inspiring
Than his more famous idea
Of absence
And his famous idea
Of an uncertain relationship of the words
In a line to make it memorably *fugace.*

Absence and I were often in my room
Composing. When I came out you and absence were wielding a broom
Which was a task I hadn't thought of in my absence
Finally absence took over
You, me, the broom, my writing, my typewriter,
Florence, the house, Katherine, everything.

Well, I don't know—those were great moments
Sometimes and terrible moments sometimes
And sometimes we went to the opera
And sometime later the automobile squeaked
There is no such thing as an automobile, there is only a Mercedes or a Ferrari
Or a Renault Deux Chevaux is that a Citroën
There is What do we care what kind of car but
Often in the sunshine we did. That's
When we were traveling I wasn't writing.

You've got to sit down and write. Solved!
But what I write isn't any good. Unsolved!
Try harder. Solved! No results. Unsolved!
Try taking a walk. Solved! An intelligent, pliable,
Luminous, spurting, quiet, delicate, amiable, slender line
Like someone who really loves me
For one second. What a life! (Solved!) Temporarily.

What do you think I should do
With all these old poems
That I am never going to even look at again
Or think about or revise—Throw them out!
But if I raise my hand to do this I feel like Abraham!
And no sheep's around there to prevent me.
So I take another look.

We asked the bad poet to come and dine
The bad poet said he didn't have time
The good poet came and acted stupid
He went to sleep on the couch
But grandiose inspiration had arrived for him with the wine
Such was the occasion.

Long afternoons, when I'm not too nervous
Or driven, I sit
And talk to the source of my happiness a little bit
Then Baby gets dressed but not in very much it's
Warm out and off we go
For twenty minutes or so and then come back.

Everyone in the neighboring houses
And in the neighboring orchards and fields
Is busily engaged in doing something
(So I imagine) as I sit here and write.

5 . DAYS AND NIGHTS

A B C D F I J
L M N R Y and Z were the friends I had who wrote poetry
Now A B and C are dead, L N and Y have stopped writing
Z has gotten better than ever and I am in a heavy mood
Wondering how much life and how much writing there should be—
For me, have the two become mostly the same?
Mostly! Thank God only mostly! Last night with you
I felt by that shaken and uplifted
In a way that no writing could ever do.
The body after all is a mountain and words are a mist—
I love the mist. Heaven help me, I also love you.

When the life leaves the body life will still be in the words
But that will be a little and funny kind of life
Not including you on my lap
And looking at me then shading your beautiful eyes.

Do you want me to keep telling
You things about your
Poem or do you want me to stop? Oh
Tell me. What? I don't think
You should have that phrase "burn up" in the first line.
Why not? I don't know. It
Seems a little unlike the rest.

O wonderful silence of animals
It's among you that I best perhaps could write!
Yet one needs readers. Also other people to talk to
To be friends with and to love. To go about with. And
This takes time. And people make noise,
Talking, and playing the piano, and always running around.

Night falls on my desk. It's an unusual situation.
Usually I have stopped work by now. But this time I'm in the midst of a
      thrilling evasion,
Something I promised I wouldn't do—sneaking in a short poem
In the midst of my long one. Meanwhile you're patient, and the veal's cold.

Fresh spring evening breezes over the plates
We finish eating from and then go out.
Personal life is everything personal life is nothing
Sometimes—click—one just feels isolated from personal life
Of course it's not public life I'm comparing it to, that's nonsense vanity—
So what's personal life? the old mom-dad-replay joke or
Sex electricity's unlasting phenomenon? That's right. And on
This spring evening it seems sensational. Long may it be lasting!

It helps me to be writing it helps me to breathe
It helps me to say anything it gives me
I'm afraid more than I give it

I certainly have lost something
My writing makes me aware of it
It isn't life and it isn't youth
I'm still young enough and alive
It's what I wrote in my poems
That I've lost, the way Katherine would walk
As far as the tree line, and how the fruit tree blossoms
Would seem to poke their way into the window
Although they were a long way outside

Yes sex is a great thing I admire it
Sex is like poetry it makes you aware of hands feet arms and legs
And your beating heart
I have never been inspired by sex, always by love
And so we talk about "sex" while thinking a little about poetry

There are very few poems
Compared to all the thought
And the activity and the sleeping and the falling in love
And out of love and the friendships
And all the talk and the doubts and the excitement
And the reputations and the philosophies
And the opinions about everything and the sensitivity
And the being alone a lot and having to be with others
A lot and the going to bed a lot and getting up a lot and seeing
Things all the time in relation to poetry
And so on and thinking about oneself
In this somewhat peculiar way

Well, producing a lot, that's not what
Being a poet is about, said N.
But trying to do so is certainly one of the somethings
It is about, though the products I must say are most noumenous—
Wisps of smoke! while novels and paintings clouds go belching over the way!

Poetry, however, lives forever.
Words—how strange. It must be that in language
There is less competition
Than there is in regular life, where there are always
Beautiful persons being born and growing to adulthood
And ready to love. If great poems were as easy to create as people—
I mean if the capacity to do so were as widespread—
Since there's nothing easy about going through a pregnancy—
I suppose we could just forget about immortality. Maybe we can!

Z said It isn't poetry
And R said It's the greatest thing I ever read
And Y said I'm sick. I want to get up
Out of bed. Then we can talk about poetry
And L said There is some wine
With lunch, if you want some
And N (the bad poet) said
Listen to this. And J said I'm tired and
M said Why don't you go to sleep. We laughed
And the afternoon-evening ended
At the house in bella Firenze.

In Bed

MORNINGS IN BED

Are energetic mornings.

SNOW IN BED

When we got out of bed
It was snowing.

MEN IN BED

All over Paris
Men are in bed.

BEAUTIFUL GIRL IN BED

Why I am happy to be here.

LONG RELATIONSHIP IN BED

The springs and the bedposts
Are ready the minute we come in.

DOLLS IN BED

With little girls.

HAMMER AND NAILS IN BED

To make it better
They are making it a better bed
And a bigger bed, firmer and larger
And finer bed. So the hammer and nails in the bed
And the carpenter's finger
And thumb and his eyes and his shoulder.
Bang! Bang! Smap! The hammer and nails in bed.

SHEEP IN BED

The sheep got into the bed
By mistake.

BUYING A NEW BED

One of the first things you did
Was buy a new bed.

WINDOW IN BED

I looked at you
And you looked back.

MARRIED IN BED

We'll be married in bed.
The preachers, the witnesses, and all our families
Will also be in bed.

POETRY BED

Whenas in bed
Then, then

OTHER POETRY BED

Shall I compare you to a summer's bed?
You are more beautiful.

ORCHIDS IN BED

She placed orchids in the bed
On that dark blue winter morning.

LYING IN BED

Bed with Spain in it
Bed with Gibraltar in it
Bed of art!

LOVERS IN BED

Are lovers no more
Than lovers on the street.
(See Picasso's "Pair of Young Mountebanks," FC 533,
Greuze's "Noces," or hear Mozart's "Fleichtskausenmusik," Köchel 427).

SOME BED

Once
Held
This
All.

GOD IN BED

Christ
Was not
Born
(And did
Not die)
In a bed.

LÉGER IN BED

Above our apartment
In 1955
Lived Fernand Léger.

SHOUTING IN BED

We wake up
To the sound of shouts.

FRIENDS IN BED

Sleep well.

ANGELIC CEREMONY IN BED

Putting on the sheets.

MYSTERY OF BED

She takes it for granted
That he will stay up all night long.

WORKMEN IN BED

With workmen's wives
And workmen's girl friends
And other workmen
And dolls.

ACAPULCO IN BED

In Mexico, with blue shimmering water,
Acapulco is in bed.

MY INTOXICATION IN BED

Was not long-lasting.
Was fantastic.
Did not lead me to be very well-mannered.
Wasn't completely romantic.

BASKETBALL IN BED

The basketball is thrown on the bed.

EXPENSIVE BED

At the Lutétia 500 francs a night
In the Hôpital St-Antoine 1000 francs a night.

THEATRICAL BED

Exceeded expectations
And received applause.

SIRENS IN BED

My face is plastered to the window
When the sirens come.

COURTSHIP IN BED

"Please. Tell me you like me."
"How did you get in this bed?"

WET DOG IN BED

There is nothing like a wet dog in bed.

DOG BED

In the dog bed
I cannot sleep.

ATOMIC BED

Billions of—uncountable—electrons
Compose this bed.

BEING IN BED

Belongs to everyone
Bed with Spain in it
Bed of art!

SNOW IN BED (LATER)

When it stopped snowing
We still hadn't gone to bed

PHILOSOPHY IN BED

(I)
Plato says this bed
Isn't the real one.
What did Plato know
About beds?

(II)
Spinoza constructed a bed
Which was slept in by Alfred North Whitehead.

(XLIV)
You say, "Let's go to bed"
But those words have no meaning.

SOUTH AMERICA IN BED

Brazil, Argentina, Ecuador, and Peru
Are in bed. The first thing you did
Was to buy a new bed.

AS WE LAY IN BED

We saw the stars starting to come together
As we lay in bed.

POLIZIANO IN BED

Angelo Poliziano
Never went to bed
Was it he or Castiglione—
The perfect Renaissance man?

LUNCH IN BED

It's late! Get up! The roseate fruit trees
Are blushing with the nape of new-frocked day!
Awake! The modern breeze of spring
Is pulsative through nest-caroming branches!

COWARDS IN BED

Afraid to turn over. Come on. Come on, turn over. Cowards in bed.

CHOPIN'S ÉTUDES IN BED

Here is the bed
Of Chopin's Études;
Over here is his Préludes' bed;
And here is the bed of his Mazurkas.

PRÉLUDES IN BED

There are no préludes in bed
Today.

LET'S GO TO BED

When the tree
Is blossoming. It will be
A long time
Before it is blossoming again.

STONES IN BED

In the bed are stones
From Egypt and Etruria
And some magazines and a pouch of tobacco.

BED

I'd wake up every morning
And look out the window across the park.

WOODEN MECHANICAL FIGURE
INDICATING A BED

With a mighty smile
And a mighty gesture
He discloses the bed.

Y. SICK IN BED

Said, If there is a heaven
I want it to look
Like what is out there.

MORNINGS IN BED

Are pensive mornings.

SUICIDE

I was unable to tell you any reason
To get out of bed.

248

A BLUE AND WHITE BED

Became a yellow and gold one,
Then was green, pale green,
Then violet, then onyx,
Yes onyx, then it was an onyx bed.

BALCONIES IN BED

When you lean over
When you fall
When you speak

BEDS IN THE GARDENS OF SPAIN

To the sound of a guitar
When you enter the room.

POETRY IN BED

Do you remember how this started—
With "Mornings in Bed" and "Snow in Bed"?

RISPETTO

Good-bye to bed.
The ceiling loses its chance
To see you smile again
In just that way.

LUXEMBOURG BED

The bed flies past
Like a swing.

ADVANCE BED

Advance arm. Advance stairs. Advance power.
Advance bed.

CHILD BED

You had two babies
Before we met

ABSTRACT BED

There is paint
On the abstract bed.

ORCHIDS IN BED

She placed orchids on the bed
On a dark red winter afternoon.

AT ENDEBED

At Endebed I mett you
You go up on the lift, no, yes
Then we hearing from sounds of guitars
Americans strolling bingo hatrack in the lake.

ENEMIES IN BED

Enemies sleep in separate beds
But in the same part of the city.

PRIMAVERA

He makes up the bed
And follows her home.

ESTATE

The bed lies in the room
The way she lies in the bed.

SAWBED

In the bed of the saw
The sawdust is dying.

WINDOWBED

From henna to blue all violet is in bed.

ZEN BED

I can't get to bed.
Show me the bed and I will show you how to get to it.

LARGE SUNDAY BED

Domingo.
Domenica.
Dimanche.

SATURDAY BED

Sabato.

SNOW IN BED

When we get out of bed
There is no more bed.

WOMEN IN BED

Everywhere in Paris
Women are in bed.

MARRIED IN BED

We did not get married
In bed.

FALSE BED

There are Easter eggs
Red blue yellow and white-pink
In the false bed.

INVITING SOMEONE FROM BED

Come, let me help you out of bed.
The sun is shining. The window is open. Look!
From the balcony there is the street, which is like a bed.

THE FUTURE BED

Will be lilac in color
And in the shape of an L or a Z.

GUITARS IN BED

When we get out of bed
We hear guitars.

POST-MODERNISM IN BED

Kandinsky, Arp, Valéry, Léger, and Marinetti
Are kicked out of bed.
Then, for a long time, nobody gets back into it.

THE HOLIDAYS OF BED

Are when no one is there.

GEORGICS IN BED

Planting wheat and rye and oats—explaining how to do it
And when, what kind of sunlight is needed and how much rain.

STRANGE BEDFELLOWS

The bear got into bed
With his claws.

CHAIRMAN BED

There is a little red book
In the bed.

SHOWER BED

For her engagement they gave her a shower
And for her marriage they went to bed.

MANTEQUILLA BED

Butter bed, beurre bed, burro bed.

THESMOPHORIAZUSAE IN BED

Euripides put the Thesmophoriazusae in bed;
Then he also put in bed Elektra, Jason, and Sophocles.
Aristophanes said, Here, let me put you to bed.
No! cried Euripides. But Aristophanes did
Put Euripides into bed with the Thesmophoriazusae.

POETRY BED

To have it all at once, and make no decisions.
But that is a decision.

OLIVE TREE BED

Along the side of the hill
Amid the green and gray trees
There is a place that looks like a bed.

I AM SORRY I DIDN'T EXPECT TO FIND YOU IN BED

With me I must have misdialed the telephone oh
Wait a minute—damn! I can't extricate
Myself from these sheets yes I'm getting up what
Did you expect after such a long night at the factory
Of unexplained phenomena with your head and shoulders
Beautiful as a telephone directory but please don't talk to me about love
I have an appointment with my head with the dead with a pheasant
With a song I'm nervous good-bye. It was the end of bed.

STREAM BED

In the stream bed
The snails go to sleep.

PHILOSOPHY OF BED

A man should be like a woman and a woman should be like an animal
In bed is one theory. Another is that they both should be like beds.

WE NEVER WENT TO BED

Listen, Kenny, I think it's a great idea! said Maxine
And she helped me sell my book to Chelsea House.
It was spring, with just the slightest hint of white and pink in the branches.

MALLARMÉ'S BED

An angel came, while Mallarmé lay in bed,
When he was a child, and opened its hands
To let white bouquets of perfumed stars snow down.

PSYCHOANALYTIC CRITICISM IN BED

What are you trying to avoid talking about
When you talk about bed?

STORM IN BED

It was such a bad storm
That we were hurled out of bed.

FLEURUS BED

There were flowers on the wallpaper,
There was loss and present excitement,
There was hope for the future, anxiety about the past, and much to come,
As I lay in my bed on the rue de Fleurus.

CARTOON BED

The door swings open and the bed comes in
Making a tremendous racket and bumping around.

OWL IN BED

The owl flew into bed
By mistake.

DAY BED

When I loved you
Then that whole time
Was like a bed
And that whole year
Was like a day bed.

DENIED BED

We were not in bed
When summer came.

LE FORÇAT DU MOULIN À GAZ IN BED

The convict of the gas mill is in bed.

SNOW IN BED

Vanishing snowflakes, rooftops appearing
And sidewalks and people and cars as we get out of bed.

DISCOBOLUS IN BED

The discus thrower
Is still in bed.

From Impressions of Africa

THE CONGO AND ZAIRE. RIVER

Quoi? said Matila
Sudi (écrivain congolais),
You mean to say
There are poets
In the contemporary U.S.?
Pour nous vous êtes le pays
De Vietnam, de Watergate, et de la bombe hydrogène.

The moon seems floating, high, tonight
Above the frames of Brazza–
Ville in which I arrive after a flight
Through the bedtime air over half of Africa.

Henri says
She came to his room
Ambassador of the Ambassador
All the French stay
Put up lamp posts, little enough
Says Jean-Jacques
(Embassy driver)
For what they've done
The Chinese on the other hand
Build hospitals
("With those people we get along well")
And live simply
Not in expensive houses.

I thought, venereal disease, bankrupt,
Father, mother, stymie, stump,
Stunned. This is where the Russians eat
Imperial Café. At night they sleep at the Cosmos.

Take me round Congo
Three hours all day. Goat side

And head. Merci. Why Henri
To the white-coated consular eventuality deeply thinkingly costlily friendlily
     frostily (by this time
The pamphlets start arriving, F.A.H. enraged, red
Face from auto emerging) said Zaira moosa be-a
Freedom offa Congo. Oltremong
Ze hull world eez een trap. So Unmbala Lavinia Black stopped
Shortly front his hotel door. Now, his head's
On around actually, winking and winked at, somewhere else.

More my village sleeping onward
Into the bush it goes. These fragments
On dead rocks, stone. Animals are chased from here
To make the city. Lilies come floating down. Big river.
Big Congo rushing and going and coming—
Said Michel, I'd make ze treep just for that!

Yes, hope
Springs always in our souls
As we cross the Congo
In search of girls.

Bastards! he said. Stupid
Sons of bitches! Jesus!
These fucking people! Christ!
I said,
How did you happen to get
In the diplomatic service?
He said for Christ's sake
Look at those cocksuckers
Standing in the middle of the road
Fuck! Squeal! go the brakes
Meanwhile Henri
Is photographed
For the Brazzaville *Express*
Standing in his white suit with his hand
On Kronemann's *Legal Briefs and Excise*
"When there is no justice in the Congo,"
Says Henri, "there is no justice
For any man or any woman anywhere!"

Shit-heads! said Deak
Of the Embassy. I asked
Why did you
Choose the diplomatic service, anyway?
Henri escaped
The Authorities. The
Black woman stayed in his bed.

I am perhaps foolish
To stand here just looking
And smiling
And saying Bon jour.

All the same in the middle of life
Some white houses in Brazza
Ah, we were all beautiful
Once she said
And cut them and
Gave them to me in my hand
By William Carlos Williams
Look at the view!
Sturdily through the garbage I seek the view.

Jean-Jacques said, Here are the boats.
One woman out in her pirogue
All alone. Later in the day
There are poets to talk to.
My kiss to you (in a letter—"Dear Z.")
Was the main part
Of this three-to-five-part day
I hear Jean-Jacques honking outside
The black and white of bees
N'Zambo's wife, the Congo, confusion extreme
She keeps
Walking down a "street," until—bush!

Funghi, growing under the bridge—
Eating the very small orange (tangerine?)
And spitting out the seeds. A bird, in its nightgown,
Goes spinning by. I've got to get out of this hotel.

Whole days stretch in seconds and then into minutes.
I do come out, and then—like water!
Smile of someone—I don't have to eat or drink!

And so are oranges, amnesty-like sweet;
Oysters are absent. And
There is no flirting in the Congo! Deak says,
I noticed that—
These god-damned cocksuckers have nothing!
Oooof! Can you imagine balling one of their women?
I imagined, I balled, I paid the rent.
I am the African, I suffragette, iron hair.

A lack of plan. A plan. Chinese men over there,
Governors of the world—"Governors of Paradise,"
"Governors perhaps of nothing, not
Even of their own souls." When I get up next morning and am advised
About which way to walk
I see the sun, silver-white.

I'd better get out of here—shore
I'll put some wings on—flamingo
I don't want to die—by the river
This way to the television station—come on
You're due there at five o'clock—the apples of Tikastra.

Sur les trottoirs de Brazza
Pays where the Com-
Munist government, like all governments, gets fat
But opens up new territory to the Chinese
Who are building the hospitals, I think
Of that (which is not much), while Jean-Jacques
Goes to get something to eat.

"Some, some, some time!" the birds seem to be singing
While there is a tremendous amount of dirt as we pull up.

O television program celebrating the fortieth birthday of *Pravda* (in
    Brazzaville)
Celebrating it as an organ of freedom, how much the dusty streets

Around the azalea bushes reminded him of Norman, Oklahoma,
And how little she thought of anything in the huge dumb station
That was the building inside which was the program that he was on.
First they read the letters—then this celebration of *Pravda*.
D. H. says, "How did it go?" "It went splendid," I cockneyed,
Hearkening back against lamp posts to frail the dust
Cameos against frock-born ceintures Africa seemed heading for my toe.
It was an absolute waste of time, I added,
While George Bernard Shaw went on being dead, and Wallace Stevens,
     and the author of *Hernani*
In Brazzaville "la nuit."

I've got to get out of here! I sat
In a big white chair
In the lobby of the Meridien Hotel.
The next day
I got out of there
Or one day after that
Of l'Hotel Meridien.

However, getting out of the Congo is not easy.
You need a pass and transportation and also
"Fucking Bastards" comes along, cursing the natives
But buying me my ticket, finally, so I can get on the boat
Which is taking me to the "Devil's Disneyland," Kinshasa—the Congo
Becoming very, very wide just here.

The wide Congo
Rushing
Trying to get on the boat
The men crippled by polio
In wheelchairs pushing
They get to carry duty-free
Merchandise to
Brazzaville from Kinshasa!
A gift of the Congo's government
To lifelong victims of this disease.

N'Zambo is his name
He hails from the village of M'Gambutenmhumo

He works for the American Embassy
His wife has rigid wires in her hair.

What a huge river
The Congo is!
But if it were named
"The Wink"—
The Congo, or "The Wink,"
Pushing endlessly down toward the Atlantic.

At the dock, boys,
Men, women, old
Men, old women, even,
Fighting to get at something, or someone,
With the city of Kinshasa behind them,
Ten or fifteen times a day.

Hoongam! says N'Zambo and he takes my briefcase
And leaves it on a shelf where Customs won't throw it away.

In Kinshasa the head
Of the driver. In the village the abdomen and the legs.
In the dog, bark.

The Zairian poets, in Kinshasa, were very good-natured and smart.
Romance seemed to play a relatively small role, I thought, in their art.
To get a book published in Kinshasa, you have to
Publish it privately or have a Catholic or Protestant mission house do
It, but you may have trouble if it is violent, sexy, or if you are a Jew,
The latter not being the case with most poets of Zaire
Who tend to mix Victor Hugo
And African drum-repetition types of sounds and to
Write works that sometimes seem to me aesthetically unclear.

In Kin-
Shasa at the
Cultural at-
Taché's place
I
Said to Su-
Maili of
Zaire: Where
Are your
Older writers? Ha!
He said,
Tomorrow
You are going
To see them
And I did
One (the young-
Est of them)
Was only
Forty-five years
Old. But why are they the old ones? Why
Are they the old ones? Because
Of publishing before l'Indépendance.
They are, he said, les Vieux!

With a big country around him
And a lot of other writers around him
A life behind him
And a life ahead of him
Odd to talk to, as if we were going slantways
Or sideways
But I like Sumaili of Zaire
Though neither of us may know (ever)
In fact, what our real "subject" is.

If I set out in my pirogue
And you in yours, we're quite the vogue
Floating on the river, yet we notice
Very, very, very little lettuce
Is being grown on either shore
And there's no magic anymore,

At least none that we know of, on the river,
Which doesn't change the strange way we feel, either,
At daybreak, when a gaggle of flamingos
Starts twisting us to shore.

N'Zambo now comes down to check
If one's to get one's baggage back. Not.

With a big packet of Zaires (the paper money
Of Zaire, which is worthless
Outside of Zaire) you can pay
For your room for one night.
I take off the rubber band
And look out the window
At the dazzling white cars—mostly Renaults.

It is regrettable
Announces the Kinshasa *Soleil*
That a letter
Mailed from Kinshasa
May not be delivered
For up to four weeks
Or four months
Or a year
To someone who is
Living just kilometers away
(In the bush) and so
This newspaper
Warmed by the morning sun
If mailed, may never get to
A reader in Oon-ga-bu-Dun
Before it is uninterestingly out-of-date.

At the Ambassador's house, the flowers are sitting
In glasses on a table. Tonight he is not the host
But some young woman who is crazy about going into the bush
On a small airplane, landing, and settling local disturbances
That stem from the chaotic ungovernability
Of Zaire, made up of so many tribes, with multifold languages and
Three times as many wives (for each man) and they come down

263

Over the mountains and
Slaughter each other. "I want to do as much of this as I can
While I'm still young—before I'm thirty-five!"

This is—I forget the name. The
Thing the people eat all the time. Without much food value. Cassava (manioc).

You bake there—and never did you fill me with desire
Except when you were young, very young—
Fifteen? sixteen?—and
Your breasts! which that day I hold in my hands, then
Marriage, and a mysteriously useful son.

To fundamental questions
Africa me brought. That's what they all like about it. The excitement
And the illusion of living at the beginning of thought.
Even old Rep told me about it. While I napped
He went out riding on his bicycle, into thought!

Now it is time to go
But I can't mark
The place exactly where a chief took down
A mango from a tree and gave extremely
Small boy deadly smiles to me
To other kinds of look.
That one is all.

A smokiness is rising from the fire flakes
Old woman crouching there a hand shakes
As I go by. "Veloum!"

You can tell which house is the chief's said Will
There is the chief knocking down a mango from his tree
Before becoming Protestant he wore the antelope mask
To the puberty ceremonies, a screaming and a thumping hid the ground.

The elephants came
They were easily overpowered
The dogs came
And barked. The more fertile parts of the ground area flowered.

It was dark. Zaire
Means River. Mobutu
Is King. This means nothing
To the grass. But to the people who pass
This way, it means something. Hip bone
Thigh bone and chest bone, it may come to pass,
Pass into subservience under a moon
That shines equally on Paris and on Gaboon.
The hill wears the mask of a traitor. Will
Drives around and then up and down this hill.

Being here
Gave him a sense of his "destiny," I think,
In a way that
Being in Chicago would not—being
In these dried places, with no place ever to go,
To arrive at, to drive to.

The air
Is faded
Has faded
Is fading
Away
From the river
You see
Dissociated houses
Also very rich Belgian rush
Residences but not
As from the other side (Brazza)
Do you have the Congo right there
To walk up to
And the woman in the boat and the grass.

"They appeared on the scene immediately.
I was handcuffed and knocked about.
They carried me away;
I was not even allowed to walk.
From the prison to the truck
They tossed me about like a stick of wood.
I was taken to the airfield

And immediately thrown into an airplane.
They twisted my neck.
I was badly mistreated.
I arrived in Elizabethville
And came out of the airplane
Like a common bandit—"

Independence brought a lot of death with it.
It brought Lumumba with it and threw him away.

"There are no more tribes in the Congo
There are no more Bakongos or Bangalas
There are no more Wagenias
We have only one free people—"
Tshombe, on the other hand,
Refused, even, to let Lumumba's remains
Be sent to his family.

The insects!
The insects of the Congo and of Zaire
Some known, some still being studied, some
Probably still unknown, are terrifying—
Landing, biting, and leaving, like a traveling death zone.

I cannot deem the rough of this hotel!
The speaking into a welled tube at night.
The grouch of linen. Movimento di windows. Outerness
Wearing masks
The mask of a maiden with a pointy chin
And narrowed but widening eyes, a thin
Fragile smile. The elevator
Takes me up instead of down! Il faut
Partir! Valery Larbaud's *Journal
de A. O. Barnabooth,* and, as well,
Henri Michaux's *Ecuador,*
I fling into my bag.

N'Zambo says, I don't carry baggage.
His wife carries the baggage.
I do not carry the baggage. I am no and have no wife.

And I have a bad back. Into the
Cool air, in an orange cotton dress, goes N'Zambo's wife
With one suitcase under her arm
And another in her other hand.

Everybody will read these
Verses in Zaire. Everybody will talk about
The statements they hold dear. But
What about Bird Africa? what about Luck Africa?
Angle Africa? Eat Africa? and Sunk Africa?

N'Zambo has arrived at the airport,
The airport of bella Kinshasa. Here, as the night heaves
And coughs gropingly, fifty-five persons
Are fighting at the same place
To get tickets at a hornets'-nest-like window.

Here, you wait here, says N'Zambo. His wife
Waits here. And I wait here. Jillian
Is standing in the middle of the vast
Airport hall.
Burundi, Upper Volta, Côte d'Ivoire, and Nigeria
Are places you can't go to from here
Because of political conditions, explains N'Zembi.
However, here, look at this ticket. Your
Plane should be coming in any time now—in three or four hours.
To the balcony (airport terrace) we rise
Shined on by the warm night eyes
Of Zairian stars. Jillian has her own "security group,"
A man from the Peace Corps to help her get on the plane.

The Colonials came
With disorientation
With exploitation
With aggression
With contempt
With no caring
With thinking
They were the people
They were the earth

They were the men
And theirs was the space
And the time

And, often, the Africans let them
Drooping in the sun
Not knowing what
They were up to

And by Colonial standards
The Africans were terrible
By African standards
The Europeans, as magic, existed.
But the Blacks weren't part of a magic world
For the oil-spattered-pants-scattered Belgians,
Germans, French (and English). They were "gooks,"
They were part of a White nightmare, they could be put to use.

Meanwhile these Europeans
Educated some Africans
Built up cities
Brought them a language
And a universal religion—
No more thunder in the cheekbones
No more crocodile knees.

Proferring, too,
A cash-crop economy
They fucked-up the old village-
Self-sufficiency economy, ploughed
Young men into the cities
And, finally, granted Independence

After the other life was almost gone—
The tribe, three wives, old man,
Manioc, dancing in the straw, saying
Gandara saloum to make the crops grow—
Almost, but not completely—

Civil courts still hand down convictions
For witchcraft. Leaders do monstrous
Things, unable to rule if they're not devils.
Christianity affects the lives, as
Do politics, and the city, but it is
Hard to tell where anything really is
Or where it is going.

One thing Africa has, it's plenty
Of that kind of thing! is help,
Extremely interested help from every Left and Right party
Of the European, Asian, and American world,
Each of them wanting its minerals, its land, and its support,
Its "voice" in U.N. assemblies
Before the final war—
Those four over there, in blue
Suits, heading for the Cosmos—ce sont les russes!

Nel servizio diplomatico
Esiste una categoria
Chiamata "hardship." You get extra dollars
Hundreds of thousands of additional Zaires
For living and working in Kinshasa
Or other Zairian cities or its bush.

"What you get is the naked, raw thing in Africa—
Life without sheets, or blankets. You see it in the market
In Kinshasa, where everything is cheap.
People are lying around and walking around. They are
Squatting and begging around. (We sleep in the street.
Under us, the street sleeps.) In the village each family has a hut.
This city is their one big hut. And the city is the scene
Of behavior of the kind you find in village and hut." Jillian comes to my hotel
Because she doesn't have any place to stay. She
Opens the window and won't close
The shutters. A hot, wet
Heat shine comes in. What
Happened to her Black boyfriend? "He was at the University,"
She says, "and, well, Mobutu closed it down
And sent all the students back to their villages—he is

Hundreds of miles in the bush now, no way to come back
To Kinshasa, and to me. . . . Well,
The part I really like, I lived
On this courtyard, it was actually a sort of market,
Everybody always talking,
And always lying around—African, really African," she said.

We didn't bring our wives because they weren't invited,
Confided N'Jombe. And, besides, we poets don't
Marry literary girls. Those girls, they are other
Ones, who like the writings. We prefer
A woman who takes care of the home, at least those
Are the ones we have married—not the literary
Roses who come serving me the dangerous prose of
Food and drink at the Zairian Club des
Écrivains, girls, not married, and in the
City, and doing all right—calm, like
Everyone else, in an ambience, all the same, of physical excitement.

On the Edge

Sleeping one day beside the Zuyder Zee
Dan was awakened by a noise of honks—
A situation quite unknown to me:
I spent my childhood in a sort of Bronx—
I placed a goldfish bowl upon my knee—
Angelica was packed inside my trunks.
At Harvard I wrote home "I'm coming back!"
And did, and through the country like a crack

The train sped home. Dan took a blossom down
From off the blossoming tree. I slept all night
Then spent the next day walking through the town.
Angelica woke up to Roland, light
And bright and fair. Dan sighed and looked around.
He couldn't see Roberta anywhere.

As in—Crete, near the ditch—old grave spot (gray spot) as
By the Greece's Acropolis's invisible waters—Parthenon—
Agh, what vents!—and you too, monopolistic
Bypath-or-street-ways, little Merkaton
Of old Athens plus light blue shimmers from the cliffs
In other places and I couldn't explain
What I felt at Heraklion, I'm sorry, or with
My nose pressed to the train—everything else stubbing
And stumping. I'd planned—but wanted to know. Reading,
In the day, complaining, stormed, red and blue lights
Until traffic, I think, is right here in the chains
Of what's holding all these chairs, this
Stuff together—up in the air, I think.
Zett calls, and now I have a drink.
Cold is the kitchen sink.

Forms to feel it out
Quietness to bring it in
As someone "felt friendly" Stendhal pushed the door

Egg was inside, the Easter Egg of Monsieur Montelfior
Who made the wind his messenger
Outside, in the penniless air
Of the warm white sidewalk and the street, thinking
Whether I am in the cloth with her or not
Then suddenly to think

Finger in the beehive
Harry says Watch out!
A drove of French novels
Particularity of stone-dead windowpane, without charity
Or trump—esthetico indeed! why, I'll
And so you—one minute—are falling, it is orchids

Paris, C's apartment
Claudio on the phone, the receiver
Tucked between his chin and his shoulder

A panther has escaped
From Nankra's Zoo! I lay confidently
Embedded in the light green grass of the Bosco
While A. A. de Celestin smoothed out her thanks
Blouse sleeping softly and mandarinly toward me
No sensations but in commands, you too
Storm and confusion. Roberta? Angling—whom?

She lifts a shoe. Where is the other one?
Jean-Claude came to dinner, etc. Sitting here, it's a café

Summery Sunday, Notre Dame des Champs,
Noel and Joanne come to take us both
Out riding to the forest. You have *gants,*
Being *frileuse* as I am not. We wear coats
Because it's, after all, the winter *temps*

And no one's in the Bois in little boats.
Ekstasin apodêmias. Première acte.
Mutas mutanda. Life in love lungs locked.

The scene is—writing—but remembering the buffering strums
Memories of a de-cupola'd Hotel de Fleurus
Triggered with leaves sidewalks a fluttering
I say something as red clouds and you said
I remember the name—going forward

Now I want to. Forces! yelled Jim Dine, and
Fairfield Porter, surprised, "Maybe! Let's just go and see."
These extreme persons of the time
And the forward and back—
To café! a cold university

Thanks for your criticism
I am thinking
Feeling my way across the yard
B-Zunk doesn't write me I figure she's
Having a love affair with Arc
Having had not much going but making love to each other
Our relationship soon fell apart

Dan is a hero of a different nature
The Colossus of America, England, and France
He is of an ordinary stature
Remarks someone at a dance
Dan dances with her and then he goes away.

The mountain of roses and the dog. What is that ripple?
Happiness, a street vine, and the nude
Weather forecaster, now dressed and out, it's day
For this monument, as if life
Depended on it, lilac, that scent, so many times!

The water fills with flowers—hibiscus, waterlilies. Ventur-
Ing then when Jan and I got in the boat
My parents objected, Haven't you got to the wrong hot spot
Of water if what you're really going after is adventure?

Adventure of the third kind
Desire driven from the mind
To the Greek statue arm muscle
We floated and then
Five years later it's of a doctoral order
Board walls of a house
And flowers tacked onto it. Hey, shining.
And Bart said You're not a scholar but a jeweler
And Schlumberger said Keep talking—until guns fired.
She hangs the wash on hooks, outside.

"What's the matter, anyway?" I say
To my friend
Toujours plus pessimiste
A quality I find assez adorable
I thought if he could just
Now we are racing toward the dust
Quality of a friend with the trace of a suit on it
Blue-brown, a necktie, red, yellow, compromising
Avec ze style of ze time, so Wallace Stevens said
"You should keep the same style," this little guy
Said A. W. jokingly, partly, has done more
For the philosophy of—Jesus! If we had time—The green ledge
Walking sideways on it without
But full of, interest, by being purely
Physical, Leger, at the age of thirty-three, a finite hem
Explaining things to me
As another always interpreted. I don't,
I said snobbishly, like it much, but

Well, you know, and everything
He liked Spring, the sweet spring
Then backing down the water (alley) with a blot
With friendship talked a lot
And was indifferent
However, there he is!

And other Elizabethan literature
I said: It's great!

Oh, it's great
        all right,
                said he
But would you read this? I'm so
Depressed!
        What?
            We—after death
And his passing—but
           also ours

Reading what I was reading, like the girth
Of that building—from the *Four Quartets*
To the *Macchu Picchu* of Neruda, neither
There nor in between was there to answer
The inevitable brio of light
Not surreal, not fragmentary or anything but
A white sidewalk—do you think?

If I had known then, in nineteen-fifty . . .
There was one introductory class at the university
And others at various places and times. The *u* was difficult.
The noses of cars kept dodging on the street
With knowledgeable humans inside them—
Not simply having experiences and growing up
And trying to judge the various stages of joy
And ecstasy and how do I get published? but
Actually participating in the crescent
And crossed edge of Being—I thought.
Sometimes, eating with you, I'd drop my plate
Or glass. You said, They are infinite. However
Just this morning I see the old man, presumably a worker
With shellfish, I don't know!
What I did the chairs were bunched
In each café. "Get out of the way." Ovvero, climb with me, the play *Truck*
Is being presented. So many girls then
Sidewalk hitting with its cement
The fabulous others who gradually fade into myself
Like the Epidaurus Theatre, starring Acts One and Three—
Act Two is your own revolution.

275

To deal with frost-bites
Into the old earth, on the surface of which all
Societies lived: French bourgeois society
Bon soir, Tante Adélie, ed entra la cugina Karamazov
On the edge
Of the cup,
Of the street,
Of reading Mallarmé
The door opens on the same spaces again.
Bird news was strafing past the window
Full feather time. I opened it and went out
Into the car.

And then last night (198?) the A.M. air was sharp
Outside the bar, Place de la Contrescarpe
And I walked home alone, not wishing to
Get in the car, since Hugues was drunk. I thought
Being alone quite the best thing to do—
And with my small red guidebook's help I brought
Myself to where I lived, cette jolie rue.

Our modern—fragmentary—Dan stands up—it's about time—reason
Sunrise—he is going to start
White sleeves
But day puts its finger in his eye
Eyes. The white vagary temple is starting up
Aislewards—
The waves were coming home! against a tree
They wash. Fifteen
Years it lasts, and no end in sight, and no
Beginning. A topic is pink white pink stripes.
Drunk. On gin, lemonade, and fizz
White as the cover of the book and of the pages inside.
Fifteen years, or is it ten or twenty that it lasts. Sexual forces,
Greek logic, Aphrodite, in statue form, born Irish girls, smiling
And removing a blouse, beginning
To snow in here, writing out notes
And flying down the street, noble as far as
Bed could be commanded by what's outside.

Or he was writing, sitting amidst the unpacked trunks
In a state of composition, while the trunks, then, are in a state of
Saturday afternoon position, as at the Mayor's house

What she was then—what a beautiful bloom!
And people sitting round their desk for hour
After hour could only exclaim, "Well, fine, boom, to hell with it,
Let's go to Tahiti, anywhere,
Out of this worm-eaten building!" At last
You wonder about the filtering down of consciousness
Till even the moth, so sensitive to light,
Is stepped on, on the stairs. The band plays
Full out—

Sometimes the feeling was so strong it came out
Sometimes was dancing or "rage" (being mad)
Biting and sleeping and then in the beautiful morn-
Ing, when to be young was very heaven,
The yellows, light on buildings' separate heaven
Of warm apartments, not too warm, now, open
A light-bulb light—
The limping man and the doctor—complements
The drink and the thirsty girl—oxygen

In questo momento scrivevo poesie
A proposito di un grande industriale
The subject is not in the world—the subject's
A limitation of the world. Thus, no true subject.
The Hotel de Fleurus was of the world
Now vanished, literally said Bob
It's turned into a private house, of many apartments
No more the door unopenable from inside
It wasn't a "subject" however. The nature
Of hotels is a subject—whose thigh?

Red bird, white bird, jumping around the house. "When you're not
Inspired, when you feel 'dry' just write anything!" False
Scholarship, false Solomon's Seal
Am I the height of Heaven or is blue the thrust
Of some addlepating ecstasy that's flooding me? Cancel

277

Your bills, believe in me. Proud to be Representative
Of Frock-White-Flowering Day appeared on doorstep
With Russian Moods and Count Weight. If only someone had told me,
Some intelligent man, said Stendhal,
To write two hours every day, whether
"Inspired" or not, I would have saved ten years of my life.

Sitting in a tiny café I read Mallarmé's *Le Livre*
I don't know whether or not this is something I want
I wasn't happy but I was absorbed and I was curious
I felt on the brink of something,
I kept reading, and in the book there was nothing doing
It may have been all just a laundry list but something was taking place in me
Did I have a mistress? Maybe. Had we been to bed? Well, not quite.

Thursday, three in the afternoon. Learning
Dutch. . . . Five minutes
Sandwiches . . . the fury in the hall ninety-nine francs
Don't like Like it Madame
Dantonville return four chemises front
Window alive serenities festive
Remember call BO 6–2279 Magyars
A visit in the sea . . . cruet . . . vast availability . . . five sleds—shirts
And then a tremendous space
Then space space space
Following: a list
Of debts?

Tears to remember again
One fourth or one sixth part of it

So I went dancing out into those streets
But on knees and on my knees it was the day
Lying catalyzed, a book. I'm not a roof if also if you mean that!

He actually made a mistake said John. It's wrong.
"Gyrene" but we continued. But Mallarmé
Fippery ovoid subject but I didn't pay
Attention. Loaf. Lilac book.

Martin McScrumbold who controlled the sedge
For fifteen companies of marble fusions
Clambered aboard the high financial towers
To make himself the toast of sanctity,
Seeming to be more holy than he was
By manufacturing gimmicks propped galore
Against the definite walls which adversaries
Totalled between themselves and him in vain.
Sunday he smashed the sleep. . . .

Summer on the folding step
And somewhere on the other.
A side step. Sunlight. Perhaps it would phone me
To be so ablution inseparable
Twenty-five years
Before nineteen-eighty. And bright
Flocks of automobiles go past
Green flight
Of centimeters, one, and up and down.
In the morning to look for
Blisters in the sidewalk Egypt of Their Time

The Journal of I forget
Virgil's Eclogues how they connect to the life
The show-business falseness is carrying on.
The bed is stored over where the light
Was, with futile and inconsistent flight. O "scatalogue" that gives me
Rushing around from feuding hours of the night
To spirited activation of the doll
Speaking in the morning
Huge halls. Not nearly buffered very long.

An ideal book for me was also that
I wanted to have and give up every subject
And I suspected it would end in about two seconds

So many painters were cracking their plates in the seminary
Of other persons' kindness while a large snowflake,
Faintly and intolerably slowly, falls. Flirting and courting heartbreak.
The Greeks—A brick blockade
Is knocked down. If I'm to be a painter, help me with your tears!
He said. Then I sat down.
Is it this—a historical
Meaning—out of your control
I crossed the wave
Of pink cement
Dawn! and study not far away!
With Eleanor, containing the football
Its footfalls, its stories of cinema'd scorn.

Bear—
Alone I think
It's
A laundry list
But still happy

Here are a few phone numbers, too

Ulla said Don't came to visit me in Sveden
Badly I threw myself as if from out of a
Bucket onto the train. Hallo goodbye said she
My boyfriend is here. I will not see you. But her flat face
In Paris, with the light hair in her eyes, her capacious
Be–loving-me sexitude, hunh, what's happened
To that? The Stockholm railway station loomed
With mounds of produce in a bag
Of each it held

Writing
Saving ten years

A blouse (blue)
Came in the entryway, drama
To perception
Instantaneously and in light

Of the moving seconds
I'm sitting and talking
Or else, exhausted, glad and sorry
Dog straining forward
Hating the seemingly automatic activity
Either language or either brain does on its their own
Wrong with so much fucking literature
French boredom bong
But as I romp around
Blonde bang bomb
Scowling
Event, climatic, and strong
How if we all came over
Or you come to my place—
Why not throw this, said Jim,
Into the fulminating fireplace? Giggled, savagely aft
While maturity stole a scarf and took her place
Beside Janice who was dreaming of a plan
For a whole season. Stanley: We displace
So many phantoms. Jean: Garage.

The ecstatic muddle does, didn't it, take place
February seventeenth nineteen-fifty Samothrace Tuesday immense

Dan walks around. He waves
His hands above his head.
Upon his tombstone it shall be engraved
He did what no one else could do instead.
He was a morning slasher. He engraved,
Summarily, upon a day of red,
The melancholy taxi of a kiss
Upon a sidewalk edge, for emphasis.

We walk out
And at a desk
On a bridge
Popular leafy upstairs
A form oh to go
Pink and white
Rose "oceanness"

I'm sympathetic to animals and all that, said.
Rescuing the fly flew into
Above water splat. Sit looking at
Specific gravity on its wings.

Crossing my sleeves with hers
Nineteen-fifty
Prepare
The quilts, mattress, bed-covers
Circa nineteen-fifty-four
Larry says Why don't you stay there
Another bluish bit
Of sidewalk and her hair
Human feather

Window, diamonds flashing
A. hard at work
Extemporaneous fingers
American Claw is reading about Van Gock (Go)
Pages of Keats (*Endymion*) This side of the cluck
Is belted with sunshine, G. Entwery
Also is recommending movie junk
And class ("I don't know why de Mourneville
Doesn't get off his ass and make more films . . .")
All the witty things we know are wasting
That used to be the center of the world.

Harry walks with me through the show of roses.
We talk about Maxine. Elizabeth
Is dancy at my side, as she supposes
I like her. I am somewhat out of breath.
With Jean I walk along and the place closes.
We dance beside the Marne. I love my desk.
As a drowning man to a spar I hold on to my desk (F. Kafka)
Hydrangeas bloom, seen from beyond the desk (Flutsworth)

And friends call Janice sits on the bed Frank calls
The momentary euphoria of understanding
Dan, much preoccupied, steps to the landing
Doesn't free me from these feelings after all

After all she was like a bird, flown off
Seems more than I could do when I mistook
Shadowing for boxing, evening for no lights in the hall
But now a fine mercurochrome like the dog's complacent ball
Into these fire vicinities. Frank said it was like it al-
Ways was, except that we were broaching entire infinities
This time, and, if I drink any more coffee I'm going to ride
Into the sky! Janice at nine in the city, cold are celebrities.
The fire plugs are cold. While they are alive
The whistle is metal, was not foot—needing—awfully—years before.

Avenue du Maine, with that wall with the posters on it
Everywhere saying it's forbidden to have posters on it,
Where I lived in the time I was a drink student
And a clink student of all flourishing Proust-things and I went out
Into the fulminating gravel of that damp sleep. That never came out
How civilized you are! we are! I was! It is, cow in and then out.
I went "to bed" with the two Swedish girls, Ana and Svenita, I don't
        remember,
In fact, their names—
You have frightened me into these staminas
Where the different associations they come running!
The bloom of helio-plaster, "medicine of the sun,"
Will absolutely cure your solar system, clean it out
So there'll be summer everywhere and always. Huh?
I loved the following women: BLANK
Out of discretion—But . . .

Alleyed-to-interview maze. I pleaded
Guilty, saying, I'm glad you're that,
Big, thin, notable, heart-
Shaped, sweet, irregular,
Smiling, quiet, tanned,
Around. Whereupon a ticket machine goes thumping
"Air raid! O climbing ceilings!
Birds that didn't add to visiting things!"

Paris
        And nineteen-fifty-two
    Fresh air

Clean warm spring morning
And I am in love with you
           Answers!
There were more answers than there were questions
Almost—questions I had to make up—

What is a "stair person"?
Do you know what a "bid minor" means?
Do scows have ears?
How many charge accounts can fit into a building?
And so, in love with you,
I walk the streets
Pretty littered asphalt, hut to roots,
Walking, talking

One shoe
Is that October or is that March
Summery day
God says, "Don't take that drink!"
What portion is two? what sidewalk?

Accidentally
Running into her. The wave
(One second). Hello. Admired Miranda!
O wild West Wind, thou breath of Autumn's
Being! Getting into Harvard (half a minute).
The log head and the pavement, stone hotel.
Dear K., I am
Leaving (three times). Why, though?

Vanishing into the Nile this comes only once

Dan was waking up,
Finding the world, some fluff from blossoms landing on him
A short breeze ruffling his
Clothes, summering sleeves, a little sun
Greatening in the white to be a big one
And that fresh air so invigorating
That he jumped up

Feeling where he wanted to go
He turns, then, sees

Thousands—need for food—all the critics say
Almost all—leaning on a railing
And looking out far—nails in the shoes—riverbank
And the motory smell
A white horse comes up
In a non-animal civilization—
The established ruins (products of four hundred years)
While the dream of the day
Is in the arms, later
Darling wronged
Sweetheart
I bray
Like a donkey (five seconds)
And the music is then of laughs (one
Second et demie). K. K. finds a cat and feeds it
And its kittens (seven days)
This moment and then coming
Completely up to date (almost), like a bat,
Seeing a cloud and thinking "It's Cleopatra!" Two seconds.
Knowing she'll take off her clothes (instantaneous).
Realizing I can't stay in the apartment
Cold, breezy nights
A collaboration (eight years, though
For the time spent working
Actually about two hours). Percentage of days
Counting the days (one,
Approximately). Times I had to work
Instead of doing what I thought
I wanted to do, some. But times I did work
And didn't do what my "life-boast," "life-bomb," or
"Shoulders-o'-stone" wanted done—
Flowers in every window of the street
Music playing behind. Friends come around. That's an excuse
(One dog). And the times, the times
Asleep, trying to sleep, making love, drunk

I notice the sunrise—it's quite something, the day!
My desire—Eleven A.M. too
And five-thirty, just before dark

Mathilda Roberts bumped against a window
Seeing a sheep, but Dan came through the day
Walking, his white coat hanging over his arm,
Left arm, and what could she (La Roberts) say
"I have been falling asleep," he said,
"In rocky different places. Beside a peak in Gstaad
Once, and by the Ceremonial Summer Beak in Tchad
As well as of course beside the well-tamed
Sea of Zuyder
Jusqu'à plus soif. The wind is very strong!"

Another day guilt is all I'm feeling
The gloves go on and off in simple whiteness
Weather is moving, and personality
Which seems just over the horizon, Greek, and homeless
I walked around
To the back of the car—sunflowers—an April evening
Living (a while) but not living very long. Totals
Of time spent merely in the society
Of other people without improving anything
Learning anything or really
Doing anything (enormous). Time
Music was of the essence (unknown).

A leg moves
To another section of the bed
I am up
Newsily bemused and musing
On what has just happened instead
Of carrying on with it. Proust wrote the book and he was dead
On the bed table, evidence! that suddenly they become
Business men and business women
As the delicate white gloves of the sun
(So dixit Svana)
I got to get up. The gun
Of a new day is pounding got to get

On my jacket's got to get
New translating job jobs at the embassy go to
Get ready for bar tonight, get
Going, up—everything

Bathing and raving—
Classic symphony, outdoor beers. Blue awning. Capes. Stone. The flashing
    substance
Of sleeves and neck and collar and the subtle
Shade of pink in cheek and slight resistance
And then surrender! Lipstick in the puddle
At the umbrella'd table close to Customs!
I—I—you—skirt—it's my—flags—in battle—
Your—by—sleeves—listen—I'm—wait—sperm—ova—
Interest—bud—easy—luck—Vita Nuova—

Never again that Sunday in the Peugeot
Spinning to Fontainebleau! I take a hairpin
And bend it sharply till it is a bow
For a minute it seemed to be there
Small white flag
Of hard dress unburdened
As the poets say
By "time" whose neck
A sheep, buttons
Of a capacious (big, roomy)
Wedge, and then

Used at breakfast to sashay me until
Sitting, somewhat sprawled, in a chair
Reading Lautréamont. Oh for God's sake
Let's group out of here. Lieutenant,
Cross over the glass porcelain men!
Wake up said Janice dear. I was walking
In nineteen-seventy-two, when suddenly
E. L. was nineteen years old, A. R. was twenty-three
And I was almost fifty, cinquante ans—

Now it is later I have just come back
From Africa, to which for the excitement
I went, and Noel still is on his track
Of pneumonology. His wedding statement
However's changed, and Z is gone, a fact
Suggesting their first choice as not the right one.
Both middle-aged and changed by that fantastic
Chimie du temps in almost every aspect

Split seconds of a chair in a café
Time the note on a glass window
Says they are coming Change
To sarabande attire, ice of the Sixties
When to be Decemberish was the soul of claim
To interest and enticement of the muse of flame,
Forties of the gnarled How-to, Fifties of consent
To split and tower and ropes weather, islands of the
Damned insane Eighties hues cupped in flame
And no car because the secret to get out of, caught in history's game
Scattered about like furniture, too wise to be the main
Movers of things, already too dead?
Reading "Yellow violet"

Appointment with nnn hayerdresser, she says. We are to meet (met)
Later, I don't like to eavesdrop. Soap.

What pompous! what ruckus! and what creates!
The whole women of Proust! the pavanes and the flowing carriages!
The doctors on horseback, their patients behind them in stalls
In Middle Ages weeping, "Cure us, or give us our money back!"
I run and put on my ducking—
Why am I wearing ducking to this place? Whose mirror is that above the
    piano?
It is Ferdinand de Lesseps' or Fernand Léger's! Qu'en sais-je? I may not
    have Stendhal's talent, after all,
To get down what actually took place.

The adornments of these clavicles, says Rodeson
(Panoscopic visions in a multifactored box)
Presuppose an Aegean civilization. You're right! What? I love! (Mayakovsky)

Do you suppose? he said. Oh, I don't know, I—
Well, that's a thought! I'd better use the tele-
Phone! The sails seemed white forever.
It clatters down the stairs. You have a fever
But stand and walk around.

Elizabeth is glad—it isn't raining
Or snowing, but the sun's out. She has just
Become nineteen. She notices
A plan, coming off the wall. That's a MAP,
Old Chinese restaurant, with a small
Waist, back-breaking task,
While sunshine rolls around

Take me with you. You don't love me. Scowl
Blank. Go.

"The secret," Harry said, "is that eternal
Fluctuations make us workers here
On this great hill of art, where on a clear
And not-too-populous day one notes the vernal
Intemperance of carnival—we cheer
The musing flowers on their slapping way."

And Bukaku hadn't yet met him so had not yet intro-
Duced me to him I was reading, voraciously, Guido Gozzano

The pink air was guzzly a little and fashionable

Harry, in any case, now in appearance, says
"Call up!" The eternity of messengers was behind us
Scattered all over, the roses of the Bois de Boulogne.
It's very convenient to be there, the earth is a phone
So, Worm, you can call anyone—Whose are the fragrant cashews of this spring
Of Roman-Indian fragrance, out into that "cool gray dock"—of "advance"

"If only we had done something, really,
Like inventing the steam
Engine. When we do (invent something), though, it instantly dwarfs us."
I thought Rilke must be standing in that zoo,

289

Said Dan, so I went up to him, I
Thought, but it was von Spitz, inventor of the atomic stream.

A fiery bracelet. Dishes pile up later.
Don't criticize me so much
I couldn't—I will—I don't think anyone will
Remember my sensations. Sometimes it seemed
All I was doing was going to sleep
Or trying not to. Did the smokestack throw
Less fire because of hell me?
In any Etruscan I found it was all there.

If they're not actual—I mean, outside!
I don't care—or think they could be outside,
They are, I can get to them! I plan to speak
To someone—the first breasts of the sky—shush!—Go to sleep!

The house on Hydra when we lived there once
Was a small house whose whiteness was its wall.
We actually stayed there just two months
Of wide, hot summer scrambling into fall.
The waves against the stones made noise like punts
While walk along and Katherine says Good-ball
Good-bye. Goats as from a frieze
Make blunt the room.

So did my white shirt-cuffs—cow path,
Jessica stays at loops, Mycene December
And French autumn, Christmas, blackness, risky
Flower arrangements, so that above the prow
Emeritus mummies appear, clement to wake us up—
The elegant white-pink of an eggshell dusked
By damask in the magician's petrified cloth—

On the side of the sparkling
Glass sliver—something—peace
In its light-red-blue reflection.
Dan puts it to some use

This earliestness has wings, like Fra Angelicos, in cars

The bed was white
Its sheets were
The moon (or what- who-ever was there) was waiting
In the morning.
I bent, leaning
From one to another place
Vision of Macchu Picchu, God what heights! (one minute)
Botticelli's Venus—two seconds—
Three minutes, eight minutes,
Planning to go there, being there, che splendida giovane!

Do you remember the storms, the depressions, the unbelievable
Disasters? and when you think of them, can you sleep
And eat? I thought my life was going to be a scrapbook,
It turned out, instead, to be a heap.
A heap of what? Noël said, laughing. Joanne was laughing,
Her skirt was on a spot
Slightly blue-colored on her right leg, white skirt
Now her gray eyes peer at Speed across the table top
Speed! tell me, when are you seeing Dan?
As in a Yeats triptych cognitized in a dream
Skittering, warm summer morning. A day of the orange
Expense account of fragile invested sunlight
But I said Which? Orin was switching the lights
I didn't want to think about or forget
The mesh, of the subway, the powder on the table
Is blowing somewhere else.
Irganian Eskimos asked him for his life
In bondage in the snow, to which he savantly replied
Yes and no, sleeping my way out
Focusing on the pale night
Driven into the streets
Desire to find out
Dripping and edged with green and orange paint
What institutions connected to what sensations?
Law to nudity?

Bread without thought.

Advancing to the typewriter (sheep), and unboxedly looking at the sky
    (weak), the
Bones of the climate and the poles, one week
The stems in the throats of those conversations!
The strong young woman emerging—Venus, not
Music playing behind.
At other times, stunned time, time being stunned, stunned
Intervals and times of anxiety's careering like a body
Inside the regular body, with nerves
All that seem in between

In Paris there was no one. It was cold out there
But it was something. Inside you was a baby.
Inside Thomas Hardy was *Jude.* I thought
What is in me? A day of secret stuttering doors is in me

"Elle craque, tu sais, absolument, elle craque!" syzygy
And blankets of stars which would put even Dan out on a limb
Of "Unusual groceries!" whereas, touching his chin—Loves, good-bye!
However, my hat doesn't ever get away from them
Keeping so busy I had no time to go out
When anything was open or anybody wanted to go with
Me—You're lucky! said Jim. Do
Come in, said rafafafa of daisies
But necessary be welcome to this town
And sit and read

He is very encouraging, usually, in particular
For whatever you propose. Going to drink coffee
Listen! My head is going to blow off if I do
But yes, let's go, quickly! Aspects of a job
That can only be done magnetically. You've got it!
Laughing and coughing in a brightly lighted street
Or a dull gray one, away from
The bright sun I saw him—the funeral
Men and women glaring at their sleeves unhinged

Do you remember the "real writers" of nineteen-fifty?
Do you remember the pretension of that spot?
Lake Sholem Aleichem was produced off-Broadway in nineteen-fifty-seven—

Dogwoods, meant for the next year, was never done.
Do you remember the bad faggots and the crackpots?
The masses of mouldy customers and the crumps? the grumps
The unsatisfied? Do you recall the Eliot Divide?
The bad, sad, and second-rate, our souls unsatisfied?
Painters shifting a place there with the paintbrush
Ain't doin nothin, nothin that counts! And it
Was true, too—
Apartment-wall-side proposed to a flame
And kept the villains inside
Who wanted to come veering out (melodies) while
Cracking a whip above the dances (waltzes) and
Wouldn't let the moon inside
The paintings! Outside on the side-
Walk side, where time was the clout of all their canvasses,
Men walk by. Sighs
Over Garbo and Dietrich, jumping excitement over Coleman
(Ornette)? Do you remember the cordite starring in *Diaspora?* Good, and bad!
What dark red afternoon did Otto Luening
Afford my snobbery vis-à-vis Stefan Wolpe as Frank crushed
Dissension by seeing the bright in everything? It's cold in here

And it was a dawn
In nineteen-fifty-eight, firing pin on the levees.
A flood is coming! Over the hill
Dan kept moving. Reading Stendhal
La Vie de Henry Brulard in nineteen-eighty
I said my goal be that!

The celebrated "inside-outside" feelings
X wrote Y when he was only twenty-one
A cherry tree (sneeze) of precocity
Annual mump
I wonder about the fig tree
On Island Ump—Hydra
Your red silk is freezing
On this sand-of-me-beep-through-the-car day.
Why a car should talk
(Seemingly) and a head
Be blinded (for a moment) I don't know.

Why am I not a tropical man?
If I can look at all these things and not be blinded, what do I think
I think at one moment and at the next moment I don't
I am blinded
Think
I see the plate
I live in this civilization
Dumbbell

All the same, though, this sad night seemed lost
And others right then, too
Nonetheless blathering hoop-la absconding frequently
Filled my days and creepings with such abundance of regardings
And suddenly (it seemed so) glad fixations on
The non-parliamentary procedures sun
Shining to plate, I said, Dearest when all this is done
When are we going to get anywhere or know anything
Slate, faculty, and pocketbook. Bust, she regarded
The soon-maidened day. Well, we will! she said.

An upward look, which is depenetrated
Southernly, by a stretch of Freud. Oh look at the complexes
The dust road is wet
Clouds' days are climbing all around.

They roll
The top
To show
The lot
How climbed
And clean
The hill was.

But well a day
It stops to say
(The air)
My clouds
Are pillows!

So run, run!
This is not
Herrick nor John Donne
But some modern
Inky fellow's
Prized Armageddon
De syllabes.

And on one opaque filled-with-joy daylight-blue-and-pink-and-white-
        faced morning
She kissed him on the cheek
Whereupon

For five hours of which the first fifty-five
Minutes are the most intense. Joanne, stopping
And with letters

They always do find them, said Dan.
He took the manacles off Schiavona's wrists.
And went home talking about the *Alchemist*
The good the bad acting the dubious kind of direction
The musty smell of the theater and the rest.
D'you like it—them, replied.
This lunchtime. Oh, how—
Bearing secondary (or supernumerary) parts. I am on the ledge
Later the doctored-up paintings and
Alone, cold
Sitting in the bundled coats and thinking Well
It's over. The lamp went out.

The car, quel tas de junk
And U. was at the wheel, ridiculously drunk
And divided between about five girlfriends
I was so much older I should have been in the trunk
But I was there, am, now, however, edging my shoulder
Past C-Jump I could see that with every act
I was hoping and she was singling some quality out
To arrive at later with better but could not afford now
To be the one I buttoned on clothes with; still, there she was
Radiating fullness in the car,

Once home, no chill, relief, cabbage in the dawning
No those are light green cloudlets coming up the trees
So then I go to bed, it's as in the car—snore,
Raffle, awake, then back to slump, and sleep—

The wavy secretary speaks at the bend
Of the desk office, now I am met by the head
Agent. I stand up, the secretary's gone. Good-bye.

Beautiful figure
Of everything! Then
Suddenly down the sidewalk
Comes the truth
In the form of a girl
Into 35 rue Notre Dame des Champs
Hey, is this the closest place
To where I want to be? Noel says
A joke is a joke. Come on, take
The box out. We don't
Quarrel, actually. B-17,
Farewell.

Two girls
Ana and Svenita
One of them
Is studying Arabic
What do I care?
The water glass is on
The Frigidaire
An American patent
A big heavy white bird
Flown from America
To here in France
I place my
Hand on Svenita's
Shoulder—
And the white flag
Of seasonal peripheries
Is scuttering everybody
To dunk back into the beds

Whereupon suddenly
All the same

It is a force (Yeats)
A catastrophe (Quevedo)
A chase (Montgomery)
A flower (Keats)
And beauty with a graveled mace has done
I see her at the airplane counter—South

Outstretched—North-wind rubberband?
Is it religious
To dream of the Southern Cross?
The band is playing, the Riviera has walks—
Whiteness today is our special, I mean of the sun—

In Nice upon the Walk attired in whitest
Silks and linens men and women went
Forwards and backwards in what seemed the brightest
Light to earth the sun had ever sent
Baking the sidewalks white, with an excitement
Felt only insofar as it was meant
To be the belt of paradise around one,
When, striped with thirst, one stops beside a fountain

The white roadway shines ahead it is
A sidewalk! In front
Beyond the windows' cou-cou-cou. I grow up
Into these shades, white and referenced
Of slender wood, somebody being always nervous about the time

Tremulous and capsizing fresh stone in the hall
On which you stumble—I catch you—
Today is seeming, in truth, a beautiful day
"You use that word too much" is a seeming
Indifferent, well maybe not so much, distinction
And the restaurant of the animals, door, is hay
Which to them smells "beautiful" and I am out my door "beautiful"
Day, sitting on the speech stump and worrying about the door—

Comatose amidon
Hand held and then released
Stairways
Always on the edge of
Seeming to want
The book opened and then the book

What is outside—cars, windows
Abroad what is inside—aimlessness, scarves,
Or, in another view, thoughts,
First smell of cattle over the evening
The burning (hot was used as an ashtray) shell
Later evenings—it was already summer
Reflections of the outside
Taking the inside's form and making it follow

A grassiness is bursting in the light
That makes it seem more than autonomous.
A good trick, then, to be phoning. My (our) "nerves."
Visiting, it's vicious, it's long-gone time.
I walk down this sidewalk it's frappant it takes where you are

Blossomingness—and she says, You have a car, yes
We hot car have legs, shine cross, then, there
High nothingness elevator my clock "re-spaced"
Tables away, plates away, gavels away, the nothing
And something in a yellow dress while
Someone in a blue and white shirt bends over
Something made of wood with four legs. I hadn't read
Marcabru yet. Oh an
Old friend's poem, encased in a letter,
Smelling of soap,
January morning, while a truck goes past.
A word decelerated from a window. Type
Evaporated
From a newspaper. *Daily Cross.* Done
Nineteen forgotten
Centuries
Of progress, red

Shoes, white linen
The Russians are doing an experiment
In painting. Summer
Collapsed on summer like a clothes-
Pin snap on a piece of clothes.

He asked her to dance.
So Larry and I go to look at the picture
Of Z. Z. de A. pinching the nipple of Bambambomba
Dominique Celestin qu'en sais-je with the little briny street
The painters lived on, whiter than a mule of hay
And vigorous in a blank unquestioning manner

It was sixty-five degrees
Out. Perfect ("perfect") weather.

All right, let's get married. Will you marry me?
This marriage is done. I want you back.
You never had me. Bringing the suitcases around.
Bringing them back. Sitting in the Hotel de Fleurus.
This floor is sandy. With you,
The best way is to separate today

I couldn't then—Olivier says Think it over!
But lost for that holiday. It stings, it
The Greek art collection, walking
Sideways, it was hard to keep up. The greatest person ever to come in
This restaurant. Her fine-boned person
And rouge et le lipstick all around
For all anyone ever understood
About it, really

John said The hula hoop identity
Of all these straw persons interests me
Then finally he was promoted
To laugh at the bar of heaven We poets are the Jews of Literature
Scamping around at me—Especially you!

I can't believe you're doing this—not insured
Not protected by anything, I felt her hand, wristbone, of my own

The Danilova equivalent, a starring baggage—then chair
Being have brought out upon the sidewalk
The bed that Dan raved about checks in with and this suit

Printed in grey letters, on the top of the fire escape,
Look at it Guillevic said, look, look at it!
Proof that we live forever, or at least in a magazine!

Drunk in my white suit at Noel Lee's house
Taking a shower I thought
Essences, never seeing anything at all
So wrapped around me as collectedness
To cure all that
Dashing, but it won't work. Summer französisch.
These partings from some
Time

Flowers umphing around
I and the skirt the body sums
Keeping and smiling up
To walk

It's in the goat
And in the footnote.
It lamps what is not to come
As well as what is, a bannister of bones and a hat.
It felt like forever.
It feels "interrogating flat." It feels shown.
Vanning about and straggling. Why is it so unknown?
Getting out of the car and going back.

THE TOMB OF ALEXANDER

(A place in Macedon, with a tomb. ALEXANDER *is inside it.)*

ALEXANDER
    Inside here adamantly
    I sleep. I am trying to get out
    But can't.
    I am locked
    Inside the tomb of Alexander.

(Enter YOUNG MEN AND WOMEN *of Macedonia, singing gently but enthusiastically outside the tomb.)*

YOUNG MEN AND WOMEN
    Hey ho Alexander
    Gods bless Alexander
    He is great Alexander
    Alexander cinnamon tree!

AN ATMOSPHERE OF HEAVY, INTENSE (SUMMER) STILLNESS PERVADES THE WORLD OF CHRISTINE ET ÉDOUARD

ÉDOUARD

> Let's sit down
> In this blazing garden,
> Christine.

CHRISTINE

> All right, Édouard. I can walk
> No more.
> I used to be fifteen
> But now I am sixteen
> And I am tired, so tired,
> After all.

ÉDOUARD

> Have we something to say?

> (*A silvery form,* THE FUTURE, *makes a fleeting appearance.*)

CHRISTINE

> Yes, yes—Look! The Future!
> But now it's gone!

MARY MAGDALENE'S SONG

(The lines are spoken by PEOPLE *in the street, excitedly awaiting the appearance of* MARY MAGDALENE.)

Mary Magdalene's coming!

How can that be? She's long dead, in the Bible.

Nonetheless, she's coming along!
Get ready, to sing the bakery song!

Why does she like that one?

Who knows or can question
Mary Magdalene's tastes?
All we know is that she likes it
And that now she is coming along!

(MARY MAGDALENE *comes along, and the* PEOPLE *sing:*)

Bread and rolls
Fresh every day!
That's how we bake them,
The merry Magdalene way!

WITTGENSTEIN, OR BRAVO, DR. WITTGENSTEIN!

(*The philosopher* WITTGENSTEIN *is walking in the city. At each clause, sometimes at each phrase or at each word, he stops and changes the course of his walk: by turning up a new street, by crossing from one side of the street to the other, by turning and retracing his steps.*)

WITTGENSTEIN
    The only things that we can say
    Are the things that are already said
    By existing actions—
    For example: I am walking today.
    It cannot be said
    This walk is taking me forward
    Or, I am the subject, or the form, of this walk.
    Then, proscriptively,
    The only things that we *should* say
    Are those that we can say. I am taking a walk.
    What cannot be said with clarity
    Should not—and cannot—be said.
    Thus I must conclude
    That the unsayable
    Has no further chance of being said—
    And, this being so,

(*A bunch of brightly-colored balloons with large printed words on them*—GOD, GOOD, EVIL, MAN, NATURE, ESSENCE, MATTER, SUBSTANCE, FORM—*burst free and are blown into the offstage sky.*)

    Our old philosopher's dream is unattainable
    And can never come true.

SPICES *(An office in seventeenth-century Spain.)*

FERNANDO DE PLAZA

    We need three tons of spice by Tuesday next.

ISAAC RUIZ

    Solomon Rosenstein is in Paris and can arrange the transfer
    Through Abraham Blum in Lisbon. Our cousin Izzy
    Barrasch will be waiting in Madrid
    For the order. Therefore you can count
    On having what you want within sixty days.

FERNANDO DE PLAZA

    But I need it by next Tuesday.

ISAAC RUIZ

    That possibility may come only after many years.
    This is the seventeenth century—

FERNANDO DE PLAZA

    Oh—but it—

ISAAC RUIZ

    At the beginning of Capitalism
    Which some say would not exist without the Jews
    And so you should be glad you are getting this order filled at all
    You should get down on your knees and thank God
    That you don't have to live in a feudal society forever
    Where everybody dies at age twelve and where you can't get anything you
        want, ever,
    Unless it happens to be right next to you!

FERNANDO DE PLAZA

    I *am* grateful but don't like being grateful to you Jews!

ISAAC RUIZ

    Such is the lot that Heaven sends to both of us. L'chaim. Farewell!

    (He goes. Sounds of heavy shipping.)

THE FOUR ATLANTICS

WOMAN
>There are four Emilies: the Emily of her parents;
>The Emily of her childhood friends, who were many;
>The Emily of her husband, William; and the Emily of her children—
>Rick, her son, and Laura, her daughter.

YOUNG MAN
>There are four suns: the sun of the tropics—of the Caribbean tropical
>   zones, of Africa, etcetera;
>The sun of the temperate countries; the sun of the North;
>And the sun of the Planets, which holds the system together.

YOUNG WOMAN
>There are four musics: the heard, the unheard, the composed and the as
>   yet uncomposed.

MAN
>*(speaking with mounting intensity and excitement, as he indicates each of the At-*
>*lantics on a large wall map.)*
>And there are four Atlantics:
>The transversal Atlantic of England and France;
>The Atlantic that ends in Santiago de Chile, of Spain;
>Portugal's Atlantic, which begins at the Cape of Good Hope and ends at
>   the Azores;
>And the Atlantic of the Middle Ages,
>And even of Classical times, the narrow winding corridor
>That goes from the Strait of Gibraltar to Britain's northmost edge.

Seasons On Earth

There is a way of thinking about happiness
As being at one's side, so that one has but
To bend or turn to get to it; and this
For years I thought was true. Or that a basket
Of sensual sensations brings a bliss
That makes one as the winner is at Ascot.
With *Ko* I had the first idea; the second
(Some first one, too) went with the story of Papend.

With strong opinions and with ignorance,
And with indifference and with aggression,
With my own odd idea of what made sense
And being happy some sort of an obsession,
Ignoring most contrary elements
By going outside, or changing the discussion,
I used to live for it, like cows for clover—
By my hot, happy sense of things bowled over.

In spite of the real suffering around me,
And poverty, and spite, I had the sense
That there was something else. Each midday found me
Ecstatically in the present tense,
Writing. And you would have to come and pound me
Quite hard to drag me from my innocence.
That sense that now seems almost unbelievable—
I love it, loved it—is it irretrievable?

Well, now, at sixty—please, some frankness, Muse!
I think about it less. It's an accompaniment
Of doing what I ought to do; and news
Affects it, and the vagaries of my temperament,
To some degree unchanging. I find clues
In books, in actions done and statements somebody meant
To be the truth, in love, with its crescendos,
And traveling, sometimes, looking out the windows.

There's no way now I can be quite believing
All feeling will take shape and I'll go walking
Up to that place where light blue air is weaving
A cloud supply for birds to fly through, squawking,
And that each exquisite sensuous day or evening
Is an announcement of a door unlocking
Inviting me to enter. Oh, my narratives,
That kept me thinking of such kinds of paradise!

I had the thought while I was writing *Ko*
To get into the poem every pleasure
I'd ever had. The Ortopedico
Was down the hill and, up the hill, the treasure
Of arms and legs that Michelangelo
Gave to his David white and huge of measure.
Janice and Katherine, like a Perugino
Mary and Child, shared with me the villino.

I was at that time thirty-one or thirty-
Two, even then glad I had lived so long,
Long enough to influence history's verdict
(I still believed in that) by my big song
Of baseball, youth, and love. No way the Arctic
Of death, disease, or pain had bent the strong
Support floor of my being: happiness,
I thought, was what life came to, more or less.

White days above the Orthopedic Hospital!
That patients came to from all over Florence—
Some young, some not so far from a centennial,
Though few from Rome, and none, I think, from Corinth.
Three miles away, about, the railway terminal
Next to the church where the Uccellos aren't—
They're *in restauro*—gave out toots and whistles
To friends and lovers kissing near its trestles.

Down the hill this side streetcar tracks connecting,
And the Piazza, and the via Forlini
Gave someone who old Florence was expecting
A slight shock, being plain as boiled zucchini.
White hat white coat policemen, though, directing
Us cross the bridge guide us to what has meaning
Historically, aesthetically, emotionally—
Statues and Giottos known here almost socially!

We spent long minutes waiting for the bus that
Went up our hill, the M, pronounced the Emmay—
A wait it would be very hard to fuss at,
Rather the kind to put in mind an M.A.
Thesis on the Sublime, or wait till dusk at
Until its beauties vanished like a mermaid
On one side into walls, on one to sloping
Of hills around. Who could be there not hoping

That that white some-such in the air betokened
A happy state convincing as an iron is
Pressed on a shirt whose collar has been opened,
Or sight of dogwoods in the Carolinas?
Inside our house we had someone to cook and
Help care for Katherine, who was two years minus
Some months, and make our sweaters bright with Woolite
While Janice read Gozzano on her Fulbright.

We'd come there in the winter. February
Already brought warm sunlight to the shoulders
Of Perseus, and to the Virgin Mary
In Convento San Marco, as to boulders
On the long walks we took; and on one airy
Young day, while gazing at some yellow folders,
I wrote three stanzas that made me feel dizzy with
Delight, as if I wrote for Queen Elizabeth—
In fact it was an Ariostic azimuth
I tried to trace, of all things on earth viz-a-viz.

Such happiness, it seems to me, that went
Into my stanzas, paradisal octaves!
My mind from death and heart from hell were bent
Each day as I pursued the same objectives:
The getting all that primavera meant
Into my work. I heard Divine directives:
Those poets write of bones, but truth is elsewhere.
Keep at it till you get to the elixir!

It was the time, it was the nineteen fifties,
When Eisenhower was President, I think,
And the Cold War, like *Samson Agonistes*,
Went roughly on, and we were at the brink.
No time for Whitsuntides or Corpus Christis—
Dread drafted all with its atomic clink.
The Waste Land gave the time's most accurate data,
It seemed, and Eliot was the Great Dictator
Of literature. One hardly dared to wink
Or fool around in any way in poems,
And Critics poured out awful jereboams
To *irony, ambiguity,* and *tension*—
And other things I do not wish to mention.

All this fell sideways past our Florence windows—
That is, it had not much attention paid to it.
Dry, stultifying words, they were horrendous,
Inspiring in the breast a jolly hatred—
And then new lines arose, like snakes to Hindus,
That for *depressed* spelled out *exhilarated.*
O metaphors! Compelling satisfactions!
The truth might be in the right mix of actions—
Like snow in spring with lilac's blue reflections:

You can call me on Saturday she said.
The hippopotamus walked in the room
And then, with a blue towel around its head,
Ran straight to the sky-mirroring lagoon,
Sank to its knees, rolled over, and played dead.
Meanwhile, Ceylon experienced a monsoon—
Such sequences, perhaps, if gotten right,
Might find the truth, as flowers find the light.

Outside the house, azaleas in a clump
Where I pick Katherine up and set her "walking,"
With hopes that she may reach yon mossy stump—
Jan, in cucina, con Erzilia talking—
All this to whirl in one poetic lump
To make a shape of with a heart knock-knocking.
Domestic trials, quiets, and disturbances,
Tourism, friendship, love and its observances.

Other days, I took some days off, some pesky
Insect or sound might drive me out, I'd stare at
The Foundling Hospital of Brunelleschi
That in my Blue Guide was one-starred for merit,
Or was it two? It very much impressed me—
Early straight Tuscan columns that a parrot
Could fly among and find no place for resting.
And in its laboratories there was testing.

Confusing and mysterious places, clinics
With stars in guidebooks, landmarks, like the Hôpital
Saint Louis in Paris, art and its gimmicks
In serious places, as if in *Das Kapital*
Marx had included flowery script and comics!
Dark streets and light all part of my occipital
Amazement, and where Dante, pre-Inferno,
Stood and saw Beatrice on the Lungarno.

Writing my lines, I felt them close as skin-tight:
What I did in the shiny afternoon,
When I was walking round, was part of insight,
And when I ate, or looked at a cartoon.
Whatever happened fell in place. I'd think I'd
Run out of lines, but then I'd see the moon
Running across sky's Arno like a searchlight
To shine for me some thought upon a churchside.

My life was in the poem and just outside it.
Nothing was written as it "really happened"
But all took place as rhyme and chance decided.
My typewriter was there, my pencils sharpened.
Ko pitched and made the team and was delighted
And threw so hard the grandstand beams were opened;
Exit the old ex-catcher. I spent hours
Walking around in the all-kinds-of flowers

That gracious grasped the hillslopes with their sweetly
Beguiling selfness. Doris looked at Andrews
And knew now she could love someone completely.
April then May came fluttering through the branches
Of peach and pear tree all around the neatly
Landscaped young villa two miles from the campers.
You, six months pregnant, lost the baby: it was
The saddest thing that ever happened to us.

You almost died. They tried to give you oxygen
In the wrong way, in the bare-beamed Municipal
Hospital. I helped save you. They were lax again
With blood. Good God! All life became peripheral,
A mess, a nightmare, until you were back again.
My poem had not a trace of these things medical;
But it was full of dyings and revivings
And strange events, that went past plain connivings—

Such as the thrust of Asia to the east
And men turned into statues. There was also
My whole past that came fizzing up like yeast—
Joy in the fact that Ko could throw a ball so
And Pemmistrek a hog. Good health increased.
I wrote some things for *Poetry Chicago*.
Alouette went to Asia, doing well
With an enormous, new resort hotel.

Life in the work? It is as if two orchestras
Played separately and sometimes simultaneously—
One from inside, deep down, where García Lorca says
Duende dwells, which sometimes intravenously
Gets fed by that outside—thus, metamorphosis!
Lamp into day. Or else a drumbeat famously
Heartlike inside turns snowflakes on the windowsills
To sounds like cries, and then abstracter syllables.

Should one be ignorant? Did I have knowledge
Instinctively I don't have now? Is knowing,
The kind one gets from every kind of college,
The opposite of the ecstatic showing
Of what life is in the amazing sandwich
Of art? Is wisdom sun? Or is it snowing?
And how much of one's life and where it's going
Gets in the work? How is it filtered? altered?
What paths through clouds rise from the chocolate malted
One drinks on a hot day and feels exalted?

Is that truth truth still now that all is older—
I, Tuscany, our language, Katherine, tutto?
Truth now that I come to experience colder
Than ever I did then, less absoluto,
With more "good sense," with decades in my folder
Of proofs that quite a lot of things are futile—
What's left? what lasts? Does it make sense to bring out
Old poems again? O bells that ring ding ding out

There in the air and do not have this problem!
Give me advice; or you, convulsive air!
You, hill; you, field; you, tree, great candelabrum!
New, nature still exists, but what is *there*—
There, I mean, in the words I wrote while Katherine
Was sleeping and her mother stitched her bear?
Then some years later when all strong sensations
I had I hurled into *The Duplications*?

The Duplications! Hardly is that word out
When a vast image out of Spiritus Mundi
Reminds me of what it was all about:
Life as a violent wild event-packed Sunday
That makes the people scream and makes them shout
And ply the sky as if in search of funding—
Venice and Samos, Stockholm and Peru,
London and Athens, gardens in the blue.

There was no Florence anymore, however,
And no sweet feeling of a Quattrocento
Harmonious mix of you, me, and the weather—
No Poliziano and io mi rammento,
No tutte cose coming all together
And intimacy springlike as Sorrento—
The street was gray and modern; and our marriage
Was more than I could mend with my then courage.

My writing now was more investigation,
Or, better yet, a sort of archaeology
Set out to find the great civilization
That once existed, maybe; an apology,
Also, for what I couldn't do. Sensation
Was what it rode on, action its theology—
Away from all that troubled you and me so,
In a sort of poetic paradiso.

That *Ko*-like bliss—I had grown so attached to it,
Could use it writing, it was even practical—
Made me think bliss could be mine with no catch to it,
No fear, no fret, no nothing but sabbatical,
As if it were my, not I its, constituent.
Anxiety, any strain, seemed unaesthetical:
Not now, I felt, I thought, Don't pain, don't tire me!
I'm in a state, and that may disinspire me.

Now fifteen more years later, looking at them,
These poems, of different times and different systems
Of using life as if one had a patent
On its effects without regard to wisdom,
I feel sometimes delight—and sometimes flattened.
What is there, that I am at sixty, in them?
How can I ever hope to get in synch with
What they're about? What do I have to think with?

What's here if I'm not that same sensual Kenneth
Of years ago, nuts for exhilaration
And always willing to convene the Senate
Of nudes and nights and nerve-ends of the nation
For one great further push through the impenet-
Rable Castello del Realization,
To its high hall where, on the gods' advice,
Is painted the true face of Paradise?

What is, I want to know, the truth if there is
Truth in the view of things I had, and what is
The source, if it's mistaken, of its errors?
Do we come into life with minds and bodies
Ready to live in some ecstatic Paris
Or is the limit of our lives more modest?
Is there a seed in us? are we the pod? Is
The blossom pleasure, and the fruit the goddess?
Did you too ever feel it, like a promise,
That there could be a perfect lifetime, Janice?

I don't know. Don't know any of this. My decades
Six now, with the beginning of a seventh,
Counsel me, sure, to dance to slower records
But I'm still trumped and bumped by glimpsed-up heavens
And think they may be true—but just for seconds.
Two words, one word, it used to be a sentence.
Nothing has come of this except my wonder
What it's about, before I'm shoveled under.

Is its being vaguer, harder to put trust in
At sixty odd, proof that it's false? or that I,
Its register, am wearing down or rusting?
Is it not, some may say so, slightly batty
To dote upon this carnival combustion
Amidst so many things that really matter?
And what about the threat to all this fluction
And fragrant life, the goddamned bomb's destruction?

They're right. You're right. I'm right. I'm wrong. I have no
Answer except the one that poets often
Sport occupationally like an Afro,
That what we give is what we have been given,
And hope we are of use that way, as Svevo
Has helped me live since I was thirty-seven.
I've been concerned with various things, and active,
But this one makes me radiantly reflective.

The question stays, for me, and in my reading
These poems again, and stays outside such study;
If I'm a house, I feel that house is leaning
And soon may fall. I want to ask somebody
What it's all been about, but not believing
I'll find the answer my young years made ready.
With things another way, might one come stumbling
To the sweet sill of truth—and get to something?
Is there a City? Was there? And a Woman
To go through death with, even, like Tutankhamen?

O sun! exhilaration! and regret!
Am I advance, or am I cataclysm?
Do I believe this anymore? Has it
Gone down, away, oh have I lost my vision?
It may be here, for I'm still hit hit hit
By what seem its surprises more than wisdom.
But—what here's mine if I'm no more that wit
To whom the academic world was poison
And every modern critic full of shit
(And all their works a spilled-out shaving kit)
And wished most poets would by dogs get bit

And was content with one good friend to sit
Or with another, in the fading glit
Of twilight, happy as a catcher's mitt
And full of futuration? In such status
How could we, I, dream of time's splintering lattice

Which would take Frank away, and Janice later,
Turn John into an Eminence—though now
We get along all right, our verbal Seder
Reconstitutes, but not those times, O Cow,
O Holy Hathor, Egypt's Cultivator,
Not those delicious moments on the brow
Of Tuscan hill, when, happy as gardenias,
We gave our souls up to the evening's genius!

It's nineteen eighty-six, or eighty-seven,
Depending if you're reading this in holograph
Or in the book. The past, that seems quite often
To be false, or fantastic, like a hippogriff,
Or to be a huge book we have been given
Of which we've hardly time to read a paragraph,
Is in these poems, I hope, some way, at random—
Story and past as if they were in tandem—

All in these stanzas that remind to clumsiness
By needing rhymes that interrupt one's quietly
Attending to one's intellectual business;
Demanding, make one feel one can't entirely
Say what one wants, and profit from this funniness
By mixing things that in states of sobriety
One would not mix, and give the proper airiness
To what is neither chance nor arbitrariness—

Stanzas still here! how strange it is you're present!
Stanzas I wrote upon the via Susini
Where Ottavino, saying "I'm a peasant,"
Io sono contadino, pressed the greeny
Latch of the gateway, smiling as he entered.
That was fifteen years after Mussolini—
A long time past. Now, as I read you over,
There's something new I'm trying to discover.

Here it is May again. And the wisteria
Smells sweet, and there's still tape splat on my window
From last year's storm. I've planted a huge area
Of wildflowers, perennials, with no end to
Their coming back, it says. What fond hysteria
Our writing, our remembering! Where to send to
To find out what's the truth, when living tramples
Down everything it gives us as examples!

It's gone but in the head it stays and sizzles,
It's gone but in the heart it stays and sings.
It's gone, sometimes, like boomeranging missiles
And it comes back, and makes, and breaks up things.
It's past. You cannot find it. Yells and whistles
Help not at all. But when the spray first springs,
Watch out! you've got it in your pectoral muscles
And in those colors first eye-closing brings.
Is this the past? Or life's sure force, in purity,
Without the mask of memory or futurity?

Some years ago when I went back to Florence
Up past the Ortopedico to where
We'd been, I found it cluttered with deterrence—
New buildings, not quite a suburban smear,
And filled with smiling children and their parents.
Sad, I let all my sadness disappear
Going back over where we'd walked, then driving
To a new town while thinking of arriving.

O bed and base and breakfast of these times!
To work, love, and good actions the cadenzas!
O possibility, sweet chance that there is
A wholeness only hinted by the stanzas
(Struggling into existence like raspberries
Or, in the Caribbean mold, garbanzos!)—
Do you remember, Janice, the sweet Jerez
We drank ten thousand years ago in Spain when
We picnicked far from Barcelona's pavement
And you were pregnant, wearing your pink raincoat
(Which Spanish men found puzzling or hilarious,
Your being so big and garbed in such a color)
And we walked uphill talking to each other?

I want to dedicate to you these rhymes.
I know it now, it's not made of sensations,
Happiness, nor of Florence and its treasures—
Can there be something greater than all pleasures?
And true? Oh, was it ever yours and mine?

NOTES

The Brassiere Factory. Fleeing from the factory arm in arm was suggested by the French word for life jacket, *brassière*—something that goes over the arms.

Your Fun Is a Snob. The perhaps unrecognizable subject of this poem is a friend standing in front of a cigarette machine on a winter day.

Pericles was written after I heard a silence-filled piece by John Cage at the Cooper Union. After the first performance the conductor decided to repeat it.

When the Sun Tries To Go On is a poem of one hundred twenty-four-line stanzas, of which these are the first six. The poem is dedicated to Frank O'Hara.

En l'an trentiesme de mon eage. The title of this autobiographical summing up is from Villon.

In Love With You. The short story "Relations" in my book *Hotel Lambosa* is about writing this poem.

Aus einer Kindheit. The title is from Rilke.

Collected Poems. I was interested in the relationship between poems and their titles. After writing this poem I sent it to Frank O'Hara, who sent me an "answer" to it, called "Collected Proses."

Hearing. The idea for a poem like this came from a series of paintings by Jan Brueghel in which each canvas was filled with things perceived by one of the five senses—one was called "Hearing."

The Artist. A monumental sculpture in the Arizona desert by Max Ernst gave me the idea. A way to write the poem I found in Stendhal's *Journal Intime.*

Fresh Air. At the time *Fresh Air* was written (1956) the kind of "academic poetry" described in it was everywhere. Later the situation improved slightly.

Variations on a Theme by William Carlos Williams. This poem was meant as an homage to a certain wildness and sensuousness in Williams's work. More strictly a parody was my (much earlier) version of Robert Frost, "Mending Sump":

> "Hiram, I think the sump is backing up.
> The bathroom floor boards for above two weeks
> Have seemed soaked through. A little bird, I think

Has wandered in the pipes, and all's gone wrong."
"Something there is that doesn't hump a sump,"
He said; and through his head she saw a cloud
That seemed to twinkle. "Hiram, well," she said,
"Smith is come home! I saw his face just now
While looking through your head. He's come to die
Or else to laugh, for hay is dried-up grass
When you're alone." He rose, and sniffed the air.
"We'd better leave him in the sump," he said.

Ko, or *A Season on Earth* is a poem in five cantos written in an ottava rima inspired by Ariosto's *Orlando Furioso.* There are a number of stories going on at the same time principally the story of Ko and his troubled but spectacular career as a Dodger pitcher, the star-crossed love of Andrews and Doris; and the deadly pursuit of Huddel, seen in Canto One, at the Coronation, and the powerful financier Dog Boss, whose obsession is to control all the dogs of the world.

In Ko's first game, he throws the ball so hard that he knocks down the lower grandstand and injures an old former catcher who has been living there in a cottage. Overcome by guilt, Ko is unable to throw his fast ball and is mercilessly pounded by the Cincinnati batsmen. The game is delayed, Ko pitches, and the Dodgers win. Toward the end of the poem, the continent of Asia begins moving east, and the champion Dodgers are transferred there. Andrews and Doris, after being thrown in the sea in a coffin, are separated from each other. Andrews, after crossing the ocean astride a magic fish, is hired to track down the criminal Dog Boss. His search leads him to the Acropolis where he at last finds Doris; they embrace and he instantly dies from a disease he has contracted that turns him into a statue. Dog Boss and Huddel also end up as statues. At the very end of the poem, however, the Huddel statue begins "flaking at the knees," a suggestion of more change to come. The circumstances in which Ko was written are part of the subject of the poem "Seasons on Earth" (pp. 307).

The Railway Stationery. This poem was suggested by Raymond Roussel's poem *"Le Concert,"* a sixty-page poem in rhymed alexandrine couplets entirely devoted to describing the scene that forms the logo on a sheet of hotel stationery. *The Railway Stationery* is in sonnet stanzas, though one is (inadvertently) only thirteen lines long.

Poem: The thing to do. The idea of a magically-controlled boat comes from Dante's poem beginning "Guido vorrei che tu e Lapo ed io."

The Pleasures of Peace. This started as a poem about the Vietnam War, but the best parts in it kept being about the Peace Movement. Madame Lipsky's is a modified version of the New York bar, Max's Kansas City.

The Duplications. Like *Ko, The Duplications* has a number of simultaneous stories, among them that of the enormously rich Commander Papend who builds a replica of Venice in the Peruvian Andes as an ideal place in which to enjoy making love, and that of the great automobile race between Mickey and Minnie Mouse, representing Canada Dry, and Terence and Alma Rat, representing Schweppes, over all the roads of Greece. The beginnings of these two stories, from Part One of the poem, are given here, along with part of a long digression (from Part Two) written three years later, concerning the summer in Kinsale when I was writing the first part of the poem. "Zacowitti" is identified elsewhere in *The Duplications* as "the Beljab God of Death who smiles at nothing." "The Spaniard" is a pub in Kinsale.

The Circus (II). The earlier poem "The Circus" referred to here is on page 49.

The Art of Love is a poem of about thirty pages in four parts. For the shortened version in this volume I've included a few pages of the first part of the poem and almost all of the last. Part One is largely concerned with ways to make love; Part Two with ways to meet women; Part Three with what to say to women. Part Four is an attempt to answer all remaining questions on the subject.

To Marina. Some of the poems mentioned, "West Wind" and "In Love with You," are in this book (pages 34 and 36). Another version of the events in "To Marina" is in the story "The Interpretation of Dreams" in *Hotel Lambosa.*

The play *The Red Robins,* an adaptation of my novel of the same name, has action and characters like those of an old-fashioned boys' adventure book. The Red Robins are a group of young aviators who fly around Asia in search of romance and adventure and particularly in hope of finding the earthly paradise, Tin Fan. They are led by a powerful older man, Santa Claus, and have, as implacable enemy, the evil Easter Bunny. Included here are a eulogy to the air by Bob, one of the Red Robins, from Act Two, and the last scene of the play, almost an epilogue, in which the characters come on stage, mostly in planes, and suggest what their true identities might be.

The Green Step is in eight parts, of which this is the first. Each part—the others are "The Brook," "The Stone," "The Train," "The Book," "The

Music," "The Woman and the Man," and "This Story"—tells more or less the same story from a different point of view.

Days and Nights. The stanza with the line "Sweetheart cabooses of diversity" refers to the style of *When the Sun Tries to Go On;* so does (earlier in the poem) "Orpheus chasms trireme hunch coats melody." The poet X mentioned in the second stanza of Part Two is Yeats. The other poets who appear in the poem are friends.

Impressions of Africa was written a year or so after a trip to French Black Africa. The poem is in five parts, of which "The Congo and Zaire.River" is the fourth.

An inspiration for *On the Edge* was Stendhal's *La Vie de Henry Brulard.* Reading it made me want to write an autobiography, but I ended up writing instead a record of a succession of highly excited, seemingly significant moments at which I felt I was on the edge of discovering what life, or my life, was all about. The character "Dan" in the poem is a kind of heroic alter ego.

Six Avant-Garde Plays. This is a selection from *One Thousand Avant-Garde Plays.*

Seasons on Earth was written as a sort of preface to the republication in one volume of two long poems written much earlier, *Ko* and *The Duplications.* See pages 81 and 142.

"the story of Papend" (stanza 1) is *The Duplications.*
"Gozzano" (stanza 11)—the poet Guido Gozzano, author of, among other poems, "La Signorina Felicita."
Stanzas 21–24 refer to various events in *Ko.*
"Io mi rammento" (stanza 30) is from Leopardi's poem "Alla luna."
"Svevo" (stanza 38)—Italo Svevo, who wrote *La coscienza di Zeno.*

A NOTE ABOUT THE AUTHOR

Kenneth Koch lives in New York City and teaches at Columbia University. His books of poetry include *On the Edge, Seasons on Earth, Days and Nights, The Burning Mystery of Anna in 1951, The Art of Love, The Pleasures of Peace, When the Sun Tries to Go On,* and *Thank You.* His short plays, many of them produced off- and off-off-Broadway, are collected in *A Change of Hearts* and *One Thousand Avant-Garde Plays.* He has also published fiction—*The Red Robins* (a novel) and *Hotel Lambosa* (short stories)—and several books on teaching children to write poetry—*Wishes, Lies and Dreams* and *Rose, Where Did You Get That Red?*

A new book of poems, *One Train,* is being published at the same time as this volume.

A NOTE ON THE TYPE

The text of this book is set in a film version of *Ehrhardt,* a type face deriving its name from the Ehrhardt type foundry in Frankfurt (Germany). The original design of the face was the work of Nicholas Kis, a Hungarian punch cutter known to have worked in Amsterdam from 1680 to 1689. The modern version of Ehrhardt was cut by The Monotype Corporation of London in 1937.

Composed by Graphic Composition, Inc., Athens, Georgia
Printed and bound by Quebecor Printing, Kingsport, Tennessee
Designed by Harry Ford